CITY STATE

Richard Roberts and David Kynaston have spent the last two decades studying the City. Between them they have written histories of many key City institutions, including the *Financial Times*, Schroders, Cazenove, Phillips & Drew, Henry Ansbacher, the financial futures market LIFFE, and the consortium bank Orion. Together they edited a book to mark the tercentenary of the Bank of England in 1994. Richard Roberts is also the author of *Inside International Finance* and has written widely on international financial centres, while the final volume of David Kynaston's four-volume history of the City of London (1815–2000) was published in 2001. They have both made a speciality of the City's contemporary history, on which they have written extensively in the press. Richard Roberts is Reader in Business History in the School of Social Sciences at the University of Sussex. David Kynaston is a visiting professor at Kingston University.

To Sarah and Lucy

Contents

Preface – A Foreign Country   ix

 1 Not in Bratislava   1
 2 Conspicuous by its Absence   4
 3 Money – New Lingua Franca?   18
 4 Getting and Spending   37
 5 Markets, Markets, Markets   60
 6 The World's Playground   82
 7 The Mighty Markets   111
 8 City 1 Industry 0   133
 9 Public Places, Private Finance   163
10 Global Portal   180
11 A Triumphal Note?   193

    Notes   202
    Acknowledgements   218
    Index   219

Preface

A Foreign Country

The City is a foreign country. It is a place whose inhabitants speak an unintelligible tongue, practise mysterious customs and worship a god called money. A benign deity, that makes many of them rich – that is the one thing everyone *does* know about the City.

Debate about the City is hampered by unfamiliarity with its activities and widespread trepidation about the subject of money. Just as a guidebook is useful when venturing abroad, *City State* provides a tour of the landscape of the City and its principal landmarks. Couched in accessible language and shorn of technical jargon, it offers a panoramic view of simultaneously the most important and least understood phenomenon in Britain today.

First and foremost, the City is an economic entity whose activities have big implications for government and industry. More and more it is the City that calls the shots. More than ever, governments are constrained in their conduct by fear of the judgement of the financial markets. 'I used to think that if there was re-incarnation, I wanted to come back as the President or the Pope,' one of Bill Clinton's advisers famously observed. 'But now I'd want to be the bond market – you can intimidate everybody.'[1]

Playing host to the world's top international financial centre has had more than just economic consequences for Britain – especially over the last twenty years, as money and the financial markets have moved to centre stage in national life. There have been social, cultural and even moral ramifications: upon welfare and social harmony; upon outlooks and horizons; and upon values and ambitions. Never has the City been as powerful or its influence as pervasive – 'Labour runs Britain as if it were the City State of London,' rebukes the *Observer* in echoing phrase.[2] Never has money been such a yardstick of achievement and approbation – 'This obscene worship of money and market forces is now the most powerful fundamentalist religion in the world,' inveighs Tony Benn.[3]

Why and how has this happened? What have been the consequences? What are the implications at the turn of the twenty-first century?

London, February 2002

1

Not in Bratislava

A generation ago the City gent, the archetypal 'something in the City' on the 8.35 from Weybridge, was male, English and public school educated. Journalist Paul Ferris spotted a splendid specimen in Threadneedle Street in 1960:

> I saw a middle-aged man with a florid face, rippling watch chain and striped trousers, a dying cigar between his red rubber lips, stop on his way back from lunch to buy a copy of the Evening Standard. He stood looking at the financial page, then made a sour face, crumpled up the paper and let it fall to the pavement, squashed the butt under his heel, and headed for the Stock Exchange.[1]

Today the City professional is as like as not to be female, foreign and global in experience and outlook. Meet Daniela, a fund manager at a European asset management house who has been working in the City for five years. Mid-thirties, trim and poised, she is dressed in a chic steel-grey suit with her dark, shoulder-length hair held neatly in place by an ultramarine hairband. She grew up in Stuttgart, the daughter of a manager at IBM, and took Business Studies and Japanology at the University of Tübingen. Thus she is fluent in Japanese, as well as English and French and her native German.

Upon graduation, Daniela joined the local branch of Deutsche Bank as a trainee. During the training programme she was sent to Tokyo as an apprentice analyst of Japanese small companies, covering an exotic variety of businesses. Memorable moments include being assigned to run a slide-rule over a specialist mushroom grower in rural Niigata. 'It was a very good business,' she says smiling. Returning to Germany, she became personal assistant to a Deutsche main board director, which gave her useful insights into the bank's overall operations and top-level management. But she hankered to get back into the business, and so accepted the offer of a job on the asset management side and moved to London.

Weekday mornings, Daniela's alarm goes off at 6.15. Then it's a quick breakfast – toast and jam and a cup of Earl Grey – and out of the door. On the tube she scans the *Financial Times*, taking in both the macro picture and company news relevant to her work as a fund manager specialising in European equities. At 8.00 she arrives at the office, a handsome post-modernist building in the Broadgate complex with soaring windows of pine-green glass surrounded by biscuit-coloured marble. Clutching a cappuccino from Pret à Manger, she swings past the security desk and makes her way through the gleaming chrome-and-glass turnstiles to the lifts. Stepping out at the fifth floor, she walks across the ice-blue carpet through the open-plan trading floor – just a mite smaller than Texas – where she works along with 200 colleagues.

Her desk, like the others, is sleek and modern, with a light wood surface and sky-blue drawers. On top is a neatly stacked rank of analysts' reports on the media sector, her speciality, and a diptych of computer screens: on the left, a high-powered PC on which she downloads data, crunches numbers and communicates by e-mail; on the right, a Reuters screen with all the latest share prices and dealing facilities. Taking a seat, she starts to deal with the day's e-mails ...

Meetings begin at 8.30 with the International Morning Meeting, a daily gathering of maybe seventy fund managers and marketing people at which they report on key points or research trips. At 8.45 it is the European Fund Managers Meeting, a smaller assembly of ten to fifteen people lasting half an hour, at which everyone comments on significant developments in their specialist sectors. There will be several more meetings later in the day, lasting about an hour each. Probably, there will be an internal get-together with colleagues focusing on administrative matters. And then a couple of visits from outsiders, either an analyst at a brokerage firm pitching the latest, the snazziest, New New Thing, or a road-show by a European corporate. 'The advantage of being in London is that the major European companies come here to present to us,' says Daniela. 'That doesn't happen in Frankfurt or Paris or Bratislava.'

In between meetings there's plenty of desk work to be done: there's the foot-high pile of analysts' reports she receives every day to be sifted through; there are 120 e-mails and twenty-five voice-mails to be answered or ignored; there are market developments to keep abreast of via the Reuters screen; there are cash flows to be invested in the market; and there are the weightings of investment portfolios to be adjusted …

Not so long ago, in the era of bowlers and brollies, leisurely, boozy lunchtimes were the order of the day. But not for Daniela's generation – it's a quick visit to the staff eatery or a sandwich at her desk.

She finds the job stimulating and challenging and enjoys working in the City. 'Just occasionally, there is a problem with a small minority who see you as a female, not a fund manager,' she says, identifying some of the older generation of British merchant bankers as among the culprits. 'But they also have a problem with Europeans and with the euro. They have so many problems, I wish them well.'

Daniela's working day draws to a close at 6.00 or 6.30. That is unless she's visiting companies next day, in which case she is off to the airport for an evening flight that will take her to Munich, Milan, Marseilles or wherever, in time to check in at a hotel around 11.00. The following morning, the first meeting takes place at 9.00. With three or four more such encounters during the day, at chief executive or finance director level, lunch is an abstract concept. And when all the meetings are over, it's back to the airport – and home to snatch enough sleep to be ready for that 6.15 reveille …

2

Conspicuous by its Absence

efore Starbucks, even before Pret à Manger, there was a City of London. The Romans established it (at the lowest bridging point of the Thames), essentially as a trading centre with northern Europe. A millennium and a half later, at the end of the reign of Elizabeth I, it was the largest port in the world. The City became an ever more prosperous commercial centre during the seventeenth and eighteenth centuries, mainly on the back of British naval power and the start of the British Empire, before, in the nineteenth century, it entered its golden age, decisively supplanting Amsterdam as the leading international financial centre. This was sterling's heyday, as in an era of unimpeded capital flows the City willingly – and lucratively – serviced the needs of a rapidly expanding global economy.

In 1914 the guns of August changed all that. The First World War was a devastating blow to the City, and in the event it was not until half a century later – the 1960s – that it was able to begin to mount a challenge to the new international champion, New York. Not everyone then, or even thereafter, grasped the point, but the unambiguous lesson of history was that the City's prime destiny lay in fulfilling a fundamentally *international* role.

During these ups and downs, the Square Mile retained a distinctive culture: male, clubby and conservative, but for the most part deeply trustworthy. 'My word is my bond' was a boast that actually meant something. The Anglo-Saxon middle class (whether upper middle class in the form of partners or lower middle class in the form of clerks) that comprised the backbone of the City seldom displayed any great creative streak, but was usually very reliable at the prosaic but all-important task of doing what it said it was going to do. The clubbishness reinforced this reliability: on the Stock Exchange, or at Lloyd's, or in the discount market, City men were happiest doing business with people with whom they had been at school, or played rugby, or who at the very least spoke the same kind of language and tacitly shared the same values and assumptions.

But the City would not have flourished as it did if it had been a wholly closed society. The cardinal fact was that over the years it was willing (albeit grudgingly) to admit into its ranks a series of gifted outsiders, often Jews. Samson Gideon in the eighteenth century, Nathan Rothschild and Ernest Cassel in the nineteenth, Siegmund Warburg in the twentieth – each brought something new and important, thereby quickening an otherwise sluggish bloodstream. The super-patriots may have grumbled, but in truth their comfortable lifestyles owed far more than most of them ever realised to these and other iconoclasts from outside the charmed circle.

Nevertheless, *everyone* in the City would have agreed about three things: that the City mattered; that its importance was underestimated; and that it was misunderstood. Over the *longue durée* – the last three centuries – we ask if they were right.

The City mattered?

The City played a vital role in Britain's rise as a Great Power – the ability to finance wars made Britain the most successful military and imperial power since the Romans. The key event occurred in 1694, when opportunistic City merchants established the Bank of England in order to fund William III's Nine Years War against France. By 1713, after the even longer War of the Spanish Succession, the National Debt, managed by the Bank of England, stood at £36 million.[1] A semi-organised stock market, based in the City's coffee houses, dealt (and provided liquidity) in the government securities created by that debt. Over the rest of the century there were few pauses for peace, and during the French Wars of 1793 to 1815 successive governments were almost abjectly dependent on loans raised by the City, where in 1801 the modern Stock Exchange was established. By 1815 the National Debt stood at £834 million,[2] while the Bank of England further served the state by having conclusively emerged as the government bank and the dominant note-issuer.

The next hundred years were more peaceful, though both the Crimean

War and the Boer War saw the City organising large loans on behalf of the British government. Meanwhile, the City played an important part in financing the continuing growth of the British Empire, both formal and informal. The First World War was a greater financial challenge, involving significant American help, but as usual government looked to the City to mobilise the nation's savings. 'Every Cheque,' as one headline put it, 'Is a She££ Fired At The German Trenches.'[3] The Bank of England conducted three enormous issues of War Loan, and by the end of 1918 the National Debt had reached £5,872 million.[4] The Second World War was financed on a rather different basis, mainly through Savings Bonds and National War Bonds, though the Stock Exchange was important in terms of keeping these bonds liquid.

Welfare even more than warfare was the voracious engine of public expenditure in twentieth-century Britain – expenditure that would have been impossible without the City's well-rewarded services. This was especially the case after the Labour government of 1945–51 had created the modern welfare state, most notably the National Health Service. In 1950 only 14 per cent of Gross National Product (GNP) was devoted to public expenditure on the social services; by 1979 that proportion had almost doubled to 27 per cent.[5] Much of this expenditure was funded through the issuing of government (gilt-edged) stock on the Stock Exchange, where the nominal value of gilts rose over the same period from less than £15 billion to well over £70 billion.[6] At any one time the government broker (by custom a member of the stockbroking firm Mullens & Co.) played a crucial role in trying to secure an even flow of gilt sales to the market and the investing institutions, and the knighthood he invariably received at the end of his term of office was one of the more deserving honours dished out to City worthies.

For all its predominantly international orientation, the City was also a fulcrum of British economic development. Between the mid-eighteenth century and the early nineteenth the commercial and industrial revolutions that transformed the socio-economic landscape relied heavily on trade credit provided by the mechanism of the bill of exchange. From the 1830s the rapid development of the nation's infrastructure – especially its railways – would have been impossible without a strong London capital market, susceptible though it was to speculative fever. By the late nineteenth century that capital market was expanding in range, with household names such as Guinness, Bovril, Schweppes and Dunlop all being floated on the Stock Exchange. A century on, it was launching new industrial stock at the rate of at least £1 billion a year. Meanwhile, through the nineteenth and twentieth centuries, an enormous variety of British businesses continued to benefit from the trade financing and bank lending facilities that were available from the City, where increasingly the clearing banks had their head offices. Even in the crisis-ridden mid-1970s it was estimated that British manufacturing industry had overdraft, loan and trade credit facilities of over £10 billion agreed with the banks.[7] Not all of those borrowing facilities were used, but it was of vital importance to industry that they existed.

In monetary matters, another key area, the City had significant influence. During most of the nineteenth century and up to 1914, the classical period of the gold standard, the British government simply subcontracted monetary policy to the Bank of England. 'In pre-war days,' a senior Treasury official recalled, 'a change in Bank rate was no more regarded as the business of the Treasury than the colour which the Bank painted its front door.'[8] From the 1920s the politicians apparently wrested control over monetary policy – a process eventually symbolised by the nationalisation of the Bank of England in 1946 – but the long-run reality was more complicated. In 1968 the government's economic adviser, Sir Alec Cairncross, reflected that he 'couldn't recall a specific case where the Bank had been pushed into cutting the rate against its will (or even into increasing it when it didn't accept the need to do so)'.[9] Historically the Bank was close to the financial markets, and its advice to government on what would or would not play well there tended to be accepted.

Indeed, between the 1930s and the 1970s the financial markets exercised a profound if negative impact on the parameters of economic policy-making generally. The sterling crisis of August 1931 that led to the fall of Ramsay MacDonald's government, the convertibility crisis of summer 1947, devaluation in September 1949, the sterling crises of November 1964, July 1966 and November 1967 that culminated in another devaluation, the dramas (Chancellor Healey's about-turn at Heathrow, the IMF called in) of 1976 – all these were famous, instantly mythologised episodes in the martyrdom of Old Labour, as dreams of expansion and/or egalitarianism foundered on forces seemingly beyond control. The markets, above all the foreign exchange market, also made life difficult for Conservative administrations. The notorious 'stop–go' cycle that bedevilled the post-war British economy was arguably at its most malign during the Tory rule of

1951–64, and invariably it was a sterling crisis that made the lights turn red. Even in the era of the managed economy, markets – and therefore the City – could not be discounted.

The underestimated City?

Perhaps reflecting the City's own penchant for secrecy and even the deliberate cultivation of mystique, British history books and encyclopaedias have given over the years a remarkably light weighting to the City. Certainly the City is conspicuous by its absence from the narratives by popular, best-selling authors like the Hammonds, Winston Churchill and Arthur Bryant; more recently, the same applies to David Thomson's influential – because so widely read – volumes on the nineteenth and twentieth centuries for the Pelican History of England. Importantly, the picture is similar among more academic treatments of modern British history. Even specialist economic historians have tended almost automatically to give a higher priority to the history of manufacturing than that of services – a priority only just starting to change as Britain becomes ever more a service economy, spearheaded of course by financial services. In terms of broad-sweep surveys, two examples help to make our point: each is by a top historian, each has been deservedly acclaimed.

A. J. P. Taylor's *English History, 1914–1945* has enjoyed the status of a classic ever since its publication in 1965. Yet a glance at the index reveals that the five entries for Montagu Norman, governor of the Bank of England for almost the entire period, are bizarrely only one more than for Lord North, the eighteenth-century prime minister. Moreover, while acknowledging that the largely Norman-driven return to the gold standard in 1925 soon 'took on monstrous proportions of decision and error', Taylor devotes less than two pages (out of 600) to the decision itself. In general, his coverage of the City as a whole is nugatory: when, for example, he does make a rare passing reference to the Stock Exchange, it is merely to note that it was, like the Church of England, a 'quaint exception' to the trend towards greater access by women to the professions.[10]

Happily, the City comes a little out of the shadows in Peter Clarke's *Hope and Glory, Britain 1900–1990*, published in 1996 in the new Penguin History of Britain series, although there are only two mentions of Norman and none of any other governor. Indeed, his treatment of the City as such more or less stops in 1939. Thereafter, although he dutifully covers the major sterling crises, he has little to say and almost completely misses the City's spectacular recovery and re-internationalisation from the 1960s. In sum, it will probably require a further generation of surveys and textbooks before the City receives its appropriate historical dues.

Not, of course, that the historical profession is solely to blame, for what is equally striking is how few political, social and even economic commentators paid close attention to the City – indeed, often did not include it in their analysis at all. That was less the case in the eighteenth and early nineteenth centuries, as the Tory 'country' critique hammered the London-based Whig plutocracy and its moneyed, unpatriotic supporters in the City. In his dictionary, Dr Samuel Johnson famously defined the stockjobber as 'a low wretch who gets money by buying and selling shares in the funds' (i.e. British government securities), while the 'cit' he dismissed as a 'pert low alderman or pragmatical trader'.[11] These and similar attacks culminated with William Cobbett, who in his *Rural Rides* of 1823 could hardly have been more contemptuous of the City's pioneer commuters: 'Great parcels of stock-jobbers stay at Brighton with the women and children. They skip backwards and forwards on the coaches, and actually carry on stock-jobbing in 'Change Alley, though they reside at Brighton.'[12]

By this time the industrial revolution was an established fact, and not surprisingly the 'dark Satanic Mills'[13] (as William Blake had memorably called them in 1804) acted as a magnet for often horrified fascination. The wealth and power of the Square Mile may have been increasing apace, but industrialisation and urbanisation on a Promethean scale had the greater sex appeal.

Take those two Victorian prophets, Thomas Carlyle and John Ruskin. Carlyle was appalled by the increasing commercialism that he saw all around him – and coined the term 'the cash nexus' to encapsulate what was happening as a result to human relations – but the City, that ultimate cash nexus, remained a mystery to both him and his many readers. It was much the same with Ruskin, though himself the son of a City man. He made many searing attacks on the laissez-faire orthodoxies of Victorian political economy, yet never really confronted the City full-on. In 1867, in a public letter to a Sunderland workman called Thomas Dixon, he seemed about to. 'While real commerce is founded on real necessities or uses, and limited by these,' he declared, 'speculation, of which the object is merely gain, seeks to excite imaginary necessities and popular desires, in order to gather its temporary profit from the supply of them.' However, Ruskin did not then go on to examine stock market speculation, but instead gave as his example 'the architectural decorations of railways throughout the kingdom', which he characterised as unwanted, ugly, and purely for the financial convenience of the builders. Of 'the millions upon millions' spent, he concluded, 'not a penny can ever return into the shareholders' pockets' – a spirited defence, in fact, of shareholder value.[14]

Ruskin liked to call himself 'a violent Tory of the old school',[15] but the failure to engage with the practicalities and implications of the financial system was shared on the Left between the mid-nineteenth and early twentieth centuries. Although Karl Marx did indeed call his magisterial treatise *Das Kapital*, the workings of the capital market were almost entirely absent from what was essentially an analysis of a closed economic system, quite different from the reality of Britain's pivotal investing, trading and generally entrepôt role in an increasingly seamless global economy.[16] Just as that economy was breaking up after the start of the First World War, Lenin's account of *Imperialism* did acknowledge the forces of internationalisation; but the City of London itself – the greatest international financial and commercial centre that the world had ever seen – remained the empty chair at the ideological banquet.

So too on the British Left. William Morris (alongside Ruskin the major influence on the first generation of Labour MPs elected in 1906) castigated 'the World-Market' as 'this ravening monster' in his most famous work, *News from Nowhere*.[17] Yet despite that Utopian novel's quite concrete sense of different parts of London, the City was almost perversely missing. As for the other major strand of British socialism, the Fabians under Sidney and Beatrice Webb, their orientation (largely inherited by their creation, the London School of Economics) was mainly towards government and the state, and it is only a minor exaggeration to say that they tried to pretend that markets did not exist, least of all financial markets.

To an extent the deep economic and monetary problems of the interwar period, symbolised by the fiasco of Britain's brief, disastrous return to the gold standard, did make the British Left rather more conscious of the City. Yet even such a clear-sighted thinker as G. D. H. Cole was inclined to play down its importance. In 1929, looking ahead to *The Next Ten Years in British Social and Economic Policy*, he did not deny the necessity of the nationalisation (or, as he called it, 'socialisation') of the Bank of England and the main clearing banks, but he insisted that such a move would be only 'a subsidiary instrument of national progress'.[18] As for a more moral critique of the City, one might have expected plenty of thunder from R. H. Tawney, the other leading socialist commentator of the period; yet whereas in his best-selling *The Acquisitive Society* (1921) he inveighed against the rentiers in their comfortable villas and hotels, he let off scot-free the brokers and the jobbers, the bankers and the money market men.

By this time, the Age of Keynes was almost under way. His great writings appeared between the wars, and from the early 1940s to the mid-1970s the British economy was for the most part run along consciously Keynesian lines, above all through the use of demand management. Keynes himself not only was personally familiar with the City and wrote penetratingly about it, but also accorded a high importance in his thinking to money, the rate of interest and capital markets – peopled, he believed, by short-term operators possessed of abundant 'animal spirits'.[19] However, the post-war Keynesians (whether economists, journalists, Treasury mandarins or even politicians) saw things rather differently: markets were at best a regrettable necessity; monetary policy was a redundant relic from the discredited era of Montagu Norman; and the City was so backward-looking as to be almost beyond redemption.

A small but symptomatic example of this Keynesian mindset was the condescension-cum-contempt felt in the 1960s by the high-flying young journalists at the *Financial Times* (most of them Oxbridge graduates) for their older colleague Harold Wincott. A self-made financial writer who had a strong following in the City, Wincott believed passionately in free markets and was an unashamed 'sound money' man. 'In the private sector the violence of the market has been tamed,' Andrew Shonfield, one of the high priests of the new orthodoxy, asserted confidently in his 1965 survey of modern capitalism. 'Competition, although it continues to be active in a number of areas, tends to be increasingly regulated and controlled.'[20] Five years later, on the eve of the break-up of the Bretton Woods system of fixed exchange rates, the legendary Chicago monetarist Milton Friedman gave the first Harold Wincott Memorial Lecture.[21] Few realised it, but the era of monetarism was about to dawn.

The City occupied an even more marginal place in the worldview of the post-war British Left, where for many years there was a far higher quota of intellectuals than on the 'stupid' Right. In Anthony Crosland's *The Future of Socialism* (1956), an immensely influential treatise, the Bank of England commanded only four references in over 500 pages. On sterling – so traumatic to Labour governments past and, indeed, future – there was only silence. Crosland, even though a practising politician, was a charismatic intellectual; so too in spades was the historian and polemicist E. P. Thompson, whose celebrated essay nine years later, 'The Peculiarities of the English', was a memorable attack on those in the New Left who wanted to mould the natives into the latest thinking from Paris.[22] One rather important peculiarity, though, Thompson completely missed: the existence in this country's bottom right-hand corner of a once again flourishing international financial centre, enjoying closer links to much of the rest of the world than to the rest of Britain.

During the turbulent 1970s the City was in the Left's sights more than before, but at least as big a target were the multinationals.[23] And when in 1979 (the year that Margaret Thatcher came to power) Tony Benn published *Arguments for Socialism*, his treatment of the City did not go much beyond the bald, unelaborated autobiographical statement that what had radicalised him in the mid-1970s had been discovering 'how the immense power of the bankers and the industrialists in Britain and world-wide, could be used to bring direct and indirect pressure, backed by the media, first to halt, and then to reverse, the policy of a Labour Government that both the electors and the House of Commons had accepted'.[24] For the British Left as a whole, it was not until the Thatcherite 1980s – rather late in the day – that the City's importance at last sunk in.

Perhaps it would all have been different if over the years the City had played a greater part in the country's creative imagination. Of course there were exceptions: the stockbroker Sedley in Thackeray's *Vanity Fair*, Dickens's *Dombey and Son* ('Retail, Wholesale and for Exportation'), Trollope's *The Way We Live Now*, the prosaic Mr Wilcox in Forster's *Howards End*, Eliot's haunting lines in *The Waste Land* about crossing London Bridge and coming up King William Street. Since then, however, the City has hardly featured in serious poetry and after 1945 was almost wholly absent from the novel. Even Martin Amis's consciously zeitgeisty novel of the 1980s, *Money*, had practically nothing on the City. So it was too in other genres. 'The Dull Life of the City Stockbroker' was Monty Python's last word on the subject; while in films, the wave of social realism that hit British cinema in the late 1950s and early 1960s was about altogether grittier, more northern milieus, with no equivalent of the scene set on the Milan Stock Exchange that featured in Antonioni's neo-realist *L'Aventura* (1962). When that director came to London a few years later to film *Blow Up*, presumably he did not contemplate sending David

Hemmings to snap his pictures along Throgmorton Street: it was hardly the happening place.

The misunderstood City?

When John Prescott was embarrassed in 1999 by his transparent ignorance about the EU withholding tax and its possible repercussions for London's Eurobond market, he had at least an honourable precedent. Hugh Dalton, Labour's chancellor after the war, was the author of an often-reprinted textbook on *Principles of Public Finance*, yet his grasp of the City was at best sketchy. By the time he took office he still did not understand the functions of the government broker, let alone the difference between brokers and jobbers.[25]

Dalton's ignorance was widely shared – indeed, for many years there seems to have existed a stubborn collective mental block about the City and its doings. So much so that in 1952 a survey conducted for the Stock Exchange found that no less than 96 per cent of the British population was 'apathetic' to that institution's affairs.[26] The likelihood is that at any one time there prevailed a perception or assumption that the City was simultaneously boring, incomprehensible and somehow distasteful. The very phrase 'something in the City' had the effect of pulling down the shutters, while the intelligentsia's rather disdainful attitude was nicely evoked in 1961 by the Bloomsbury diarist Frances Partridge. 'Few people want to spend the whole evening laughing heartily at someone else's capers,' she noted about a disagreeable dinner-party companion, before reaching for the ultimate put down: 'It was like a night out with stockbrokers.'[27]

Why was the collective block so immovable? The City hardly helped its own cause through its abiding reluctance until at least the late 1950s to explain itself; but there were other causes, going beyond the general lack of enthusiasm for business life rightly identified by Martin J. Wiener in his well-known 1981 survey, *English Culture and the Decline of the Industrial Spirit, 1850–1980*. Up to and including the 1950s, press coverage of the City tended to the staid and uncritical; thereafter (as a broad generalisation, with important exceptions) the trend was towards an undue emphasis on personalities and sensationalism. In both periods, more could have been done to promote an accurate understanding of what the City did and did not do.

Arguably, though, the culpability of the press was mild as compared with that of the broadcasters. The extent of coverage given by BBC Radio to City news (including stock market reports) fluctuated wildly between the 1920s and 1960s, before Radio 4 at last stepped up its game in January 1974 by initiating *The Financial World Tonight*.[28] On television, whether BBC or commercial, the City was virtually a non-starter. In general, the shortfall was not only that there was an inadequate awareness of the City's functions, but also that very few outside the City even began to understand what the City was like as a place: how it instinctively mistrusted anything that smacked of ideas or theory, how its deepest desire was to be left alone, and above all how it held together so effectively – and *contra mundum* – as a dense network of family, social and other connections that with uncanny exactitude repeated themselves down the generations.

Yet before the late 1950s there was literally no sociology of the City, while afterwards the sociology that was attempted was far from complete or indeed always convincing. Popular writers such as Paul Ferris and Anthony Sampson made notable, pioneering stabs,[29] but the shame was that during the 1960s and 1970s hardly any sociologists (at that time a proliferating breed in British universities) had the imagination and resolve to tackle this alien world.[30] Perhaps they feared the scorn-cum-incomprehension of their peers, or perhaps they were simply worried about going native. In any event, the 'history man' failed to address what historically mattered.

In two key areas the City did *not* escape attention, sometimes even examination. Nevertheless, in both these areas there were profound and disabling misunderstandings.

The first was the vexed matter of the City's relationship with British industry. Here the angle of inquiry – or often attack – was far from constant. Before 1914 the main criticism, articulated by the radical economist J. A. Hobson, was that industry at home was starved of investment by the capital market because the City channelled so much overseas. During much of the inter-war period it was the banks that were under fire for allegedly inadequate lending policies, leading to the Macmillan Committee on Finance and Industry. Its report in 1931 identified the so-called 'Macmillan gap' (concerning the provision of finance to medium-sized companies), which helped to move attention back to the capital market. After the war, the City/industry controversy was relatively quiet for a quarter of a century, with instead an increasing focus on the government/industry relationship – until it returned with a vengeance in the 1970s.

Edward Heath was convinced in the early 1970s that his expansionist economic policy was being foiled by the City's unwillingness to give industry (as opposed to the property sector) the necessary financial backing; the City itself was at the same time being increasingly seen as the playground for unproductive asset-strippers like Jim Slater; and once Labour returned to power in 1974, it was almost a turkey-shoot. 'The short-term outlook of City decision-making is incompatible with the needs of restructuring our economy for stable long-term growth' was a fairly typical assertion from the Left, made in 1975 by the prominent trade union leader Clive Jenkins.[31] Eventually, in September 1976, the only way that James Callaghan was able to counter demands for nationalising the clearing banks and controlling institutional investment flows was by promising a wide-ranging inquiry (the Wilson Committee) into the whole subject of the finance of industry. By the time it reported in 1980, its anyway tame conclusions had been rendered redundant by a larger sea-change in political life.

The City/industry debate has generated a sprawling historical literature, much of it negative to the City, but we wish to make three broad corrective points about the reality of the City's role. First, that its exporting of capital (with the City rationally chasing the highest returns) not only often benefited British industry through accompanying or ensuing contracts, but also frequently involved a substantial proportion of foreign capital, with the City merely fulfilling an international financial centre's entrepôt function. Second, although the British banking system was often castigated for its apparent refusal to engage in medium-term lending, all the empirical research reveals that its preferred method of making short-term rollover credits amounted in almost invariable practice to the provision of medium-term finance.[32] Third, far too little emphasis has been given in the literature to the way in which the City helped to generate a high level of international exchange, undeniably beneficial to British industry, by playing an indispensable part in the world's trade finance, insurance, shipping and commodity markets.

None of this is to deny that the City at times could display a certain unattractive arrogance and detachment in relation to the problems of British industry. Nor is it to argue that the City's firms and markets always gave their industrial clients – and beyond them the national economic interest at large – the most discerning, the most cost-effective service as financial intermediaries. Yet anyway, irrespective of these judgements, the larger truth is surely that in terms of explaining Britain's relative economic decline after about 1870 it is merely naïve to try to pin all the blame on the City. Management, labour relations, education, cultural values – it is not hard to round up the usual suspects. The City is one of them and should neither be let off without a caution nor demonised. After all, as Cole observed in 1929, 'if the bankers were really engaged in strangling the industrialists, and were the causes of industrial depression, the captains of productive industry would long ago have had something to say about it'.[33] Half a century later the Wilson Committee gave another generation of industrialists every chance to pour out their woes, but their criticisms of the City proved notably muted. No doubt they did not wish to be associated with an anti-City campaign coming from the Left, but even so it was a reticence that said much.

The other significant area where the City has been put in the historical spotlight concerns the so-called 'nexus' between the City and the Bank of England on the one hand, the Treasury and the political class more generally on the other. The multifarious social and other connections between these two worlds has, the argument runs, given the City an unduly privileged place in British economic policy-making, in sharp contrast to largely excluded other interest groups, such as manufacturers or organised labour.[34] Undoubtedly at a top level those close connections did often exist, typified by the long-standing convention that a retiring Conservative minister almost automatically qualified for a remunerative directorship in the City. Yet to make the jump from that to a charge of systematic excessive influence is more problematic.

For a start, none of the main historical examples usually given to substantiate that charge quite stands up. In 1925 industry was almost as happy as finance about the return to the gold standard; there is no evidence that the City six years later intended to bring down MacDonald's Labour government; after the Second World War the City was far from alone in not questioning the assumption that strong sterling meant a strong Britain; while the series of sterling crises that did so much to undermine Labour governments during the 1960s and 1970s owed at least as much to the negative perceptions of holders of sterling worldwide as it did to the admittedly atavistic anti-Labour attitude of the City.

Indeed, one could argue that, so far from exercising undue influence, the City was just as likely to back the wrong horse. Certainly that was the case in the first half of the nineteenth century. The return to gold in 1821, the move to free trade, the Bank Charter Act of 1844 – these were the major policy decisions that between them did so much to ensure the City's extraordinary prosperity during the rest of the century, yet the City itself initially opposed each of them. There was an echo of this faulty judgement in the background to the Thatcher government's momentous decision – of huge positive significance for the City – to abolish exchange controls in October 1979. '"Steady on", I was told,' Thatcher would scornfully recollect about encountering City opposition to the idea. 'Clearly, a world without exchange controls in which markets rather than governments determined the movement of capital left them distinctly uneasy. They might have to take risks.'[35] There is, furthermore, no evidence that her government had the interests of the City particularly in mind as it reached its decision. Notions of an automatic, smooth-working 'nexus' are wide of the mark.

In large part this overestimate has derived from a flawed reading of how the so-called 'mind of the City' worked – or rather, did not work. Our strong sense is that at any one time the great majority of City people were primarily interested not in policy questions, but in making money; and that, apart from a dislike of high personal taxation and a fear of war or anything interrupting the money-making machine, there was seldom a coherent 'City view'. Indeed, we would go further and argue that governments historically have been at the mercy *not* of City conspirators or of influence-hungry central bankers and others, but *rather* of financial markets. It is markets that have been powerful (as demonstrated in the recurrent sterling crises of the mid-twentieth century), *not* individuals and firms, which have usually made their money on an agency basis and, even if they liked to pretend otherwise, have had little more idea about what would happen in those markets, let alone the wider world, than the man in the street. The fact that two of the greatest City names, Barings and Warburgs, came unstuck in the mid-1990s largely or entirely through ill-judged trading on their own account, speaks volumes.

This distinction between markets and players is crucial. They have always been very different, and the way that 'the City' has so often been assumed to mean one or the other, or both, without making that distinction, has badly skewed historical understanding. Just as importantly, it is a distinction that helps to make sense of the City now – at a time when the City has never seemed so short of individual 'giants', but its markets have never before been so powerful.

3

Money — New Lingua Franca?

How was the 1980s for you? That in essence was the question that in spring 1990 the long-established social survey Mass Observation asked its panel of several hundred people — none of them newspaper columnists, television interviewers or other metropolitan opinion formers. Most agreed that the decade they had just lived through had witnessed a revolution in British behaviour and assumptions:

> My impressions of life in this country are of a society which has been legislated into greed and selfishness which our political masters have called 'Freedom' of choice. (Computer operator from Bristol)

> Through the eighties I think we continued to become more materialistic and a large proportion of our population became less caring. (Engineer from Bracknell)

> People jumped on the band-wagon, made piles of cash, and others lost out to the most heartless set of people to ever run a country. (Civil servant from Morecambe)

> The re-appearance of overt beggars on the street, the destruction of much of the existing social care network, the enshrining of Mammon as the One True God ... (Graduate from Scunthorpe)

Many of the friends I once regarded highly now talk incessantly of mortgages, pension schemes and job security ... (University research assistant from Stafford)

The exaltation of naked greed and self-interest, the worship of the power of money, the lack of concern for the less fortunate, the cultural philistinism have been revolting to behold. (Social development officer from Stevenage)

The only source of privilege now is money; even land and property is only assessed in market terms. (Librarian from Nottingham)

Strikingly, many of the panellists, while reviling Margaret Thatcher and all her works, noted that at a personal level they had done rather well out of the decade. 'I don't like Thatcher's Britain on principle,' a school secretary from Aylesbury reflected, 'but I have to admit it's been very good for me.' Most, however, preferred not to confront this uncomfortable paradox.

Where was the most visible manifestation of greed and selfishness in daily action? The answer was obvious:

It was a decade in which the Stock Exchanges of the world made Monte Carlo and Las Vegas casinos look like Presbyterian churches, with John Knox still in charge. (Banker from Bexhill-on-Sea)

The complete dishonesty of our financial establishment, with all the Yuppies going 'ga ga' for instant cash without production to back it up ... (Sales promotion manager from Pinner)

Although the claims that greed and selfishness flourished were the slogan cries of Mrs Thatcher's political opponents, there is truth in the claim insofar as it applied to the City of London. Changes there, starting with what became known as the 'Big Bang', brought the culture of the street market into the Stock Market floor and the Money Exchanges. Vast salaries were paid to youngsters of little or no merit who made money simply by shunting it around ... (Civil servant from Orpington)

*Even the Chairman of the bank that holds my account had to
resign! The City behaved probably worse than it ever has since the
eighteenth century. (Shipping company manager from Chalfont
St Peter)*

*Many ordinary people have bought shares, people who never
owned shares in their life before. I know when I went on a walk
with my rambling group at the time of the British Telecom
privatisation, there was a lot of talk about share-buying, which
seemed to me rather sad, as we were supposed to be looking at the
countryside and observing the scenery! (Shop book-keeper from
Stockport)*

*The amount of people with shares is large now ... I have some
myself, they are shares in British Gas, only about a hundred but
still it's quite interesting to see how they go up and down ...
(Housewife from Birmingham)*

*The eighties heralded the Yuppies – I've yet to meet one in
Lincoln – but they seem to stand for greed ... (Secretary in
probation service from Lincoln)*

Perhaps the most eloquent assertion came from a middle-aged woman
from Ipswich working as a part-time clerk at a dental surgery: 'Everything
seems to have become dominated by one word – profit, and short-term at
that ... Where is the respect for learning? Museums coupled with the history of an area are now part of the Heritage Industry. Is the whole country
becoming one vast commodity on the Stock Exchange?'[1]

It is an important as well as fascinating body of testimony. Values, attitudes, social and moral criteria – these are not readily quantifiable matters,
but clearly something happened in the 1980s and clearly the City was more
than just a bit player in the process. Equally clearly, it was a process to
which far from everyone signed up. Not surprisingly, it would take the best
part of another decade before some sort of resolution was achieved.

Serious money

Thatcher rode to power in May 1979 on an explicit agenda of wealth creation and the abandonment of post-war egalitarianism. By 1981 cuts in direct taxation, the abolition of exchange controls and moves to limit the power of the unions had all happened or were in train. That spring – as industrial Britain endured its deepest recession for half a century – the journalist Ian Jack smelled money in the air when he went to Oxford to research a piece about 'The Return of the Bright Young Things'. 'What has changed in Oxford is that it's fashionable again to be rich and smart,' Tina Brown, editor of *Tatler*, had already told him. 'In the sixties and seventies the rich and smart went on existing but were rather more on the defensive.' The bright young thing whom Jack found was William Sieghart, an Etonian reading philosophy, politics and economics at St Anne's. He had been interviewed that very day by Morgan Guaranty, and he coolly informed Jack that he wanted to be 'a millionaire within ten years – I'm blindly ambitious on that score'.[2]

Happily, the City's streets were about to be paved more deeply with gold than at any time since 1914. The great Wall Street bull market began in August 1982, with London following in its footsteps soon afterwards; while in July 1983, a month after the Tory landslide, the agreement between Trade and Industry Secretary Cecil Parkinson and Stock Exchange chairman Sir Nicholas Goodison set in motion the 'Big Bang' process that in effect opened up the London securities market to all-comers and meant that the City did not squander the potential for a hugely enhanced international business that had been created by the abolition of exchange controls. Between 1981 and 1984 London lost 90,000 manufacturing jobs, but generated 45,000 jobs in the financial sector: the contrast could hardly have been starker.[3] The City benefited from the Thatcher government's increasingly ambitious privatisation programme, where the key breakthrough was the successful almost £4 billion flotation of British Telecom in late 1984 amidst bitter political controversy. By just over two years later, following the £5.4 billion British Gas ('Tell Sid') flotation in December 1986, the number of individual shareholders had jumped from some 3 million at the start of the decade to about 8.5 million, almost one-fifth of the adult population.[4] The much-touted 'popular capitalism' (aka a 'shareowning democracy') had – apparently – become a reality.

A raging bull market (accompanied by a series of bitterly contested takeover battles), Big Bang and privatisation had the cumulative effect during the mid-1980s of putting the City in the centre of the national picture – and indeed discourse – to an extent it had not known since the

South Sea Bubble and its aftermath way back in the 1720s. 'The High-Tech City of High-Speed Cash' was the title of a lengthy piece in the *Sunday Times Magazine* in April 1985, heralding a rash of newspaper and magazine profiles of the Square Mile and its inhabitants.[5] Press coverage generally increased, including the start of the *Sun*'s 'Sun Money' page in 1987, and television and radio news bulletins now began regularly to include stock market updates on a systematic basis through the day. In March 1987 Caryl Churchill's play *Serious Money*, satirising the financial futures market, opened at the Royal Court and proved an instant hit, soon transferring to the West End. Perhaps most tellingly of all, Nigel Pargetter in *The Archers* temporarily left Ambridge and migrated to the City, where he proved an enthusiastic if less than gifted stockbroker.

Crucially, the City that was cast into the unfamiliar spotlight during these two or three hectic years was *itself* changing so fast that almost inevitably it became in some way emblematic of a whole new way of life and set of values. For so long a rather stuffy, unfashionable backwater, the City now suddenly found itself at the very cutting-edge. It did so in four distinct ways:

1. *Greed is Good.* Fittingly, the apposite phrase is American (Gordon Gekko in Oliver Stone's 1987 film, *Wall Street*), for as the American banks swiftly took advantage of deregulation to become big players in London, so the City's character began rapidly to be Americanised. 'We like to be seen as nice people,' a British corporate financier had observed on the eve of the revolution. 'To talk about something as dirty as money at one's first meeting with someone is regarded as bad form.'[6] Such inhibitions were soon superfluous. Driven first by the American demand for qualified personnel ahead of the October 1986 Big Bang, and then by shameless poaching between firms, City salaries and bonuses rocketed from the second half of 1984 onwards. By July 1985 the going annual rate was £250,000 or more for top gilts dealers, up to £300,000 for Eurobond dealers, £200,000 for experts in American equities, £250,000 for currency dealers and £150,000 for swaps specialists.[7] Thatcher herself memorably told *Newsnight* at about this time, 'Top salaries in the City fair make one gasp, they are so large.'[8]

For years there had been an entrenched City tradition of loyalty to one's firm and of not 'crossing the street', but this now crumbled almost overnight. In a highly publicised episode, also in summer 1985, Kleinwort

Benson lured away eight BZW market makers, who received between them £1 million to defect and upwards of £2 million for their first year's salaries.[9] The era of the 'golden hello' had arrived with a vengeance – as it had also of the City headhunter. One, Carl West-Meads, put it aptly in summer 1986: 'It's now a recruitment-premium salary market, and greed is exponential.'[10] Another, Rupert White of David Sheppard and Partners, spoke frankly to a Sunday colour magazine just before the Big Bang: 'I don't come cheap, and I'm expected to produce results – so I'm not recruiting people who've merely got the taste to buy the right sort of stripy suit. They've got to be able to make money – a lot of money – for the client.'[11] Understandably, he did not express a view on whether there might be a downside to the rapid erosion of the ties that used to bind. Presumably, if pressed, he would have agreed with the head gilts trader quoted in *Liar's Poker* (the entertaining, highly instructive memoir by Michael Lewis, an American who worked at the London office of Salomon Brothers for three years from 1985): 'You want loyalty, hire a cocker spaniel.'[12]

2. *Lunch is for Wimps*. Gekko again – and again appropriately, as directly under American influence and example the once pleasantly civilised, clubbable City day became simultaneously longer and sterner. 'I have to get in at 8 a.m. now – before the Americans arrived the working day started at 9.15,' Neville Wood of the stockbrokers L. Messel & Co (in the process of being taken over by Shearson Lehman) ruefully noted in January 1985. 'I arrive before the tea lady now.'[13] Shortly before Big Bang the stockbrokers of Haslemere, unhappy about the 7.15 being their first train to Waterloo, managed to persuade British Rail to run one at 6.44; at the other end of the day it was claimed by one British broker that it was now impossible to get a taxi in the City at 8 p.m., because everyone else was also working late.[14] Eating habits changed too. The American 'power breakfast' – a strictly working affair – came in a big way to the City, while sandwiches and spritzers at the desk increasingly replaced the time-honoured ritual of the long alcoholic lunch. According to Peter York, probably the most acute social commentator on the 1980s, it was the newly Stakhanovite working habits of the City that helped to sell the American deal to the wider British world:

> *First of all, you could admit that money was the be-all of life*: at last you could say it. *And secondly, you could see that vast*

> *quantities of money and vast quantities of work not only went*
> *together like ham and eggs, but was suddenly better than sex.*
> *And you understood: this is what America had been on about all*
> *those years. If you worked hard and made what looked like an*
> *absolute fortune, you felt good about it. And if, in sordid, run-*
> *down Britain, there was some way you could work hard and*
> *make a packet, then a new world of possibilities opened up*
> *around you. Of course, Mrs Thatcher had been expatiating on*
> *every citizen's duty to toil away and be productive and make a*
> *good living for one's dependants, but that sounded like no more*
> *than a headmistressy way of telling you to do your best on sports*
> *day. No, this City stuff: this was the proof, the reality behind the*
> *flannel ...* [15]

3. *New Blood*. Many of the people working these increasingly intense, manic hours were of working-class or lower-middle class background, with no previous City connection – in caricature, the 'barrow boys' from Essex. The big new trading floors of the American investment banks (which had no hang-ups about the British class system) were a favourite playground, but it was on the floor of LIFFE (pronounced 'life') that they really captured the public imagination. Explicitly modelled on the Chicago futures markets, the London International Financial Futures Exchange began in September 1982 at the long-empty Royal Exchange, right in the heart of the City. From the start the colourful jackets and loud, gesticulating antics of the traders attracted widespread media attention, as did the rapid fortunes that many of them were reputed to be making, especially once this market in arcane derivatives began to take off from about 1986.

One of Thatcher's stormtroopers, more articulate than most, was David Kyte. 'I trade anything that moves' was his philosophy. 'If I lose £10,000 now, there's plenty more where that came from. If I make £10,000 it's not going to make such a great advance on my equity. I don't think of it as money any more. It's just points. If I'm up it gives me more to play with ...' Kyte was still in his mid-twenties as he explained himself to the *Sunday Times Magazine*, the cover of which said it all: 'City Gents 1987: On a good day the man on the left [Kyte, in coloured jacket] makes £100,000.'[16] Back in the late 1950s, in the film *I'm All Right Jack*, the shop steward Fred Kite (memorably played by Peter Sellers) had seemed to hold the key to the future, but the world had moved on.

4. *Spend, Spend, Spend.* The red Porsche, the cellular phone in the restaurant, the bottle of champagne (usually referred to as 'shampoo') bubbling over – all these in the mid-1980s became the almost instant clichés of the lifestyle of the City yuppies. Ten years later, the television series *Naked City* was an opportunity to recall a brief era of breathtakingly rampant conspicuous consumption:

> *People did develop this idea that in some way they were masters of the universe – that they could tread over anything, and that if they couldn't tread over it they could buy it. (Christopher Bodker, British merchant banker)*

> *Classically on the Monday morning there'd be a huge competition, especially on the trading floor, where everyone said, 'So, what did you do this week-end?' Someone said, 'Well, I stayed at the Hermitage in Monte Carlo', or 'I stayed at the Crillon in Paris', or 'I flew Concorde to New York' ... (Linda Davies, London-based American investment banker)*

> *As well as having a fast car to drive and a smart apartment, perhaps overlooking the Thames, they wanted to furnish that apartment with bright colourful pictures, and so they came to the auction rooms ... They looked upon pictures as another commodity, a way of making a few quick bucks in a short space of time. (James James-Crook, art auctioneer)*

> *Big Bang blew the whistle for the capital that these people had suddenly accumulated overnight to squander out in the country. They bought anything that they liked and saw, and country houses was a big statement to their friends that they had made it. (Tommy de Mallet Morgan, estate agent)*

> *These people were having their salaries increased quite dramatically. They went off and bought their large estates in Hampshire, Wiltshire and Dorset. That led to one of the biggest transfers of land since the Reformation. (Alastair Ross Goobey, fund manager)[17]*

Metropolitan prosperity had always been the engine for property booms, but never so graphically as at this time. As house prices doubled nationally between 1985 and 1989, there came to seem no other possible subject of conversation at the dinner-party table – a coarsening, all-consuming obsession in large part directly attributable to the wealth visibly pouring out of the City.

Unsurprisingly, many young people joined – or attempted to join – the gold rush. A delightful, almost Jamesian episode, set in summer 1984 just after the Americans had decided to expand in a major way their London operations, is told by Michael Lewis. It captures perfectly one culture's apparent surrender to another:

> Two vaguely uncertain American investment bankers found themselves sitting on one side of a long conference table, facing on the other an applicant from Cambridge. Why, the bankers asked, did an Englishman want to work for an American investment bank?
>
> 'I admire your firm's track record, and its commitment to excellence,' said the student. 'The people here are clearly exceptional.'
>
> The American bankers agreed. They nearly forgot to be surprised by how eager – how American – the kid sounded. 'Any other reasons?' asked one.
>
> 'I thrive on doing deals,' said the student, 'and on working long hours. I would view working here not so much as a job but as a way of life. Frankly, working here would put me on a very fast learning curve.' Learning curve, he thought to himself. That was the American phrase, wasn't it?
>
> 'Isn't there something else?' suggested one of the bankers.
>
> 'Well,' said the student, racking his brain for the crucial lie. The winning lie. 'Well,' he said, 'I suppose I could use the money.'
>
> The bankers looked at each other. There was this awful pause. Then they began to laugh. 'Yes,' says one, 'there's only two groups in town that pay this kind of money. There's us. And there's the Rolling Stones.'
>
> I heard many versions of this vignette, but always with the same punch line. I'm told it was all over Cambridge in a week, Oxford in two ...[18]

A little over two years later, in late 1986, Lewis himself went to the London School of Economics (still in the popular mind imbued with the revolutionary spirit of 1968) to give a talk on the workings of the bond market. He did not expect a large gathering for this esoteric subject, but over a hundred students turned up. 'When one seedy-looking fellow who was guzzling a beer in the back shouted that I was a parasite, he was booed down. After the talk I was besieged not with abuse, and not with questions about the bond market, but with questions about how to get a job at Salomon Brothers.'[19] The stampede continued – so much so that by the following autumn the proportion of Oxbridge graduates joining industry was reckoned to be the lowest ever, prompting thirty-three of Britain's biggest companies to come together to try to persuade this would-be gilded youth not to go into the City.[20]

Importantly, it was not just about the cash nexus. Retrospectively assessing how things were by the late 1980s, Peter York surely gets it right, at least in terms of a particular generation (born, say, between the late 1950s and early 1970s) living in or near London:

> The City had taken hold of our minds: City buildings (now thrusting, futuristic) lurked in the backgrounds of car promotions, insurance commercials, moderne electric cooker ads – symbolising wealth, power, tomorrow. City practices – up-all-hours work sessions, spontaneous deal-making, eating and drinking and wassailing in the smartest environments – set a benchmark by which the rest of us decided what kind of lives we were living. The financial Square Mile had become a magnet for people's dreams and demonologies. It even set clothing fashions ...[21]

The City was also a magnet because of its newly found demotic qualities. Suddenly the fortunes of nations seemed to depend not on statesmen, or thinkers, or economists, or even central bankers, but instead on untutored, brash young men in flashy braces who alone could decipher and interpret the banks of flickering screens that stretched out as far as the eye could see. The American commentator Thomas Frank has coined the term 'market populism' – the axiomatic assumption that the will of the people and the will of the markets are identical – and this process was already at work in Britain in the 1980s.[22] Businessmen like Richard Branson and Alan Sugar may have been the entrepreneurial heroes of Thatcherism, but even they stood or fell by the verdict of the markets. Now that those markets were apparently run not by constipated toffs but by 'people like us', how could anyone complain about the judgements they reached?

The June 1987 election – no overmighty unions fomenting a winter of discontent, no jingoistic aftermath of a victorious war in the South Atlantic – was the acid test of whether the British people *as a whole* chose to endorse the Thatcherite/market dispensation. Contrary to notions of City values infecting the nation's bloodstream, all the evidence during the lead-up was that 'popular capitalism' was only a skin-deep phenomenon – in the sense that the great majority of new shareholders had got involved in privatisation issues strictly on a one-off, eye-to-a-bargain basis, not in order to become serious private investors. Indeed, in the 1986 report of *British Social Attitudes*, the psephologist John Curtice noted (on the basis of almost 2,000 interviews the previous year) 'a clear shift to the Left', citing as evidence the fact that whereas in 1983 as many as 49 per cent had wanted to see less state ownership in industry, by 1985 only 31 per cent subscribed to that view.[23]

In spring 1987 the same annual survey asked over a thousand people specifically about their attitude to the City. Although fewer than one in ten disagreed with the proposition that 'the success of "The City" is essential to the success of Britain's economy', almost two-thirds of respondents saw the City as out for quick profits at the expense of long-term investment. No doubt with the Guinness scandal that had recently broken partly in mind, the survey also asked whether the City could by itself be relied on to uncover dishonest deals. Only one-third thought that it could. Strikingly, almost two-thirds of the graduates in the sample took the more jaundiced view, in comparison with less than a quarter of those with no qualifications. Indeed, the survey found, 'even Labour identifiers trust the City more than graduates do in this respect'.[24] Presumably the moral was that the more one knew about the City, the fewer illusions one had.

Yet two or three months later, despite these apparently encouraging straws in the wind, Labour under Neil Kinnock lost the election resoundingly. 'Guilt did badly,' commented the television interviewer Brian Walden three days afterwards. 'People do not like being lectured by powerful fat cats about the state of their conscience ... By the end of the campaign the humbug was so rank that steam was rising from it. The voters smelt it for what it was.'[25] From a standpoint more sympathetic to

Labour's central pitch that indiscriminate tax cuts and naked market economics were destroying the social fabric, Martyn Harris reflected glumly in *New Society* (its title ever more anachronistic) on the implacable implications of a 21 per cent rise in real incomes over the previous eight years: 'The reality is that the electorate has said, not once, but three times, that it prefers money in its pockets to ashes on its heads, and if Labour is ever going to win again it is going to have to take note.'[26]

For the big dealing houses, election night was a time of wild, exultant celebrations, presaging a further few months of the most exciting bull market in anyone's memory. At the end of September the traders at LIFFE celebrated in inimitable, take-no-prisoners style their market's fifth anniversary. It was perhaps the very apogee of the counter-revolution against the paternalist, men-of-goodwill, managing-decline, more-important-things-than-money post-war consensus.

In denial

Barely a fortnight later the world's stock markets (including London's) suffered their most severe crash for over half a century. Nigel Lawson's hubristic tax-cutting budget and another year of sharply rising property prices still lay ahead, but the 'high eighties' were over. For most of the young men who had scooped the City jackpot over the previous few years, it would never be glad confident morning again. At an emotional level, a clear line connects the pervasive mood of *Schadenfreude* in October 1987 to, almost ten years later, the electorate's therapeutic, cost-free purging of collective guilt on 1 May 1997.

'What's the difference between a pigeon and a stockbroker?' went the joke in the immediate aftermath of the crash. 'The pigeon is the one who can still put a deposit on a Porsche.'[27] The *Daily Mail* headline, with no great gnashing of teeth, was 'Party's over for the Yuppies', while from an almost eighteenth-century 'Country' perspective Peregrine Worsthorne argued that the crash could positively strengthen Thatcherism: 'Nothing in the Thatcherite world is easily come by. Everything has to be worked for. Until last week, share-buying had been the exception that disproved this central Thatcherite rule. Now it, too, has been brought into line – and if we soon hear Norman Tebbit telling yuppies to get on their bikes, instead of into their Porsches, that will be no bad thing either.' Indeed, Worsthorne anticipated with undisguised pleasure the sight 'of seeing yuppies on the dole', in which case 'the sounds of bourgeois triumphalism will be stilled at least for a time'.[28]

But for Simon Jenkins, also writing that October on the Sunday after the dramatic events of Monday the 19th and Tuesday the 20th, the reaction that he characterised showed the natives at their worst: 'Oh, the yuppies had it coming to them! Now let's watch them pawn their Porsches, drown in their champagne, rot in their second homes. Thank goodness the monstrous horde had only a year of glory before its demise ... There were moments last week when I thought the media were going to choke on their own glee.' Condemning on the one hand the old, cosy, risk-averse City as 'a haven of restrictive practices and insider dealing', on the other the snobbishness of Churchill's *Serious Money* with its 'working-class entrepreneurs' as 'pastiche villains', Jenkins claimed great things for his anti-heroes:

> The yuppies projected into stardom over the past year were in
> direct line of descent from the Tudor privateer and Victorian
> railway kings. Their ships may be swivel chairs and their iron
> horses video screens, but they work phenomenally hard and have
> ensured British financial services a pre-eminent role in a global
> growth industry ... The young men and women of the City have
> been the advance guard of Britain's overdue capitalist revolution.
> They have assaulted reaction's strongest citadel and breached its
> walls ...[29]

Assiduously rooting out cant, Jenkins had a point – but in the weeks and months after October 1987, there were no stories reported of hats being passed round for yuppies down on their luck.

The late 1980s and early 1990s were a difficult time for the City. Markets were patchy, trading volumes were chequered, and amidst undeniable overcapacity in the securities industry many well-known City firms were closed down, decimated or stripped of their identity by their new (mostly foreign) owners, who during Big Bang had acquired them in haste and were now repenting at leisure. There was also an unpleasant whiff of recurrent scandal about the City. Both the Guinness scandal (eventually coming to court in 1990) and the Blue Arrow scandal apparently involved heavy City complicity in share-support operations. July 1991 saw the recordbreaking collapse of Bank of Credit and Commerce International (BCCI), with its headquarters at 100 Leadenhall Street. Four months later the sudden death of Robert Maxwell led to a series of invidious revelations about City banks and individuals who had kept the great bully financially afloat. And perhaps most damagingly of all, it was starting to emerge that, in the wake of change in the rules in 1988, there had been mis-selling of personal pensions by the life insurance companies on an appalling scale.

Not surprisingly, the City was no longer quite the fashionable magnet it had been in the mid-1980s. The symptomatic moment came as early as 1989. Shane Longman was the name of the investment bank in *Capital City*, one of ITV's showcase drama series that autumn, and all the by now familiar accoutrements were present and correct: youthful traders in enormous, open-plan, screen-dominated dealing rooms; clocks on the wall showing the times in different financial centres around the world; much talk of swapping securities of all types and provenance ('swap back into Chilean paper … steel plant in Hungary …'); and, most importantly, esoteric, Americanised sandwiches being ordered by phone for lunch.[30] But the mood had changed – the series flopped.

Even before Thatcher fell in November 1990 the conventional wisdom was that she had failed to convert Britain to the enterprise culture. In 1989 the annual edition of *British Social Attitudes* confirmed earlier findings about widespread support for a strong welfare state and adherence to broad notions of social equity.[31] The following spring, of course, the Mass Observation survey was entirely in line. When Britain's most 'conviction' prime minister since Gladstone reluctantly departed for Dulwich, there was on the part of many Tory supporters as well as others a profound sense of moral relief. Even *The Times* reflected that her 'evident distaste' for the welfare state had 'left her vulnerable to the charge of lack of compassion, not caring enough for the losers in society'.[32] By this time the South of England was moving into a protracted recession and negative equity loomed. Flexible labour markets had sounded fine when the economy was booming; job insecurity for oneself was a quite different matter.[33] In that context – the whole Thatcherite deal not only suspect but virtually shot to pieces – Labour *should* have won the April 1992 election. In fact, fear of tax rises and lack of confidence in Kinnock gave John Major a narrow victory. But there remained an emotional bill to be paid for Thatcherism.

Over the next five years, even as the economy and the stock market recovered (in large part thanks to Britain's enforced but fortuitous ejection in September 1992 from the ERM), all the mood music pointed to an eventual, belated act of popular catharsis. The astonishingly charged public reaction to the pit-closure programme announced in October 1992 can only have been an act of remorse for the passive endorsement of Thatcher's humiliation of the miners in the mid-1980s. The media campaign against 'fat cats' in the newly privatised industries – notably the hapless Cedric Brown of British Gas – struck a long, sustained chord. The City also took some flak, as bonuses once again rose sharply, and in January 1997 William Rees-Mogg caused a certain frisson when his column in *The Times* was defiantly headed 'Why Nicola Horlick was underpaid', shortly after Morgan Grenfell had suspended its star fund manager on full pay of about £1 million a year.[34]

There was also one of the publishing phenomena of not just the decade but the century. 'This is a book of political economy' was the unpromising first sentence of the preface to Will Hutton's *The State We're In*, published in January 1995.[35] In over 300 energetically argued and often morally passionate pages, he put the City's failings – and in particular its inadequate servicing of British industry – at the heart of his analysis of what needed to be done to improve what he saw as a generally lamentable state of affairs. His treatise sold a staggering 200,000 or so copies, by far the most for a book of that kind since Keynes's *The Economic Consequences of the Peace* shortly after the First World War. For months it headed the non-fiction bestsellers, ahead of Alan Bennett's *Writing Home*, Nelson Mandela's *Long Walk to Freedom* and even Rosemary Conley's *Complete Flat Stomach Plan*.

What was going on? About the time that Hutton's treatise appeared, Peter York started talking to people in preparation for a book and television series about the 1980s:

> *What emerged was that many of them were in denial ... They didn't want to think about it and they almost didn't want to admit they were there. They'd all heard about 'the greedy decade', about 'selling the family silver' and the victory of hype over substance and they tended to parrot it back at me – and the more educated, media-junkie-ish the more so ...*[36]

Had there ever been such a sharp reaction against an immediately preceding decade or era? It made the attitude of the let-it-all-hang-out 1960s towards the conformist 1950s positively benign by comparison. Certainly it was a repudiation that demanded the skills of a psychologist to explain fully.

We will never know whether this almost atavistic revulsion, including a strong if unspoken sense that 1992 had somehow been the 'wrong' election result, would alone have been enough to produce a Labour victory (let alone a landslide) in 1997 if Tony Blair and Gordon Brown had not created 'New' Labour, which, along with warm words about 'community' and sharing, caring values, stressed economic prudence and no increases in personal direct taxation. Piquantly, and no doubt with deliberate symbolism, it was at a LIFFE lecture at Guildhall that Blair in September 1996 made his most unambiguous pro-business, low-taxation speech prior to the election; while in spring 1997 itself, he went to the Corn Exchange building in Mark Lane on 7 April and spelled out how his party's tectonic plates had shifted: 'We accept, and indeed embrace, the role of free enterprise in the economy. There will be no retreat from any of that.'[37]

By polling day, with opinion polls predicting a Labour landslide, share prices had soared to new heights – a moment of intense irony for the historically minded. Happily, for those who imagined that 2 May 1997 would usher in a kinder, gentler, market-transcending world, there was reassurance during the campaign in a much-publicised news story. It concerned a controversial, widely criticised attempt by the financier Andrew Regan to break up the Co-op, with the particular City twist being that he was being backed by Hambros. Eventually, after a High Court judge had condemned his unscrupulous methods, Hambros (under considerable fire) was forced into a humiliating apology to the Co-op. City grandees grovelling to the Rochdale pioneers ... It made a perfect backdrop to the velvet revolution.

Back to the future

Yet four years later, in spring 2001 on the eve of Labour's landslide re-election, money's stranglehold seemed complete. The personal finance sections in the weekend press got ever fatter, not least in the *Guardian* and the *Observer*. The circulation of the *Financial Times* rose inexorably. Magazines with such titles as *Moneywise, Money Observer, All About Making Money, Money Management* and *Your Money Direct* took up unconscionable space on newsagents' shelves. The BBC had its first-ever full-time business editor (Jeff Randall, former editor of *Sunday Business*). The high-profile exhibition at the Royal Academy, 'The Genius of Rome 1592–1623', was sponsored by an international investment bank, Credit Suisse First Boston. In one of the final scenes of the latest box-office smash,

Bridget Jones's Diary, the eponymous heroine ran down Cornhill chasing her heart-throb, catching up with him just outside the Royal Exchange. The television programme *Who Wants to Be a Millionaire?* not only won the ratings war, but gave Carlton the sort of high-spending audience that advertisers want. Six years after the start of the National Lottery, a Warwick University study suggested that only a windfall of £1 million or more could give a significant boost to psychological well-being.[38] The *Sunday Times* published its annual Rich List, established in 1989 and spawner of many imitators. The curiously innocent face of Nicola Horlick ('A head for figures') stared from posters asking us to invest in the fund she manages. Sonique in her acceptance speech at the Brit Awards (sponsored by MasterCard) thanked her accountant. And, unblushingly, BBC 2 ran a ten-part retro series on Saturday evenings, *I Love the Eighties.*

One thing above all over the previous four years had further tightened money's grip – the internet boom. 'Age of the day trader' proclaimed the *Financial Times* in February 1999, at a time when Wall Street's capitalisation of Yahoo!, the world's leading internet company, had appreciated by 3,800 per cent since 1996, making it worth more than Texaco or Merrill Lynch.[39] But if the dot.com stock market mania started in the US and was largely driven by American firms, by the end of 1999 it had reached Britain with a vengeance. 'The New Klondike' was the apt title of a *Financial Times* series that December, charting how thousands of new individual investors were not only pouring money into anything to do with the apparently all-conquering e-economy, but also using the internet to trade enthusiastically across the market as a whole.[40] Within a few months the value of shares traded online in the UK more than doubled, up from £1.5 billion in the last quarter of 1999 to £3.2 billion in the first quarter of 2000 – a spectacular bubble of excitement climaxing in the much-hyped flotation of lastminute.com.[41] Last minute indeed, as by summer 2000 it became painfully (or deliciously, according to taste) clear that the heady days of the internet boom were over, with many among the first generation of day-traders soon ruing not having got out earlier. Even so, some big fortunes had been made, and the bitter-sweet romance of the stock market had permeated the national consciousness in a way that it seldom had before, arguably not even during the height of privatisation in the mid-1980s.

Of course, the City itself played a full – and almost entirely indiscriminate – part in pushing the internet boom. Moreover, the City generally flourished during these post-1997 years, culminating in the bonus season that began shortly before Christmas 2000. Yet public outrage at this and similar City bonanzas in the late 1990s was strangely muted. There were stories in the press about country pads, Princess yachts, Ferraris and the rest, but on the whole the conspicuous consumption was not quite as ostentatious or self-aggrandising as it had been in the by now mythic yuppie era. It also made a difference that the City had become a much more anonymous, much more professional, much more international place. As the great dynastic names disappeared or became an irrelevance, their replacements – above all the big international investment banks like Morgan Stanley, Goldman Sachs, Merrill Lynch, Deutsche Bank and CSFB – seemed to most people impenetrably remote and beyond criticism.

Inasmuch as there was by the new century a consistent external impression of the City, it was of an important, necessary place where highly qualified people worked incredibly long hours in a harsh, brutally competitive environment, having in effect made a Faustian pact to trade in most of life's normal pleasures (such as watching one's children grow up) in return for a crock of gold. For anyone outside the City who actually knew a stressed-out City high-flyer, pity was as much the predominant emotion as envy. It was a pact, though, that the cream of the nation's youth was more than willing to make. By autumn 2000, of those graduates taking a job straight after Oxford, almost a third became a consultant, banker or accountant in the City.[42] The prospect of becoming a Treasury or Foreign Office mandarin, let alone an academic or teacher, no longer held its old allure. Amidst the dreaming spires as elsewhere, money values – City values – had won the day.

Undeniably the Labour government played its part. Sticking to Lawson's 40 per cent rate for higher earners, not pushing an overtly redistributionist agenda, glorying in its connections with (and use of) City and business 'leaders' – the key signals all pointed in the same direction. Yet the deeper truth was that the 1997 landslide had performed its cathartic task and that in the largely benign, mainly bull-market economic climate of Labour's first term the protracted emotional spasm against the 'greedy 1980s' was at last exhausted. By 2001 the City, once the principal focus of that reaction, was the clear beneficiary. Almost a century and a quarter earlier a Victorian politician had famously declared that 'we are all socialists now'. But *now* – with our ISAs, our baby bonds, our stakeholder pensions and our income-generating investment portfolios – we are all capitalists, otherwise known as 'high net worth individuals' (actual or would-be). The psychic shift ushered in by Thatcher has virtually become a preordained, taken-for-granted feature of the landscape. Guilt about money is little more than a quaint memory from a repressed age. This may or may not be a good thing, but at least we have shed our oldest vice: hypocrisy.

4

Getting and Spending

M ichael von Clemm had a problem. The London head of Credit Suisse First Boston was fed up with paying a king's ransom for City offices that were woefully below American standards and poorly suited to the needs of a modern investment bank. For five years he had been trying to get a new front-office location in the City, but had been stymied by unsuitable sites and restrictive planning regulations.

One day in February 1985 he paid a visit to the Isle of Dogs looking for a site for a packaging plant for the Roux Brothers' restaurant chain, of which he was a director. Although the Isle of Dogs was only three miles from the City, it might well have been on a different planet. There was acre upon acre of abandoned quayside, derelict railway tracks, desolate buildings and dank canals. But there were also some spanking new office buildings – built to take advantage of the subsidies and tax breaks provided by the London Docklands Development Corporation that had been created by Margaret Thatcher's government in 1981 to regenerate docklands.

From the barge where he was eating lunch, von Clemm spotted a disused banana warehouse on Canary Wharf and began to toy with a different idea. Why not convert the warehouse into a back office for Credit Suisse First Boston, saving some of that expensive City rental? Von Clemm pitched his idea to Ware Travelstead, a US property developer who advised First Boston on its real-estate investments. Aware of von Clemm's quest for new offices, Travelstead turned von Clemm's suggestion on its head. How about the Isle of Dogs as a front-office location, he asked, a state-of-the-art solution to the bank's accommodation problem?

'The question was breathtaking in its audacity, suggesting a 180-degree reversal of London's pattern of development,' Vanessa Houlder would reflect in the *Financial Times*. 'For generations, any institution with wealth or influence has gravitated towards the west of London, while the east has been associated with poverty, dockyards and sweatshops ...'[1]

From bricks and mortar to concrete and glass

By the time of the Great Fire of 1666, London was the largest city and commercial centre in the world, and settlement had spilled way beyond the City walls. That conflagration torched almost two-thirds of the Square Mile, some 437 acres, but within five years the City had been rebuilt, this time in brick, not wood, to avoid another fire, with Christopher Wren's St Paul's Cathedral as a lasting monument to its regeneration.

Banks, offices and warehouses supplanted residential premises in the Square Mile in the nineteenth and early twentieth centuries. By the outbreak of the Second World War, the resident population had dwindled to a few thousand while the so-called 'day population' of commuters numbered around 350,000. Then German bombing in 1940–41 flattened 225 acres, reducing a third of the City to ruins. Reconstruction was considerably slower than after the Great Fire, owing to government planning controls that prioritised the allocation of building materials to public housing, and it was not until the mid-1950s that it got under way in earnest. Prominent new buildings included Bracken House, built for the *Financial Times* and later acquired by Daiwa Securities; New Change, overflow accommodation opposite St Paul's for the Bank of England; and Bucklersbury House, a drab slab that would not have looked out of place in the Soviet Union.

The 1960s saw a great property boom in London and other UK cities. In the City, the most visionary project was the City Corporation's Barbican development of housing and cultural facilities. Much less distinguished were the cheap and nasty blocks run up along London Wall and the Paternoster Square development around St Paul's. The decade also witnessed the arrival of the high-rise office, with soaring towers being built for British Petroleum, P & O, Commercial Union and the Stock Exchange. And finally, there was the go-ahead for a fully fledged skyscraper – the NatWest Tower off Bishopsgate, built 1970–81 – Britain's then tallest building.

The economic downturn of the mid-1970s led to a lull in City redevelopment, though the replacement of riverside warehouses with office buildings along Lower Thames Street proceeded. The 1970s also saw a conservationist backlash against the destructive vandalism of some 1960s developments and against banal system-built block houses, such as Bucklersbury House and along London Wall. The City Corporation's conservationist-leaning Draft Local Plan of November 1984 responded to these sentiments, extending the protection of the City's architectural heritage.

By this time the transformation of investment banking in London along Wall Street lines – from 1983 onwards – required a new type of bank building. Firstly, it had to be big enough to accommodate open-plan trading floors of 10,000 square feet or more, such wide-open spaces being the factory floors of a modern investment bank. And, secondly, there had to be enough free space between floors to accommodate the thousands of miles of wiring required to support the electronic trading and information platforms at which people worked. Few existing City buildings met these requirements, which meant either building anew or gutting an old building. But the City's planning regulations and its narrow Victorian frontages obstructed both courses of action. Which was why Michael von Clemm had a problem.

Yet a number of schemes did get planning approval. Several City landmarks were converted into trading-floor accommodation, notably Billingsgate (the former fish-market), the vacated City of London School, the *Daily Express* building, the General Post Office and the *Financial Times* building, the newspaper itself moving across the river to the southern end of Southwark Bridge. The most notable new development was Broadgate, the largest building project in the Square Mile since the Great Fire, on the site of Broad Street Station which was demolished in 1985. Besides offices, Broadgate had shops, restaurants and an amphitheatre skating rink, reminiscent of New York's Rockefeller Center; it soon filled up with blue-chip tenants, including Warburgs, Lehman Brothers, Security Pacific and Lloyds Merchant Bank. Other financial firms looked further afield for suitable accommodation. Paribas moved to the West End, Price Waterhouse was already in the new London Bridge City development and Salomon Brothers relocated to Victoria. The diaspora of the international financial services industry beyond the Square Mile was under way.

Canary Wharf

It was Canary Wharf that became the most important new location. The process began in summer 1985, when Michael von Clemm put together a consortium, comprising Credit Suisse First Boston, First Boston Real Estate and Morgan Stanley, with Ware Travelstead acting as the developer. They drew up an ambitious plan for the largest real-estate development in Western Europe, comprising 8.5 million square feet of office space on a 71-acre site. The unveiling of the Canary Wharf scheme, coupled with Salomons' proposed decampment to Victoria, prompted a volte-face on the part of the City Corporation. In March 1986 it announced new planning guidelines that would allow the building of 20 million square feet of new office space in the Square Mile. But Canary Wharf already had wind in its sails.

Realising that the project was out of his league, Travelstead sold his interest in it to Canadian property developer Olympia & York, the family business of the Reichmann brothers. The sons of Jewish refugees from Central Europe, the three brothers had entered the property business in suburban Toronto in the 1950s. Their first major prestige project was First Canadian Place in downtown Toronto, completed in 1975, the tallest building in Canada. Moving into New York, they built the landmark twin-tower World Financial Center that opened in 1985. By then Olympia & York, headed by Paul Reichmann, had become the world's foremost commercial property company and was estimated to be worth more than New Zealand.[2]

Reichmann had been interested in the Canary Wharf scheme since autumn 1986, when he had heard about it from Charles Young, formerly president of Citibank Canada, who had been transferred to London. So he did some personal research: 'I had meetings with twenty-nine business leaders in London to see if such a project made sense. I did not ask them if they would move to Canary Wharf. The answer would have been no. My main question was: "Are you happy with your operating premises or do you see the need to do something dramatic?" What I detected was the great majority were very unhappy with their premises but their attitude was that they had no choice.'[3]

Next, Reichmann quizzed a variety of banker friends as to whether London would continue to be Europe's premier financial capital. 'They said that they would not consider putting their European headquarters anywhere else, since even the most left-wing government in the UK had always been more beneficial to the financial services industry than the most right-wing in the US.'[4] With these reassurances, Reichmann was delighted to take over the project in July 1987, when Travelstead bailed out.

Other considerations also counted in Canary Wharf's favour. There was political support from Prime Minister Thatcher, for whom the project provided another showcase demonstrating the dynamism of the private sector over the dead hand of government. Paradoxically, handouts by that same dead hand – public money amounting to £1.3 billion – also helped. Reichmann responded robustly to criticism of the taxpayer subsidies: 'Without an enterprise zone allowance Canary Wharf would not have developed. It would still be some second- or third-rate development. The benefits were given for the whole area. At the time my company invested £2 billion, it would not have been possible without the tax policy.'[5]

Margaret Thatcher herself, wearing a hard-hat and a smile, officially initiated the project with a pile-driver in May 1988. By then the project had become even bigger and more ambitious than Travelstead's scheme. It would now comprise forty buildings containing 10 million square feet of state-of-the-art office space, 500,000 square feet of retail, restaurant and leisure space, and 425,000 square feet of residential accommodation. It was to be built in three phases over a decade.

Phase One would comprise nine buildings with 4.5 million square feet of floor space. The centrepiece, One Canada Square, was to be an 800-foot high, fifty-storey tower, the tallest building in the UK. It would have the form of an obelisk and at the top there would be a pyramid roof lit from within. It would be clad in a semi-matte stainless steel skin so that it glowed like an ember at sunrise and sunset.

From the outset, Canary Wharf's Achilles heel was transport – the roads choked and rail non-existent. From 1987 access was provided by the Docklands Light Railway, initially from Tower Hill and in 1991 from Bank. There was also a river boat service, but it was unprofitable and folded in 1993. Nearby, London City Airport opened in 1987, giving access to continental cities if passengers could reach the airport. Construction of the Limehouse Link got under way in 1989 – at £4,586 per inch, the most costly road in Britain. But it did not open until May 1993, almost two years after the arrival of the first tenants at One Canada Square.

The real solution to Canary Wharf's transport problem was the extension of London Underground's Jubilee Line to docklands. But, before committing public funds, the government demanded substantial contributions from the private sector companies whose real estate holdings would benefit from the transport improvements. There was nothing wrong with that in principle – the problem was that Olympia & York was unable to come up with the £500 million which was its end of the deal. Consequently the Jubilee Line extension stalled.

One Canada Square was ready for occupation in August 1991, only three years after the ground-breaking ceremony, a remarkable feat of engineering and project management. The first occupant, State Street Bank, was followed by Credit Suisse First Boston, Morgan Stanley and others, and soon the working population numbered 7,000. However, overall occupancy was only 55 per cent in 1991 and 1992, other firms being reluctant to relocate to what was widely regarded as an inaccessible backwater. Since much of the building was on a speculative basis without tenancy agreements, the financial strain fell on Olympia & York. Buffeted by simultaneous property slumps in London, New York and Toronto, brought about by the recession of the early 1990s, Olympia & York collapsed in May 1992.

Canary Wharf fell into the hands of eleven banks, headed by Lloyds, to which it owed £576 million. They installed Sir Peter Levene, formerly head of procurement at the Ministry of Defence, to run the show. Levene proved adept at attracting new tenants, including the Mirror and Independent newspaper groups, the European Medicines Evaluation Agency (the first European Union body to be based in the UK), and the Personal Investment Authority, a City regulator. Then in 1995 he pulled off a real coup – BZW announced that it was quitting the City for Canary Wharf, the first prestigious British bank to do so. But some of BZW's staff were far from happy at the prospect of working in docklands. 'Horror' was his first thought, recalls Mike Dyson, head of bond trading. The second was: 'Call the headhunters.'[6]

The planned defection of BZW alarmed the City Corporation. It was known that at least six large banks were looking for 'vast new offices', threatening a glut of City commercial property if they followed BZW's example. 'We can't compete on cost with Canary Wharf,' said Michael Cassidy, chairman of the Corporation's Policy and Resources Committee, who complained about Canary Wharf's 'poaching' of City institutions, 'but we have quality of environment, proximity to all the key players and transport access, particularly to Heathrow. And you can walk from meeting to meeting in the City – Canary Wharf has still some way to go.'[7]

Later in 1995, hard on the heels of the news about BZW, came the announcement that the eleven banks had accepted an offer from a consortium to buy Canary Wharf for £800 million. The consortium, which included Prince al-Waleed bin Talal bin Abdulaziz of Saudi Arabia and US media mogul Larry Tisch, was led by none other than Paul Reichmann, who thereby reassumed control of the project in which he had never lost faith.

Yet majority opinion remained sceptical. Over three years later, in March 1999 at the time of Canary Wharf's flotation on the London Stock Exchange, Norma Cohen, property editor of the *Financial Times*, noted that 'almost the only supporters were analysts at investment banks connected with the float who, perhaps coincidentally, were based at Canary Wharf'.[8] 'As a monument to non-intervention by government, it will always raise a laugh, and to the headhunters trying to lure expensive bankers down the river, it will always be a handicap,' wrote Christopher Fildes of the *Daily Telegraph*. 'In property, proverbially, only three things matter – location, location and location – and Canary Wharf has none of them. I would tow it out to sea and sink it.'[9]

But the doubters were mistaken. The expansion of investment banking in London in the second half of the 1990s led to a 'space crunch' with soaring commercial rents.[10] In November 1997, by when Canary Wharf's working population had reached 21,000, Reichmann announced the start of Phase Two, to take the project to an eventual 14 million square feet of office space. The decision of the Financial Services Authority, the new consolidated regulatory body, to locate in Canary Wharf was another feather in Reichmann's cap: 'second best to the Bank of England', as he put it.[11] Even more significant were the decisions by Citigroup and HSBC to move to custom-built towers adjacent to One Canada Square, each accommodating 8,000. Subsequently, US banks Lehman Brothers and Northern Trust, and law firms Clifford Chance, Allen & Overy and Skadden Arpos Slate Moagher & Flom LLP, announced that they would be joining them. Then Barclays Bank announced that it too was decamping to Canary Wharf, quitting Lombard Street after 300 years.

One reason common to many of these decisions to re-locate to large new buildings at Canary Wharf was the desire of banks to concentrate their staff in a single location. Underlying mergers and consolidation in the banking, accounting and legal industries is a vital factor, says Canary Wharf chief executive George Iacobescu: 'We are successful because we are helping large companies in their consolidations'.[12]

The completion of the Jubilee Line extension in 2000 – at a cost of £3.4 billion – helped too. At last there was a mass transit system capable of moving people on an adequate scale, and the West End was only 15 minutes away. Improved access and critical mass were transforming it from a remote satellite to an attractive location in its own right. It even had its own glossy 'courtesy magazine', *Canary*, published by the estate's owners jointly with Condé Nast, and an independently produced free weekly newspaper, *The Wharf*.

With the completion of the HSBC and Citibank towers and other developments, 42,000 people are now working at the 86-acre Canary Wharf estate. According to Norma Cohen, this makes it 'arguably the equal of the City of London in claiming to be at the heart of Britain's financial capital'.[13] However, new developments in other parts of town are competing hard for tenants. In the City there is the 1.1 million square feet redevelopment of Paternoster Square and the proposed Heron, Swiss Re and St. Botolph towers. Then there is the monumental development at Paddington Basin, comprising 8 million square feet of offices and flats. 'It is not as big as Canary Wharf, but it is better located,' says a bullish City property analyst. 'It is on the fringes of the West End, a short walk to Hyde Park, and the Heathrow Express means it is now just 15 minutes from an airport. If you were an American executive constantly crossing the Atlantic, where would you rather be?'[14] On the other hand, Canary Wharf has become very popular with its denizens. 'It's clean, it's safe, it's secure,' is how convert Mike Dyson of Barclays Capital now sees it. 'And with the Jubilee Line, it's easy to get to.'[15] Yet after the attack on the twin towers on September 11, such brashly iconic buildings do not convey as secure an aura as they used to.

The significance of the rise of Canary Wharf to London and Londoners was twofold. Firstly, it spearheaded the regeneration of a vast derelict wasteland in the east of the city. The investment in infrastructure that stemmed from its creation has had positive effects upon a great swathe of a neglected part of the metropolis. Secondly, at a crucial moment when the major US investment banks were expanding abroad and the international financial services industry was consolidating, Canary Wharf was able to provide the state-of-the-art accommodation they needed, or held out the prospect of being able to do so. 'If it had not been for Canary Wharf,' claims Iacobescu, 'the City could have lost a lot of financial institutions.'[16] And that would have cost thousands of high-paid jobs, casting a shadow across the whole London economy.

Bonusville UK

The City's well-remunerated workforce is plainly a significant factor in the capital's economy. How significant? Our estimate of the total wages and salaries of London's money-centre workforce of 335,000 people in the year 2000, taking account of a variety of evidence, is £11.5 billion in wages and salaries, plus £1.5 billion in bonuses, making total earnings of £13 billion.[17]

What about the earnings of individual City workers? The international investment banks, the dynamo of today's City, have a US-style five-tier hierarchy amongst the banking professionals. Graduate recruits, generally known as analysts, are paid significantly more than most college-leavers, though the hours are longer too. After a few years' practical experience and the acquisition of an MBA at business school, a successful analyst, generally in his or her mid-twenties, is promoted to associate. As associates become more adept at contributing to the bank's bottom line, their pay rises sharply. A smart associate with a couple of years' experience at that level, who may still be under thirty, could be taking home £200,000 – nine times the average British wage of £22,700.

The next step, probably in the early thirties for those who make the grade, is vice-president. A vice-president has more responsibility and will often have analysts and associates working for him. The 'v-ps' are sometimes known as 'marzipans', lying between the suet of regular employees and the icing of top management. Depending on ability and length of experience, a successful thirty-something vice-president in an investment bank might be earning as much as £300,000 plus.

Salesmen, who market the bank's products, and traders, who buy and sell in the market on behalf of clients or their own bank, are paid performance-related commissions. Their earnings may well exceed those of their bosses, depending on how much they bring in. Junior traders can expect to take home 10 per cent of the revenues they generate, which might mean £500,000 on earnings of £5 million. Senior traders can command up to 20 per cent of the money they make for the firm, and their earnings will be much, much higher. 'I took home £10 million last year,' says one of them. 'But I'm worth every penny.'[18]

Promotion to the rank of senior vice-president (the equivalent of director or departmental head) brings the assumption of managerial responsibility for some aspect of the bank's operations. At this level a salary of £200,000 or more might be expected. But actual take-home pay would usually be substantially higher because of the bonus, the level of which varies substantially from job to job and from year to year. Generally, the top firms pay better than those further down the league table.

At the top of the organisation are the managing directors, the so-called 'rainmakers', who earn most because they bring in the business. These masters of the universe – and almost all are men – tend to be in their forties or maybe their fifties, with twenty or thirty years' experience under their belt. The highest-paid are a handful of managing directors at the top of firms, such as Goldman Sachs or Morgan Stanley, in hot sectors like mergers and acquisitions, who command at least £5 million a year. On the other hand a recently promoted managing director, working for a third-rank bank in an out-of-favour sector, might have to make do with £650,000.

The bonus system is considerably more widespread in the City than in most other UK business sectors, though the practice seems to be spreading – another example of City behaviour influencing the wider community. 'The bonus round in an investment bank is the crucial time of year,' comments former investment banker Philip Augar. 'Get it wrong and the firm unravels, pay too much and profitability is shot to ribbons.'[19] In some firms the whole staff receives a bonus; overall 70 per cent of City workers are included in bonus schemes, though most of them receive only a token amount. 'Everyone in the company gets 25 per cent of their annual salary as a Christmas bonus, even the cleaners,' a twenty-nine-year-old settlements clerk at NatWest Markets told the *Evening Standard*. 'I think it's a clever ploy because it does keep you going, especially through the autumn when you've had your summer holiday and there's not much to look forward to. It makes you work harder.'[20]

The payment of a modest Christmas bonus is a long-standing paternalistic City practice. In 1980 bonuses in UK banks and merchant banks were around 3 or 4 per cent of salary and sometimes even took the Dickensian form of a turkey or food hamper.[21] Performance-related bonuses were a feature of the remuneration package at Stock Exchange firms, and one reason for the increase in the bonus dimension of City remuneration was the acquisition of firms of brokers and jobbers by the banks in Big Bang. Even more important from the mid-1980s was the competition for staff from US banks, where bonuses formed a much greater part of remuneration. Substantial bonuses were paid in the boom years 1986 and 1987, but payouts were smaller in the doldrums years of the late 1980s and early 1990s. By 1992 bonuses at investment banks and in fund management averaged 25 per cent of remuneration, though only 8 per cent at commercial banks.

During the 1990s the bonus dimension of City remuneration increased by leaps and bounds – payouts several times annual salary became commonplace. The rise of big bonuses began in 1993, when the US investment banks really began to motor. That year more than 100 top partners at the London offices of Goldman Sachs were paid year-end bonuses of more than $1 million each. In 1996, the next bumper year, City bonuses totalled £750 million. At the end of that bonus round a City headhunter reckoned that there were at least 1,000 dollar millionaires working in the City – double the number four years earlier. Another headline statistic of the day was that half of the 150,000 people in Britain earning £100,000 or more a year worked in financial services.[22] But the largesse of City firms was having a perverse effect on employee morale, engendering greed and footloose opportunism, not gratitude. Taken aback by the lack of loyalty to his firm, a senior banker caustically observed that the large payments to staff only 'increases their already considerable vanity, and encourages them to think they are more valuable than the organisation'.[23]

A much remarked-upon development of the 1996 bonus round was that classic oxymoron – the 'guaranteed bonus' – as a device for poaching staff from other firms or retaining key individuals. A future bonus guaranteed for a year, a form of signing-on present, was not uncommon before, but the scale of the phenomenon was unprecedented as firms scrambled to hire or lock-in the star players. It was a recruitment spree by Deutsche Bank's investment banking arm, then called Deutsche Morgan Grenfell, that was generally held responsible for the proliferation of the guaranteed bonus. 'Deutsche are openly boasting that they can take out who they like,' said a prominent investment banker at the time. 'The salaries they are paying can be at least two or three times what people were earning before. Their strategy is that rather than go out and buy a bank they will pay whatever it takes to pick up another's top team. In practice, we are having to promise our big hitters that if they stay with us they will earn much more than they would if Deutsche had not been nosing around.'[24]

In theory the bonus system provides City firms with a flexible cost base that allows them to weather the ups and downs of a cyclical revenue stream without having to undermine their effectiveness by laying off staff. This makes sense for the firm, but it has the effect of transferring operating risk from the shareholders to the staff. Employees tend to prefer a predictable

income, and the guaranteed bonus is a device for batting the risk back to
the boss. In the tight labour market of the late 1990s many star performers
were able to win such guarantees from their employers. This shift towards
a less flexible cost base in the boom years of the late 1990s portended problems when the downturn eventually arrived. It was a spectre looming particularly for the second-tier investment banks that had been aggressively
hiring to build their businesses. 'As a rule of thumb,' observes banking
sector analyst Kinner Lakhani of Morgan Stanley, 'two-thirds of a strong
franchise's personnel cost base is variable and one-third not. For weaker
franchises the reverse is true.'[25]

City bonus payments hit the £1 billion jackpot for the first time in 1997.
Besides being a good year for the financial services industry, it saw a vigorous recruitment drive by a number of European banks, such as Deutsche
Bank and UBS. 'Everybody is trying to reposition their business, and they
are gazumping each other for staff,' said Bernhard Meyer of headhunters
A. T. Kearney.[26] 'Our employees are a commodity,' was the no-nonsense
view of the managing director of an American bank. 'We simply look at
what headhunters have recently been offering for employees with particular talents, and then we offer them a little more if we want them to stay.'[27]
By 1997 the annual City bonus round had assumed its own ritualistic form:
'Salomons and Goldman Sachs pay in December,' a headhunter explained,
'Lehmans in January. Then the rest in March and April. Rothschilds brings
up the rear in June.'[28]

The unprecedented largesse of the 1996 and 1997 bonus rounds made
some people in the City a touch uneasy about the size of their pay packages. 'I do sometimes sit down and think "Can this be right?"' mused an
investment banking millionaire. 'My answer is that it is not wrong.'[29]

In January 1998 a debate was held at the Mansion House on the motion
'This house believes that City salaries are totally fair and justified'. The
event, which was organised by the Futures and Options Association in
conjunction with Reuters, was attended, reported the *Evening Standard*, by
'over 200 top City folk – of which two-thirds claimed to earn more than
£100,000 (with a third saying they earn in excess of £200,000)'.[30] Proposing the motion, George Cox, a director of LIFFE, argued not only that
antipathy towards City pay packages was based on 'resentment and envy',
but that 'if you cut City remuneration tomorrow there will be less available
for society at large and we would all be the poorer as a result'.

Speaking against the motion, Andrew Winckler, former chief executive of the Securities and Investment Board, declared that the Square Mile had become 'smug and complacent' about salaries and bonuses. 'The current bonus system encourages a degree of speculation that is not warranted and is rewarding failure,' he maintained. The audience agreed with him and the motion was defeated by 52 to 45 per cent, with the rest undecided. The house then voted on a second, supplementary motion: 'Bonus payments: fair reward or dangerous incentive?' This produced a clear expression of disquiet about big bonuses, 55 per cent voting that the bonus system was dangerous and only 40 per cent that it was fair.

The big City bonus payouts of 1996 and 1997 prompted speculation as to whether something more fundamental than a market cycle was afoot in the financial services industry. One proposition was that with the break-down in national boundaries to investment, the big European and US investment banks had started to compete with each other on a global basis. This had created a single elite labour market, and London pay was catching up with Wall Street pay levels and US remuneration practices.

Special factors were identified to explain the soaring remuneration of particular jobs, notably derivatives traders and corporate financiers. As financial markets had become increasingly complex, and banks were risking larger amounts of their own capital to boost earnings, highly skilled traders had become more profitable and hence valuable. But individuals with appropriate mathematical qualifications and skills to develop strategies to use financial derivatives to exploit tiny market anomalies were in short supply, so their price had risen. So had the premium on the very brightest corporate financiers, whose innovative proposals could win mandates that made a huge difference to an investment bank's earnings. This was because greater competition amongst banks allowed corporate clients to be more picky. 'The merchant banks used to have cartels and franchises, and they had to be very bad to be fired,' recalled the head of a London bank wistfully. 'These days, companies will take ideas from anywhere.'[31]

The East Asia financial crisis, the Russian default and the near-collapse of Long-Term Capital Management, cast a pall over the financial services sector in 1998. Some firms, notably Merrill Lynch, laid off thousands of staff. The gloomy outlook and a downturn in profits led to a fall in bonus payouts, which tumbled to £600 million in 1998. The 'deferred bonus', in which part of the entitlement is held back for payment in several years' time provided that an employee is still with the firm, returned to fashion.

However, firms were unwilling to be too tough on their star performers. 'Bonuses have nothing to do with outside political considerations, or even the bank's profit performance,' a senior manager at an American bank had explained even before the downturn. 'If you really paid the people who have the relationships on the basis of how well the bank had done, you'd lose them in a bad year.'[32]

His grin-and-bear-it stoicism was soon vindicated by 1999's bull market and takeover boom. That year generated record bonus payments totalling well in excess of £1 billion, some estimates pitching them towards £1.5 billion. 'Banks have had a staggeringly good year and people will be taking it home in their pay packets,' declared a corporate financier at one of the big five accountancy firms.[33] A new factor pushing the level of bonuses northwards in 1999 was desperation on the part of the investment banks to staunch the defection of staff to the booming dot.com sector, where share option schemes appeared to offer the prospect of making a fortune overnight. 'Our industry used to be thought of as a place to get rich quick,' lamented a less than gruntled investment banker, 'but the real money is being made by the internet entrepreneurs.'[34]

In the US, where the dot.com Klondike began and went furthest, investment banks experienced an exodus of staff; senior vice-presidents complained about having to spend 40 per cent of their time dealing with recruitment rather than contributing to the bottom line (and their own bonus).[35] A variety of schemes was devised to tie-in personnel. For instance, Goldman Sachs awarded 2 million shares to junior staff, while Donaldson, Lufkin & Jenrette introduced two-year pay deals (including a guaranteed bonus). Another concession was a relaxation of the office dress code, the banker's dark suit being discarded for dress-down smart-casual – as at the hip dot.coms.

As two years earlier, the record level of bonuses in 1999 resulted in a certain amount of masochistic hand-wringing on the part of some members of the industry. 'I know how this looks to anyone who has not got their snout in the trough,' a sheepish senior investment banker protested to the *Independent*. 'But in this business you have to make the most of it while you can. Some time in the next two years there is going to be a downturn and everyone knows it cannot last.'[36]

But the good times were not over yet. Thanks to booming markets and an unprecedented level of global mergers and acquisitions, the millennium year saw yet another record bonus round totalling in excess of

£1.5 billion. Tim Smith of headhunters Michael Page City boasted that it had been 'a seriously good year'.[37] 'The overall bonus results mean that the financial districts of London and New York are awash with money,' commented veteran City-watcher Ian Kerr:

> Even if being a sterling millionaire isn't what it used to be and dollar millionaires on Wall Street are considered to be just above the poverty line, there are hundreds of new members of these once-exclusive clubs.
>
> A real divide has been created between the financial services business and manufacturing industry and other commercial sectors. The City is a gold mine but when I am harangued about the 'totally unjustifiable discrepancies', I point out that the City and Wall Street are not a closed shop. You just have to be very good to get in. Then, with hard work and luck, you might become rich.
>
> Don't expect life to be a bed of roses along the way. If every employee in the international capital markets, including support staff, were honest, I would estimate that 25 per cent don't particularly like their jobs and that 10–15 per cent actually hate them. When placed under the microscope, it isn't a very nice industry because financial ambition is a far more important consideration than making friends.[38]

Job uncertainty and the toll upon personal life are perennial refrains of practitioners and their wives. 'There are more people at the top of the tree being paid enormous sums,' says a senior banker, 'and more people getting fired.'[39] 'People may be paid a huge amount, but the risks are high,' explains a manager at a US investment bank. 'If you do not perform, or your department stops making money, you can lose your job quickly.'[40] 'It's been a good year and I hope to be getting a £1 million bonus,' says a thirty-year-old Credit Suisse equities expert. 'There is a downside to this. I often work seven days a week from 7 a.m. to 7 p.m. The bonuses are not always this good and everyone is aware they might be out of a job next year.'[41]

Others draw attention to the way investment banks use money as a substitute for more subtle forms of management. 'Money is the only true measure of performance, the only way that investment banks express their gratitude,' according to an investment banker. 'They are not well-managed businesses, and they do not know any other way to please people than by giving them more money.'[42] 'It is hard work,' a corporate financier at a US investment bank comments, 'not because of the content, but because it is so relentless, and there tends to be a lot of squabbling.'[43] Perhaps this whingeing will cease now that City high-flyers can pour out their hearts at the The Priory Clinic's spanking-new City branch, Keats House.

Naturally, he who pays the piper calls the tune. 'If we're paying people £500,000 or £1 million a year,' snarls a senior banker, 'we own them. They're on call all day, all through the year, weekends included. Holidays, marriages, children must all come second to the needs of our clients.'[44] An investment banker's wife, Chantal Clarendon, is keen to 'set the record straight':

> *Investment bankers do not socialise, they cancel. The wives who organise dinner parties end up hosting them on their own …*
> *Holidays are a taboo subject for bankers' wives! They spend them alone: literally or metaphorically. Bankers spend the whole time on the phone and e-mail, if they're not called back to the office … investment bankers have little or no control of their lives. Their clients are paying for their services and they don't care whether or not a holiday was scheduled …*
>
> *To the outsider the investment banker's wife has it made: she doesn't have to work, she can hire a nanny and a cleaner, she can send her children to private schools and take expensive holidays. Even those wives whose husbands commute between New York and London know better than to whinge in front of non-bankers. As soon as money enters into the equation, all sympathy disappears …*
>
> *Wall Street and the City are not places for sensitive souls. They're battlefields, except the soldiers aren't fighting for freedom or land, they're fighting for deals. And in every war, it's the non-combatants who suffer most.*[45]

Although most people in the City receive some sort of bonus payment, the bulk of the money goes to a few thousand senior or best-performing staff. Since the disclosure of earnings is 'virtually a sackable offence' in the City, there is no hard data on the distribution of the larger payouts, but City headhunters have a feel for what is going on.[46] One such estimate for the 1999 bonus round was that 15,000 individuals got more than £100,000, amongst whom 500 received more than £1 million, and a handful even £5 million.[47] For the 2000 bonus round, an estimate was that 6,000 City workers got at least £250,000, of whom perhaps 2,000 received £1 million or more.[48]

The bonuses paid to individuals are usually highly confidential, but one case that hit the press in the 2000 bonus round was that of Brian Winterflood. A director of Close Brothers, a niche UK investment bank, he received a £3,160,000 bonus as a top-up to his salary of £290,000. 'We are thorough capitalists here,' comments the firm's pugnacious chief executive, Rod Kent. 'If you make a lot of profit, you make a lot of money.'[49]

Over at Morgan Stanley, people were also making a lot of money: it was announced that fifty London staff would be receiving payouts of £1 million each. 'The junior analysts get bonuses of up to £50,000, the traders up to £200,000 and the best-performing directors more than £4 million,' a high-spirited employee explained indiscreetly to a *Sunday Times* journalist in a Canary Wharf wine bar. 'They will spend it on property, travel and their social life – in that order.'[50]

How to spend it

Across the European Union, inner London has the highest per capita GDP of any urban region. Although the media, fashion and technology sectors are major wealth generators, the City is the single most important contributor to London's prosperity. High salaries and big bonuses make City workers – one in twelve of London's labour force – a powerful factor in the London economy – and beyond. Their spending power has been a significant force in London's boom since the 1990s.

At the top end of the London housing market, City bonuses are the oxygen that fuels prices. The 1990s saw the development of an annual price surge at bonus time, vendors being advised to put their properties on the market in January to catch the rush. Property consultants FPDSavills estimate that house prices in prime neighbourhoods such as Kensington and Chelsea rose by 20 per cent in early 1994 after record payouts in the 1993 bonus round.

According to FPDSavills, 40 per cent of buyers of prime central London properties have City jobs. Some areas are particularly sought after: the Notting Hill office of estate agent Knight Frank reports that 70–80 per cent of transactions are for City clients; and Foxtons in Chelsea say that 70 per cent of clients are bankers.

What type of property do the City high-rollers go for? Flats and houses in London's best districts – Belgravia, Chelsea, Holland Park, Kensington, Knightsbridge and Notting Hill – are the most sought after, and family houses in Fulham, Wandsworth and Hampstead. Financial sector buyers are prominent in the prime areas of docklands, close to Canary Wharf and the City. Penthouses, especially those with river views, are a favourite with single buyers who are seeking a cutting-edge lifestyle statement. 'Cash-rich and time-poor, these buyers are generally looking for places which don't need any work,' says James Wyall of Knight Frank.[51]

Out of London, the preferred counties for those wishing to acquire a £1 million plus mansion are Gloucestershire, Oxfordshire, Wiltshire, Berkshire and Hampshire. 'Most corporate financiers,' says an investment banker, 'dream of owning a huge house in the country and spending their days negotiating with English Heritage for renovation grants.'[52] But they have a problem – there just are not enough sellers of really expensive grand old houses.

Who are the purchasers of £1 million plus properties in London and the Home Counties? 'They're young, British and definitely "new money"', according to David Moulton, head of research at Knight Frank. He estimates that 62 per cent are in banking or business, while 10 per cent are highly paid City lawyers. Nearly a third of buyers are under forty: 'The number under forty is growing all the time. We may need to start an under-twenty category soon,' Moulton jokes. 'There is a whole generation unlike anything which has gone before,' says Michael Conign of the Wandsworth offices of estate agents John D. Wood, 'who have made a lot of money in just fifteen years and whose whole lifestyle is subsidised by their employer. All we can do is look on in awe.'[53]

Many foreign nationals who work in the City live in rented flats and houses. In central London's prime rental sector, more than four-fifths of tenants are from overseas and a high proportion work in the financial services sector.[54] Even more than in the purchase market, it is demand from City banks and bankers that underpins prices at the top end of London's residential rental market.

After expensive real estate come luxury holidays. 'South African safaris are particularly popular at the moment,' trills Vanessa Jones at World Wide Journeys. 'It's our most popular destination for an active holiday. Flights, a three-night stop in Cape Town and a stay at the Shamwouri Game Reserve comes to £13,000.'[55] '25 Ways to Blow Your Bonus in Style,' trumpeted the travel supplement that accompanied the *Evening Standard* of 30 March 2001 – by a rich irony, the day there appeared the DTI report into the Maxwell scandal, a testament to the myopic, bonus-chasing greed of a previous City generation. The untroubled sales pitch had 'sophisticated City folk' in its sights:

> *If money were no object, where in the world would you go? With an atlas in one hand, a passport in the other, would you opt for all-action adventure, a sporting challenge or a five-star beach and sun-tan?*
>
> *Would you swap the trading floor for your own Boeing 737 and take a few chosen friends to see the tigers of Nepal and palaces of Rajasthan? Or leave the laptop behind and board the Great South Pacific Express to the heart of Australia? Slice through Antarctic ice floes, or stretch out on a lounger and let a warm ocean wash away the stresses of work?*
>
> *We are talking Dream Holidays here. Not a short break snatched between deals or a last-minute dash for the sun. This is major-league luxury. Far flung places to relax and celebrate that bonus paycheque in style. Top-drawer destinations for sophisticated City folk who work hard, and deserve to relax hard too.*
>
> *So dig out the sun glasses, order the travellers cheques and cancel the milk … Your Great Escape from the Square Mile starts here.*

Top of the range, at £14,748 per person, was a tour of the Orient: 'Forget airline timetables, and the FTSE, when you board your own private jet … for a 15-night exploration of the East … searching for tigers and temples.' More modestly priced, at £1,829 a head, was a sojourn at a Balinese hilltop resort situated 'seductively far from Bull or Bear markets'. Or at £1,533 each, a cruise off the coast of Alaska on a liner flatulently enough called *Norwegian Wind* that featured 'everything from a jogging track to a casino'. Fittingly, the final destination was the frontier city of Skagway, epicentre of the Yukon gold rush.

'Already got your London house and county seat? Not quite sure what to do with some of your year-end bonus? What about purchasing a serious boat?'[56] This unsolicited e-mail appearing on screens at City desks at Christmas 2000 then went on to explain how the purchaser of a £1.5 million yacht could save £145,000 through the crafty use of a British Virgin Islands company. For landlubbers, or skinflints who did not want to spend quite so much, maybe a serious car is the business: it was reported that sales of Ferraris doubled after the City bonus rounds of 1996 and 1997, and BMW and Mercedes dealerships did very nicely too.

Hundreds, maybe thousands, of top-of-the-range retailers and London's 8,500 restaurants are beneficiaries of the City's high disposable income. Traditionally such emporiums were located in the West End, Knightsbridge or Chelsea, the City's own streets featuring little more than pubs, newsagents and sandwich bars. The late 1990s, however, saw the proliferation of luxury-end eateries and shops in the Square Mile and Canary Wharf, and at satellite locations such as Smithfield and Butlers Wharf. Simultaneously, as a result of the redundancy of many traditional banking halls, the Square Mile became host to an unrivalled array of coffer-ceilinged, marble-walled wine bars.

The conversion of the Royal Exchange, where two centuries earlier Nathan Rothschild had made his fortune trading bills of exchange, into a high-class shopping mall is yet another symbol of the awesome purchasing power of the bonus babes. And moves are afoot to open a five-floor House of Fraser department store in King William Street. It will be the City's first department store since Gamages in High Holborn closed way back when the bowler was still almost *de rigueur* in the Square Mile.

With over 500,000 square feet of retail space, Canary Wharf is equivalent to a sub-regional shopping mall: in fact, a recent survey revealed that 40 per cent of shoppers do not work there. As well as fashion, food and gift shops, there is a crèche, a health club and up-market car dealership HR Owen. 'Lotuses are very popular,' says Camille Waxer, head of Canary Wharf's retail complex.[57]

The fundamental reason for the transformation of the City from consumer desert to shopping oasis is the affluence of City workers, particularly the growing number of well-paid women. But these days they are so busy earning money that they have no time to travel to the West End to spend it, so the shops have had to come to the City. A more accommodating attitude on the part of the City planning authorities, rattled by the challenge from Canary Wharf, has been another factor.

Bankers whose work is so all-demanding that they do not even have time to set foot outside the office can avail themselves of the services of a 'City Butler'. 'We are there to pick up the pieces of people's busy lives,' explains Jonathan Wallace of Entrust, whose firm does anything or everything for its clients, from booking tickets for the Royal Opera House or a rock concert to organising a children's birthday party or a safari in Tanzania. 'What these people are selling is time, which is exactly what we don't have,' says a busy banker. More and more City firms are providing such services as a time-saver for staff. 'We are competing for the best and brightest,' Karl Dannenbaum, a managing director at Lehman Brothers, insists. 'This is a way of getting and keeping them.' But some are wary of using a facility that potentially allows their employer to keep tabs on them. 'This could mean that I will have no more personal life,' frets a City executive.[58]

Not quite everyone in the City is a shopaholic. After a run of good years many high earners have accumulated as many houses and shiny toys as they feel they can cope with. As one banker who had received a £500,000 bonus put it: 'I already have a house and I don't like fast cars. For reasons of principle, my children go to state schools. I just don't know what I am going to spend it on.'[59]

Crisis of affluence

Central London's astronomical property prices – City driven – now disqualify most people from living there. So too the surrounding areas, where prices have been pushed up by the arrival of affluent households displaced from the centre by even more affluent bankers. Since the 1980s, London house prices have risen by 3.9 per cent a year to an average of £180,000, but wages have grown by only 2.7 per cent. Even in relatively deprived inner London areas, gentrification means that the average price of houses now outstrips average salaries by a ratio of seven to one.

For nurses, teachers, police, fire-fighters, social workers, bus crew and other lower- or middle-income public sector employees, living near their place of employment has become financially impossible. 'We lose one in five officers because of the cost of housing,' Mike Shurety, a personnel director for the police, reports. 'The further they get pushed out by prices, the harder it is to get them in for shifts.' Moreover, such workers have no prospect of ever being able to buy a home in inner London. 'You have to be very rich, or in social housing or to have bought your house donkey's years ago,' said Christine Whatford, chief education officer for an inner London local authority, in March 2001. 'It has got markedly worse in the last eighteen months.'[60]

Some US cities have already had to confront this twenty-first century urban affliction – a crisis of affluence. When property prices rocketed in the up-market ski resort of Aspen, Colorado, owing to demand for holiday homes, the urban infrastructure began to collapse because the vital public service workers had been priced out of town. To remedy this market failure, the municipal authorities began to offer subsidised housing to low-income families – meaning around *half* the permanent population. Developers were forced to set aside up to 70 per cent of new homes for affordable accommodation. New York has the same problem, leading New York University to build 10,000 residential units in the city for staff and students in the last ten years.

The full force of the crisis has yet to hit London. Many public sector workers entered the housing market years ago when prices were still within reach. As they start to retire, affordable housing on the scale required will have to come from somewhere. A variety of initiatives are under consideration, but the likelihood is that the problem will get worse rather than better.

A headlong plunge in the level of mergers and acquisitions and securities activity began in the closing months of 2000 and continued through 2001, with the US slipping into recession, and onwards into 2002. The devastation of Wall Street on September 11 darkened the gloom further. In London, Goldman Sachs' deals for 2001 were worth just one-fifth of its total for 2000 and top City law firm Linklaters saw a drop of two-thirds.[61] The CBI/PricewaterhouseCoopers Financial Services Survey published in January 2002 showed the biggest dives in business volumes and profitability since 1991.[62]

The depressed levels of activity spelt bad news for bonuses and jobs. Reports of bonus cuts varied from firm to firm: 70 per cent at Morgan Stanley; 60 per cent at Goldman Sachs; and 40 per cent at JP Morgan Chase. Overall, it was estimated that City bonus payments for 2001 would be down 50 per cent on the previous year – although it was still reckoned that 18,000 City workers would receive bonuses of £50,000 or more.[63] Yet some were facing more than the loss of their bonus – their livelihood. There were predictions that the 2001–02 downturn would lead to 15–30,000 City job cuts, though if the slump proved to be on the same scale as the early 1990s a cull of 60,000 jobs was on the cards.

The *Evening Standard*'s much-respected City editor, Anthony Hilton, took no pleasure at the prospect, but nonetheless detected a silver lining:

> For years we have had to watch while the raging bull market created a sky's-the-limit culture in which no amount of salary and bonus was too much, but no amount of money seemed to buy loyalty or gratitude. Older employees had the decency to be embarrassed about the amount of cash thrown their way, but took the understandable line that they should grab it while it was offered because such excess was clearly unsustainable.
>
> Younger members had no such moral touchstone. They confused genius with a bull market and had the arrogance to believe they were worth it ...
>
> The reality is that few of those people who get £1 million, a handful of those who get £10 million and almost none of those who get £20 million a year are worth it, nor need to be paid on that scale. Almost all would work for a fraction of these amounts were it not that they want to get more than their peers in rival firms. Their bonuses have little to do with economic reward and a lot to do with comparative ego.
>
> The question now is how quickly salaries and bonuses will return to more realistic levels, given that life is rapidly becoming much tougher for investment banks ... They will have to cut and cut hard – not ditching secretaries and first-class air travel but chopping out whole departments that are unprofitable. Then we will see what these City high-fliers are really worth.[64]

But the likelihood is that the shakeout will be short-lived and will make little difference to the underlying fundamentals. So long as London remains the world's leading international financial centre, the City will go on being the cuckoo in the nest.

5

Markets, Markets, Markets

The City is the world's top international financial centre: more international banking and other international financial services business is conducted in London than anywhere else. The result is jobs – the biggest concentration of people working in international financial services across the globe. The international financial services sector makes a significant contribution to the British economy and has pervasive effects on its host city and on the British way of life.

Two types of financial services activity are conducted in London – 'mainstream' and 'money-centre'. Mainstream financial services are the sort found in any UK High Street; they predominantly serve a UK customer base and are largely retail in character, that is they accommodate the financial needs of individuals for personal cheque and savings accounts, loans and mortgages. Money-centre activities comprise a range of financial activities that are mostly wholesale in nature, meaning that they serve the requirements of corporations, governments and the financial services industry itself. They are also predominantly international.

For centuries, banks and other firms conducting money-centre activities clustered together in *the City*, the geographical area with St Paul's Cathedral at its heart bound by the medieval city walls, sometimes known as *the Square Mile*. But in recent years, some international banks and other firms conducting money-centre business have spread to other neighbourhoods, notably Canary Wharf. Despite the diaspora, the traditional term 'the City' continues to be used as a shorthand for London's money-centre activities; it is in this economic sense – referring to international financial

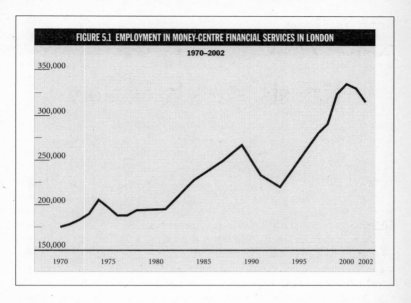

services activities in London, both inside and beyond the Square Mile – that it is used in this book.

Why London?

After the 1960s, when London re-emerged as the foremost international financial centre, employment in money-centre financial services grew from around 175,000 in 1970 to 315,000 in 2002 (see Figure 5.1).[1]

Most years saw some increase, with particularly rapid rates of expansion in the early 1970s, the mid-1980s and from the mid-1990s. But there were also short-term reverses, associated with the recessions of the mid-1970s and the early 1990s, when the City shed almost 50,000 jobs, and in 2001–02 when perhaps as many as 20,000 jobs were lost. *Overall,* employment in money-centre financial services in London grew by an average of about 1.5 per cent a year.[2]

Why has the City seen more than three decades of almost continuous expansion? It is a universal feature of long-term economic development that the stock of financial assets – deposits, loans, shares, bonds, mortgages etc. – grows faster than the rate of increase of total output. In other words,

as a society becomes more prosperous and economically more sophisticated, the ratio of financial assets to national output rises. The management of the stock of financial assets is the activity performed by the
financial services sector; thus as an economy grows, its financial services
sector expands faster than national output. Take the UK: between 1970 and
1995 the total number of people recorded by the occupational census as
working in 'banking, finance, insurance and business services' rose from
1.32 million to 2.75 million, representing an increase from 6 per cent of
total employment to 12.5 per cent.

This relationship between economic development and the growth of
the financial services sector also applies to the international economy and
international financial services; as the international economy grows, the
international financial services industry expands *even more rapidly*. The
operation of this underlying process has been the driving force behind the
growth of international financial services in London, the leading location
of the international financial services industry.

There have been four key dynamics:

- the rapid expansion of international trade;
- the growth of international financial flows;
- the internationalisation of investment;
- the increasing conduct of international financial transactions
  'offshore'.

Since 1945 the world economy has grown more or less continuously.
This expansion was fostered by the dismantling of restrictions on trade
and financial flows under the generally benign regime of the post-war set
of international economic institutions, notably the International Monetary Fund (IMF), the World Bank, the World Trade Organisation and the
Bank for International Settlements. Global economic growth stimulated
the *expansion of international trade*, which rose at a faster rate than world
output. The buoyancy of world trade provided a direct boost to several
City activities – trade finance, foreign exchange trading, ship and aircraft
broking and international insurance – and an indirect stimulus to others.

Initially, overseas lending was mostly undertaken by banks; but from the
1960s an enormous international capital market – the Eurobond market –
grew up as an offshore alternative source of funds for borrowers. The bulk
of *international financial flows* was between developed countries, but

emerging countries also began to borrow from Western banks and in the international capital market to fund economic development, not to mention the purchase of armaments or other unproductive purposes. As the leading international banking centre and the foremost Eurobond market location, London benefited greatly from these developments.

The *internationalisation of investment* has been fostered by the abolition of bureaucratic barriers to free financial flows and advances in communications. In the 1950s and 1960s many countries operated exchange controls to support the value of their currencies under the system of fixed exchange rates agreed at the Bretton Woods Conference in 1944. Following the collapse of the Bretton Woods system in the early 1970s, countries gradually scrapped exchange controls, thereby allowing their citizens to invest their money wherever they wished.

The communications revolution, meanwhile, has further stimulated the increase in both international capital flows and the internationalisation of investment by broadening perceptions of opportunities and reducing the risks. Advances in telecommunications have dramatically improved the availability of information and the speed of dissemination and cut the cost. Improvements in aviation technology have reduced the time and cost of air travel, making it easier for fund managers and private investors themselves to visit financial centres in foreign countries. Extended horizons have led to the international diversification of assets.

The rapid expansion of international financial flows boosted the whole range of the City's international banking and investment banking activities. The City has benefited from the stimulus to international fund management and securities trading, particularly of international bonds and equities that dwarf the volume of transactions in UK securities. Cross-border mergers and acquisitions work has boomed, as has other international corporate finance advisory work such as privatisations.

Since the 1960s there has been a rapid expansion in the *conduct of international financial transactions 'offshore'* – that is, subject to a regulatory and legal framework chosen by the contracting parties, not simply those of their domicile. For instance, traditionally a US corporation would finance its activities either by borrowing from US banks or through the US capital market in US dollars. Such transactions would be subject to US laws and regulations. But offshore finance offers much greater flexibility and opportunities. It permits tapping new pools of funds, which may provide cheaper finance than is available from domestic lenders. The parties to the transaction are free to choose the legal and regulatory framework of any jurisdiction, or to stick with US laws if they so wish. Even if a deal is negotiated in the USA, it can be 'booked' in a more advantageous jurisdiction. Finally, the loan can be made in any currency, which might then be converted back to dollars via a currency swap, should the borrower so wish.

There are three main kinds of financial activity that are conducted offshore – offshore banking; offshore bond issuance, underwriting and trading; and the swaps and derivatives markets. The offshore markets have trounced their onshore counterparts by providing a greater range of product types and more dynamic product innovation as well as lower costs. Not surprisingly, the volume of business conducted offshore has mushroomed. In theory, offshore financial facilities can be located anywhere and everywhere. But in reality London has been the prime beneficiary from the post-1960s offshore boom.

As the world's largest international financial centre, London has an unrivalled pool of skills and experience. This concentration of financial expertise allows City firms to reap the benefits of 'external economies of scale'. These accrue to firms when a positive relationship exists between efficiency and the size of the industry in which they operate. There are many reasons why a larger financial centre provides a more advantageous operating environment than a smaller centre. The quality of financial markets – their liquidity and efficiency – is strongly correlated with the scale of operations. These are highly desirable features, meaning lower dealing costs and diminished likelihood of market breakdown.

Moreover, the larger number and greater range of activities of other financial firms produces a more innovative environment, which may generate new business opportunities and demand from other practitioners. It may also stimulate competition, promoting keener pricing for transactions of all sizes, product innovation and perhaps the development of bespoke products for individual clients. Such factors will incline clients to place their business with firms operating from a larger financial centre rather than a smaller one.

Financial firms operating in large financial centres with a wide range of complementary activities also enjoy 'economies of scope'. The ready availability of commercial lawyers, accountants, specialist printers, information technology experts, financial public relations consultants and many other specialist services, enhances a firm's efficiency and competitiveness.

The bigger the centre, the more extensive and more varied the concentration of complementary activities.

External economies of scale and economies of scope are powerful forces in the global financial services industry, bestowing a major competitive advantage upon leading financial centres such as London. Indeed, in theory, the logical outcome of their operation is that all international financial activity should concentrate in a single centre. But centralisation can also generate 'diseconomies of scale', such as crowding and congestion, or perhaps increased information costs because of distance from clients. Moreover, in the real world, political factors and regulatory barriers and incentives exist that distort the operation of the centralising economic forces. So regional and local financial centres continue to exist.

Streets paved with gold

The City's workforce generates output valued at £22 billion: this means that on average each City worker generates output of £68,000 a year.[3] Since this average includes a substantial number of support staff – clerks, messengers, secretaries, receptionists, chauffeurs etc. – it means that the output generated by the executive echelon is much higher. 'Telephone numbers on slips of paper', in the words of Sir Howard Davies, chief financial services regulator.[4]

It is not just the stars who make a lot of money – so does the supporting cast. Unlike the acting or sporting profession, most of whose members are on the breadline struggling to make ends meet while dreaming of their fifteen minutes of fame and fortune, in the City the whole cast is better-paid than those who work in other sectors. Between 1970 and 2000 the average salary of male City staff rose from £2,256 to £47,673, compared to national average white-collar incomes of £1,856 and £27,762 respectively (see Figure 5.2).[5]

The earnings of City women tell a similar story, rising from an annual average of £1,138 in 1970 to £30,638 in 2000, compared to national non-manual averages of £915 and £18,590 respectively. Although at the end of the 1990s, City men's average earnings were 80 per cent higher than those of City women, a gender discrepancy far larger than the nation as a whole, the gender gap had closed a little over the three decades owing to the advance of women into highly paid executive positions (see Figure 5.3).[6]

Not only are City staff better-paid than workers in other sectors, over the years the pay premium has grown wider and wider. In the 1970s the

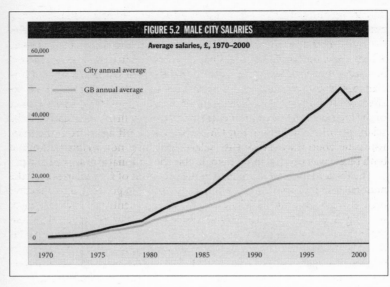

FIGURE 5.2 MALE CITY SALARIES

Average salaries, £, 1970–2000

City annual average

GB annual average

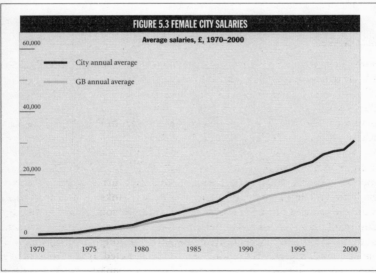

FIGURE 5.3 FEMALE CITY SALARIES

Average salaries, £, 1970–2000

City annual average

GB annual average

average incomes of City staff were around 20 per cent higher than national average white-collar earnings. The City earnings premium grew rapidly in the 1980s, rising for men from 25 per cent in 1980 to 60 per cent in 1988. These were the years of 'Big Bang', which resulted in a fundamental restructuring of the way many City firms did business and an influx of foreign banks and securities houses into London. Both processes had the effect of bidding up City salaries – the so-called 'yuppie boom'. In the wake of the October 1987 stock market crash, many City firms shed staff and the salary premium stabilised. But City salaries took off again from the mid-1990s; by 2000 the average City salary (full-time non-manual adults of both sexes) was £45,419, more than double the national average of £21,842.[7]

The fivefold increase since 1970 in the premium of City salaries over the national average, from 20 per cent to more than 100 per cent, is a reflection of the dynamism and efficiency of the money-centre financial services sector. It is consistent with estimates based on national income data that the output of City workers rose by at least 7 per cent a year in real terms over the decades of the 1970s, 1980s and 1990s.[8] This is a much faster rate of growth than the rate of increase of City employment, which has averaged around 1.5 per cent. The outcome has been the rise of City salaries and the ever-widening earnings premium.

What goes on?

Some idea of what these 315,000 enviably remunerated City people actually do may be obtained from Table 5.1.[9]

Banking and securities
Banking is the City's foremost activity, generating three-fifths of jobs. City banks service the financial requirements of governments, corporations and investors through a variety of activities. Traditionally a distinction has been drawn between 'commercial banking' and 'investment banking', though in recent years the boundary has become blurred because of mergers between commercial banks and investment banks, as well as amalgamations with securities houses and insurance companies; today the dominant players in international finance are massive conglomerate banks undertaking the full range of bank activities. Although both commercial banking and investment banking are now conducted by the same banks, they remain distinct activities. Commercial banking means taking

Table 5.1 **London money-centre employment, 2002**

	Number of people	%
Bank activities:		
Domestic head office banking	20,000	6
International commercial banking	35,000	11
Foreign exchange trading	5,000	2
Corporate finance	15,000	5
Securities: domestic equities	25,000	8
international equities	15,000	5
bonds	25,000	8
Derivatives	5,000	2
Fund management	40,000	13
Total banking	185,000	
Insurance	50,000	16
Professional services	60,000	19
Other: commodities, marine and specialist services	20,000	6
Total	315,000	

deposits, often from members of the public for whom bank accounts are convenient repositories for funds. The bank uses these funds, plus some of its own resources, to make loans. To protect depositors and try to prevent reckless lending, commercial banks are highly regulated and closely scrutinised.

The biggest UK commercial banks, the kernel of the UK's financial system, and many other domestic financial institutions have their head offices in the City. These offices often handle the bank's relationships with major UK corporate and public sector clients. They also provide support for the bank's board of directors, for instance in strategic planning and economic analysis; furnish group-wide services, such as public relations, human resources and regulatory compliance; and conduct core bank functions, notably treasury operations – the management of the bank's own balance sheet – and foreign exchange trading. Around 20,000 people work in these head office domestic banking activities in London, mostly in UK banks, though some foreign banks also service UK corporate and retail customers.

Some 35,000 people work in international commercial banking. London is host to 481 foreign banks, a larger number than any other financial centre (see Table 5.2). [10]

Table 5.2 **Foreign banks hosted by selected countries, 2000**

UK	481
US	287
Germany	242
France	187
Japan	92

The principal reason for the presence of so many foreign banks is to participate in the thriving offshore financial markets, providing access to these vast pools of funds to foreign corporations, banks and governments. As a result, London is the leading centre for international cross-border bank lending (see Table 5.3).

Table 5.3 **International cross-border bank lending, market share, 2001 (by percentage)**

UK	20
Japan	11
US	10
Germany	9
France	6

The finance of international trade is a longstanding City activity, which is undertaken by both domestic and foreign banks in the City. Most City banks conduct foreign exchange dealing, an activity supporting around 5,000 jobs. London has the largest number of market participants, some 340 dealing firms, and offers the greatest array of spot and forward market contracts. With a daily turnover of $504 billion, 31 per cent of the global total, London is the world's leading foreign exchange market by the proverbial country mile (see Table 5.4).

Table 5.4 **Foreign exchange trading volumes, 2001 (average daily turnover)**

	$billion	%
UK	504	31
US	254	16
Japan	147	9
Singapore	101	6
Germany	88	5
Switzerland	71	4
Hong Kong	67	4
France	48	3
Other centres	338	21
Total	1,618	

Investment banking comprises a set of advisory and facilitation activities for companies and governments, for which an investment bank is remunerated by fees. According to the *Banker*, in 1998 the top twenty-five investment banks worldwide handled business worth $11 trillion, of which mergers and acquisitions advisory work comprised about half, securities underwriting and private placements just over a third, and the remainder derived from international bank loans and the management of medium-term notes. Around 15,000 people work on this advisory side of investment banking in London, a handsomely paid elite corps.

Investment banks do not lend money to clients themselves but raise it on their behalf through the capital markets, organising issues of equities or bonds. Often they act as a guarantor that a fund-raising exercise will be successful – 'underwriting' the issue. The risks in the investment banking business are that fee income will be insufficient to cover an expensive cost base or that unforeseen market developments during an underwriting exposure will leave banks holding securities that are worth less than they paid for them.

The market for new issues of securities to raise funds is known as the 'primary market', while the pool of existing securities is called the 'secondary market'. The role of investment banks as intermediaries in the origination of new securities makes the buying and selling of securities a complementary activity. Investment banks are active in both the primary and secondary markets. Most investment banks bear the names of firms that were originally securities underwriters, for instance Morgan Stanley and Goldman Sachs, and diversified into securities brokerage; but others – such as Salomon Smith Barney (Citigroup) and Merrill Lynch – began as securities houses and built their business the other way round.

Securities brokerage involves buying and selling equities and bonds for clients on a commission basis. Banks' in-house securities traders execute clients' orders to buy and sell; they may also trade on the firm's behalf – 'proprietary trading' – profiting by the full amount of any gains instead of just a commission. Securities analysts with expertise in particular market sectors provide advice, both to clients and in-house, on investment and trading opportunities. Securities salesmen develop relationships with clients, such as fund managers, corporate treasurers or wealthy investors, to whom they market the quality of the team's analysts and the skills of its traders to win buy and sell orders. Around 65,000 people work in the City on the securities side.

Equities trading focuses on the London Stock Exchange, the world's third-largest exchange by equity capitalisation. Trading is conducted in a variety of UK securities, principally government bonds and domestic equities, and in international equities – the shares of foreign companies with listings on their domestic market. More foreign companies are listed on the London Stock Exchange than on any other exchange, turnover accounting for half the trading in all international equities around the world. Transactions in international equities substantially exceed business in UK shares (see Table 5.5).

Table 5.5 **Turnover of foreign equities, 2000**

	£ billion	%
London	2,669	48
New York	1,142	21
Nasdaq	844	15
Frankfurt	321	6
Stockholm	96	2
Euronext	74	1
Others	380	7
Total	5,526	

The biggest of the securities markets is the offshore Eurobond market. 'Eurobonds' are bonds denominated in a currency other than that of the country or market in which they are issued. New issues are underwritten by an international syndicate of banks and distributed internationally in countries other than the country of the currency of the bond. Thereby the issue avoids being subject to national restrictions. The 'Euro' prefix originated in the 1960s and has nothing to do with the European single currency. 'Offshore bonds' would be a less ambiguous term.

Eurobonds were invented in London in 1963 and the market has been focused there ever since. Eurobonds comprise 90 per cent of international bond issues, with 70 per cent of issuance taking place in London. It is also the focal point of the secondary market, again with 70 per cent of Eurobond trading being conducted in the City.

Derivatives is the generic term for a variety of financial instruments that are 'derived' from underlying financial products. Derivative products – options, futures and swaps – are used for hedging financial risks or for betting on movements in securities and commodities prices, currencies and interest rates. The 1980s and 1990s saw a spectacular expansion of the global derivatives market and it is one of the City's most buoyant growth activities. 'Rocket scientists' is the City term for the maths-wonks who invent new derivatives products. These are marketed to clients by specialist salesmen. Sometimes they are developed as bespoke products to meet clients' particular needs. Derivatives are traded in two ways, through organised exchanges or over-the-counter (OTC), that is directly between the counter-parties to a deal. The London International Financial Futures and Options Exchange (LIFFE), founded in 1982, is Europe's largest derivatives exchange, and second largest in the world for exchange-traded business. London hosts the highest volume of OTC trading, 36 per cent of the global total, substantially ahead of the US (see Table 5.6). Derivatives business generates around 5,000 money-centre jobs in London.

London is the world's leading centre for fund management, an activity employing around 40,000 people. The City manages a greater volume of investment funds than the next seven European centres combined (see Table 5.7).

Fund management services are provided by independent specialist firms, both UK and foreign, and by commercial banks, investment banks and insurance companies. Their clients are institutional investors – corporate and public sector pension funds, charitable foundations, educa-

Table 5.6 **Average daily turnover of OTC derivatives, 2001**

	OTC turnover ($billion)	Global share (%)
UK	275	36
US	135	18
Germany	97	13
France	67	9
Netherlands	25	3
Japan	22	3
Switzerland	15	2
Others	128	16
Total	764	

Table 5.7 **Funds under management in financial centres, 2000 ($billion, ranked by holdings of institutional equities)**

London	2,461
New York	2,363
Tokyo	2,058
Boston	1,871
San Francisco	726
Los Angeles	589
Paris	458
Philadelphia	419
Zurich	414

tional endowments – and private individuals. Funds are invested in equities, bonds, real estate or venture capital opportunities, both in the UK and around the world. Some firms focus primarily on institutional clients, but many also operate unit trusts or mutual funds which cater to the requirements of individual savers by pooling their funds to enhance returns and reduce risk. A large choice of funds is available, pursuing a wide range of different investment strategies.

Investment decisions are made by a key group of fund managers, operating within the framework of the firm's overall investment stance – its outlook about the prospects of the market as a whole and the relative attractions of different sectors. The fund managers are supported by research analysts who evaluate companies and other investment opportunities. Traders, often in-house, buy and sell the securities in which the funds invest. There may also be private arrangements between buyers and sellers of securities that do not go through the market, especially large blocks that might disrupt prices. The highly competitive market for fund management services means that firms market themselves aggressively both to win new institutional mandates and to attract individual investors to their unit trusts and mutual funds.

Advising the wealthy on investment, insurance and other money matters, a service known as 'private banking', is a buoyant City activity. The long boom of the 1980s and 1990s created a big increase in so-called 'high net worth individuals' – with assets greater than $1 million – who now number 7.2 million world-wide.[11]

The Bank of England has a special place in the City as banker to the UK government since 1694 and overseer of the financial markets. The Bank is responsible for UK monetary policy and sets UK interest rates. Being closely in touch with the financial markets, it acts as a conduit for the exchange of views between money-centre firms and the government. It has a staff of 1,800.

The Financial Services Authority is the unitary regulatory body for financial services. Established in 1997, it has a staff of 2,500 who are responsible for the supervision of banking, insurance, fund management, securities brokerage and personal investment advisers. The combination of responsibilities for both retail and wholesale financial services is a cause for concern on the part of some international bankers – justifiably wary that politically driven consumer protection may lead to encroachments on the freedom to innovate that has been one of the City's competitive strengths.

Insurance, professional and support services
Insurance is a major City activity, supporting 50,000 jobs.[12] London is host to a unique wholesale insurance marketplace, comprising insurance and reinsurance companies, Lloyd's of London and Protection and Indemnity (P&I) clubs. It is the world's largest international insurance market with gross premium income of £14 billion – over 50 per cent from the company market, 40 per cent from Lloyd's and the rest mainly from P&I clubs. It is the global leader in aviation and marine insurance, with market shares of

27 per cent and 22 per cent, respectively, and the leading centre for rein-surance. Insurance companies provide both 'general' insurance (aviation, fire, marine, motor, personal accident and property) and 'long-term' insurance (life assurance, and annuity and investment policies). Some risks, for instance oilfields, space exploration or earthquakes, involve potential payoffs that are so big that the liability has to be spread over a large number of insurers. Reinsurance, as risk spreading is called, is under-taken by specialist reinsurance companies, by the larger insurance com-panies and by Lloyd's of London.

Many of the UK's 840 insurance companies have their head offices in London and do business with Lloyd's brokers. Around 170 of them are owned by foreign insurance groups and most major international insur-ance companies maintain a presence in London. Moreover, banks and insurance companies are merging in order to offer a more comprehensive range of financial products, creating so-called 'bancassurance' financial services supermarkets.

Lloyd's of London is not an insurance company, it is a wholesale insur-ance market. Founded in 1688, it is the world's oldest and largest insurance market with a staff of 2,000. Originally the bulk of its business was marine insurance, but now all sorts of special risks are covered. Business at Lloyd's is conducted between around 220 firms of brokers, representing clients who need insurance, and some 140 Lloyd's underwriting syndicates that provide the cover. The syndicates are backed by groups of private individu-als, known as 'names', and by corporate members. Lloyd's maintains a fund to support syndicates that might otherwise default and thus damage the reputation of the institution. The business conducted at Lloyd's is prepon-derantly international, three-quarters of earnings coming from overseas.

In the late 1980s and early 1990s, Lloyd's was buffeted by a series of scan-dals and by a run of enormous losses that totalled £7 billion. Many of the names were ruined and there was a spate of litigation alleging negligence or fraud on the part of underwriting agents. The crisis led to far-reaching reforms beginning in 1993, the year which also saw Lloyd's return to profit.

The City's banking and insurance industries are serviced by specialist firms of lawyers and accountants, employing around 60,000 people. London and New York are the leading centres for international legal services. Most of this work in the City is conducted by indigenous law firms, providing a full range of commercial legal services in areas includ-ing corporate finance, corporate and commercial law, project finance, international capital markets, tax, and dispute resolution. There is also a growing number of foreign law firms, including over sixty from the US, and the legal practices of the large accountancy firms are also important.

London is a leading international centre for the provision of accounting and related services. The principal services offered are audit and tax, corporate finance, insolvency and business recovery, and consulting. The globalisation of investment banking has led leading City law and accountancy firms to forge alliances or mergers with similar firms in the US and continental Europe in order to service their worldwide clients, becoming international entities themselves.

From the seventeenth century, London was the largest port in the world. Thus it naturally became the leading centre for commodities trading and shipping services. The London Metal Exchange (LME) conducts 95 per cent of the world's traditional metals trading, setting prices for aluminium, aluminium alloy, copper, lead, nickel, silver, tin and zinc. Eleven of the fourteen dealing members are foreign-owned and 95 per cent of trades originate outside the UK. London is also the world's leading clearing centre for gold and silver trading – clearings amounting, respectively, to $6.3 billion and $600 million a day in 2001. The world prices for gold and silver are fixed daily in London through the members of the London Bullion Market Association. Cocoa, coffee, sugar and other agricultural commodities are traded at the London Commodity Exchange. The International Petroleum Exchange (IPE) is Europe's leading energy futures and options exchange and the second largest in the world. The price of Brent Crude – the key international oil price marker – is set on the IPE. Trades at the IPE, LME and LIFFE are cleared at the London Clearing House, a leading global clearing house. It facilitates the workings of these markets by acting as the central counter-party to all contracts entered into by members, thus guaranteeing contract performance. The LCH has 110 member firms, four-fifths of them from overseas.

London is the world's premier provider of maritime services. Business focuses on the Baltic Exchange where ship owners, cargo owners and ship brokers match vessels and freights. Around 50 per cent of tanker charters and 40 per cent of dry-bulk cargo charters are arranged in London. More than half the world's new and second-hand tonnage is bought and sold through London brokers. As ever, the business is thoroughly international. Less than 10 per cent of deals negotiated on the Baltic Exchange involve a UK ship owner, importer or exporter.

Information is the life-blood of the financial services industry. It was no accident that the UK's newspaper industry was traditionally located in the Square Mile in Fleet Street. New technology led to the dispersal of the press to cheaper locations, though Reuters and Bloomberg, the electronic providers of market information and trading platforms, are still located in the City. There is also a host of specialist publications serving the money-centre readership, the leading publishers being the *Financial Times*, which has a London staff of 1,000, the *Economist* and *Euromoney*.

The City's operations generate opportunities for a myriad of specialist consultants and providers of support services. These firms, together with those in commodities, marine services and financial information providers, comprise perhaps 20,000 money-centre jobs in London. Support services include firms specialising in financial public relations, recruitment, advertising, market research and information technology. Public relations firms specialising in the financial services sector came to the fore in the takeover battles of the 1980s and have thrived ever since. Moreover, the major banks now employ their own in-house corporate communications staff, as do the Bank of England and the Financial Services Authority. Between 1989 and 2001, membership of the City and Financial Group of the Institute of Public Relations doubled in size, from 200 to 400.[13]

Traditionally, City bankers worked for a single employer – or at most two – for the whole of their career. That changed decisively in the 1980s with the influx and growing power of American banks – notorious for their hire-and-fire approach to personnel, which in turn sundered the bonds of loyalty on the part of staff. 'An entire industry of headhunters has been built on this institutionalised disloyalty and the desire of firms to buy instant success rather than work for it,' comments City journalist Anthony Hilton.[14]

Industry insiders estimate that the financial services executive search industry – headhunters in everyday language – comprises around 2,000 jobs. The business is dominated by half a dozen major global firms that work on a retention basis for the leading banks. In addition, there is a score of niche players, also on a retention basis, and a host of specialist boutiques that are engaged on a contingency basis. In normal times, executive search firms smooth and speed up the operation of the City jobs market to the advantage of both employees and employers. But if a City firm gets into trouble, its problems may be magnified by predatory headhunting which can quickly strip a bank of its best people. Occasionally the defection *en masse* of a whole team or department to a rival firm hits the headlines, accompanied by furious denunciations from the erstwhile employer.

Computers and telecommunications are critical to all money-centre firms. Banks have their own in-house IT staff who develop new systems and sort out operational problems. But there is also a thriving undergrowth of specialist independent IT consultants providing services such as writing software, web-site design and maintenance, and fire-fighting all manner of electronic emergency. The management consultancy arms of the major accountancy firms are amongst the leading practitioners in the IT consultancy field.[15]

Every major bank has in-house economists who provide analysis of market and sector trends to assist traders and salesmen. There are also independent economic consultants, often specialising in a particular market sector. Actuarial consultants advise and assist not only insurance companies and pension funds about policy liabilities, but human resources departments about executive remuneration schemes. Then there are so-called strategic consultants, that advise companies on issues such as restructuring their operations. Finally, there are craftsmen, such as printers who can run off a prospectus within hours, and specialist banknote, bond and share certificate designers.

Training is a significant money-centre activity. Two business schools specialise in training for London's financial services industry, the City University Business School and the ISMA (International Securities Markets Association) Centre at the University of Reading. The London Business School and the London School of Economics also have close ties. The Chartered Institute of Bankers and the Institute of Chartered Accountants organise courses to prepare candidates for their professional examinations. Then there are half a dozen commercial financial training companies that specialise in running banks' graduate induction courses and on-the-job skills development.

The City Corporation, the local government authority of the Square Mile that hails back to medieval times, promotes the City to the outside world in a variety of ways including numerous publications. There is the pageantry associated with events such as the annual Lord Mayor's show and Lord Mayor's banquet, which attract national television coverage. The Lord Mayor himself, a one-year appointment chosen from the Aldermen, has become something of an ambassador at large for the City. During his year in office in 2000, Lord Mayor Clive Martin made more than thirty overseas visits 'promoting the City of London as the hub of the UK's financial services industry', including a tour of prospective EU new members that took him to Prague, Warsaw, Bucharest and – Bratislava.[16]

Less flamboyant promotion of the City is undertaken by the Corporation's Policy and Resources Committee, supported by research and analysis conducted by the Economic Development Unit. Then there is International Financial Services, London (IFSL), which has the brief of promoting UK-based financial services throughout the world. It works with member firms to develop strategies for individual markets. It also compiles a wide range of statistics and reports on the role of London as an international financial centre and the contribution of the financial sector to the UK economy.

The well-paid workers in the international financial services industry generate jobs in a variety of services in the vicinity of their offices, such as shops, restaurants, sandwich bars and transport terminals as well as construction sites. Around 30,000 people work in the Square Mile in such secondary employment and a very much larger number in London as a whole.

The best is yet to be?

The City's output of £22 billion constitutes almost 3 per cent of UK Gross Domestic Product and 13 per cent of London's GDP, while the 315,000-strong money-centre workforce comprises 1 per cent of UK employment. But these relatively modest macroeconomic statistics do not capture the full significance of London's money-centre sector to the economy. In fact, the chancellor, Gordon Brown, deemed the City's contribution to be so significant that one of his famous 'five tests' in 1997 for the UK's readiness to join the euro was that it should not damage the City to do so.

The chancellor's solicitude towards the City can be easily explained. Firstly, because the City contributes £9.8 billion in tax towards the public purse, about 4 per cent of total tax revenues, which is about 45 per cent of the City's GDP.[17] Secondly, because the City's overseas earnings – £22 billion in 2000 – play a vital part in the UK's balance of payments, largely offsetting the longstanding deficit in the trade in goods – manufactures, foodstuffs and raw materials. Over the past decade the financial sector's net overseas earnings have risen from £10 billion in the early 1990s to £15–20 billion in the mid-1990s to over £30 billion since 1998: a stunning achievement. 'Sustaining earnings at this level since the euro was launched in 1999,' comments Duncan McKenzie, director of economics at International Financial Services London, 'provides further confirmation of London's status as the leading financial centre in Europe'.[18]

Will the City continue to expand and prosper? It *ought* to, because the underlying causes of the City's growth over recent decades still operate. Demand for international financial services continues to grow rapidly, driven by global economic growth, trade and financial liberalisation and the shift to offshore operations. In fact, these forces may even gather momentum in coming decades as more and more countries – including perhaps Brazil, China, India and Indonesia – become integrated into the international financial system.

The ongoing dynamic expansion of demand for international financial services, coupled with the City's entrenched advantages as the world's foremost international financial centre, have led forecasters to estimate that the real output of the London money-centre sector will grow by at least 6 per cent per year over the next ten to twenty years, repeating the performance of the last three decades.[19] This is a much more rapid rate of expansion than the historic trend rate of UK economic growth, meaning that there is every likelihood that the City will loom larger and larger as a factor in the British economy and in British society and politics.

The difference between the 6 per cent per year projected rate of growth of real output and a much lower rate of employment growth, historically 1.5 per cent per annum over the last thirty years, implies the continuation of substantial increases in real output per head and hence in personal incomes. This would be consistent with other factors promoting greater labour productivity, particularly investment in computing and communications equipment and the relentless advance of these technologies. Another factor is the increasing scale of financial transactions in global financial markets – the average size of equity and bond trades, currency deals or mergers. The result will be that the already yawning gulf between remuneration levels in the international financial services industry and other employment sectors will continue to grow wider and wider. This alone will ensure that the City is continually in the headlines in years to come.

Yet undeniably there are a number of clouds on the horizon. Over most of them the City has little or no control. Take London's transport crisis: the city grinds to gridlock while the politicians posture and trade insults instead of sorting out the problems of London Underground. Or taxation, where the government's current take of 45 per cent of the City's GDP is bound to rise if recession bites at a time of ambitious public spending commitments. Then there is regulation, where the draconian powers of the Financial Services Authority make many practitioners very worried about increasing cost and inflexibility. In all three areas, London's competitive advantage could easily be eroded.

There is also the euro. So far its advent in 1999 has probably benefited London, highlighting the City's distinctiveness from rival financial centres. But if Britain joins the euro-zone in, say, 2003, additional taxes and red-tape, the diminished status of the Bank of England, an inappropriate interest rate and a refocusing away from the City's traditional global outlook may make it a less attractive place to conduct business. Such an outcome would mean – if rather late in the day – that one of the Treasury's five key tests had not been fulfilled.

Perhaps inevitably, the darkest cloud is the least easy to gauge. The City has flourished since the 1960s in a rapidly globalising world of free trade and free capital flows. Should there be any retreat from that liberal international economy, because of an anti-globalisation backlash in the West or yet another financial crisis in the emerging markets, the impact will probably be felt more acutely in London, the world's most global city, than anywhere else.

6

The World's Playground

Once upon a time, and not so long ago, the core of the City was a nexus of London-based, medium-sized, specialist financial firms. A 1978 handbook for City job-seekers, *What Goes On In the City?*, counted 11 discount houses, 20 jobbers (market-makers), 60 merchant banks and 257 Stock Exchange brokers. Two decades on, almost all of these 348 independent, British-owned firms had disappeared.

Today the bulk of the City's business is conducted by a much smaller number of relatively big firms. The investment banking and securities business is dominated by a set of fifteen large, integrated, foreign-owned banks, operating on an international basis:

- Top-tier global investment banks: Credit Suisse First Boston, Deutsche Bank, Goldman Sachs, Merrill Lynch, JP Morgan Chase, Morgan Stanley, Schroder Salomon Smith Barney (Citigroup) and UBS Warburg.
- Second-rank international investment banks: Bear Sterns, BNP Paribas, Dresdner Kleinwort Wasserstein, ING Barings, Lehman Brothers, Nomura and SG Hambro.

The top-tier investment banks account for 55,000 of London's money-centre jobs, and the second rank, with smaller City staffs, for a further 13,000. Five major British banks – Barclays, HSBC, Lloyds TSB, Royal Bank Group (Royal Bank of Scotland and NatWest) and Standard Chartered – have 22,000 staff engaged in money-centre activities in London.[1] In total, these twenty banks employ 90,000 staff, almost half of London's 185,000 money-centre banking activity jobs, and more than a quarter of the overall total of 315,000.

The City accountancy profession is highly concentrated, most money-centre work being conducted by the 'big five': PricewaterhouseCoopers, with 6,000 City staff; KPMG, 5,000; Arthur Andersen, 3,000; Deloitte Touche Tohumatsu, 3,000; and Ernst & Young, 3,000. The top City law firms ranked by number of City staff are: Clifford Chance, 2,600; Linklaters & Alliance, 2,500; Lovells, 2,500; Allen & Overy, 2,000; and Freshfields Bruckhaus Deringer, 2,000. There is also a large number of smaller, yet significant, City law firms including the formidable Slaughter and May, with 1,200 City staff.

Most of the leading UK insurance companies have head offices in the City, though only a small part of their total workforce is based there, the majority operating from cheaper provincial centres. Prudential, the largest of the UK long-term insurance companies by worldwide net premium income, has around 1,000 City staff and CGNU, ranked first in general insurance business and second in long-term business, about the same. In total, the top five insurance companies have some 5,000 City staff.

Overall, the leading thirty-five City firms – the top fifteen foreign banks, five UK banks, five accountancy firms, five law firms and five insurance companies – account for 43 per cent of City employment. An alternative yardstick of the importance of the big players in the City is that large businesses (more than 200 employees) account for 51 per cent of employment, compared to only 31 per cent in Britain as a whole.[2]

At the other end of the spectrum is a host of small undertakings: there are 2,870 VAT-registered businesses located in the Square Mile that identify finance as their area of activity. There remains a substantial number of independent operators at Lloyd's of London, the Baltic Exchange and other exchanges. Many of the 481 foreign banks are modest operations, particularly the 200 or so representative offices that have just a handful of staff, as do some of the City outlets of UK insurance companies and building societies. Somewhat larger, but still minnows relative to the big banks, are the providers of specialist public relations, human resources and information technology services, and boutique or niche finance houses, such as Close Brothers, Singer & Friedlander, 3i Group, Hawkpoint Partners, Beeson Gregory or Intercapital.

It is the medium-sized independent firms, once a distinguishing feature of the City compared with other financial centres, that have become an endangered species. Gone, save in some cases as a brand-wrapper for a mutual fund, are most of the roll-call of names synonymous with the City for generations – names such as Akroyd & Smithers, Alexanders, Bisgood, de Zoete, Greenwell, Morgan Grenfell, Mullens, Pember & Boyle, Rowe & Pitman, Scrimgeour, Smith St Aubyn, Vickers da Costa, Wedd Durlacher. The sole survivors (future uncertain) from the *ancien régime* of City firms are Cazenove, with 900 London staff, Rothschilds, with 850, and Lazards, with 600.

How was it that the City became the playground of a handful of large and mostly foreign banks? What happened to all those British firms? Does it matter that a majority of City jobs are now provided by foreign firms? Should the consolidation of business in the financial services sector be a matter of public concern?

Crème de la crème

'The Battle of Waterloo was won on the playing fields of Eton,' famously declared the Duke of Wellington, the victorious general. Wrong. It was won in Lombard Street and 'Change Alley; it was the ability of the City to raise massive loans to finance the armies of Britain and its allies that really carried the day. The benefit was mutual: the City emerged from the French wars of 1793–1815 as the world's foremost international financial centre.

The money to fight the wars was raised through bond issues organised on behalf of governments by a small band of powerful merchant banks. Pre-eminent amongst them were the firms Barings and Rothschilds. It was Barings that soon afterwards organised the massive loan raised by France to pay reparations to its erstwhile enemies in 1818, prompting the Duc de Richelieu, the awestruck prime minister of France, to remark that: 'There are six great powers in Europe – England, France, Prussia, Austria, Russia and Baring Brothers.'[3]

Thereafter, the leading merchant banks formed an elite cadre amongst City firms. Their partners, veritable merchant princes themselves, dealt with monarchs and prime ministers as equals, having the power to grant or deny them access to the international capital market. In the City itself, they were the undisputed kings of the jungle: it was inconceivable that a partner in a merchant bank would pay a visit to a commercial banker, let alone a securities broker or jobber or commodity merchant. The exception was the Bank of England, an institution whose Court of Directors included some of the most eminent merchant bankers of the day and whose governor was sometimes chosen from their ranks. In the Bank's case, it was the partners who came calling and did the waiting. This reflected the Bank's special status as the government's bank and its role as the merchant banks' lender of last resort in a crisis. By combining these roles, the Bank provided the British state with privileged access to City finance – and City firms and markets with a bedrock of institutional and public support.

As the name suggests, merchant banks were both merchants and bankers. They began as merchants conducting international trade: even Nathan Rothschild, the founder of Rothschilds, started out as a dealer in printed cottons. Trade requires credit, and it was the merchant banks that developed the business of guaranteeing sterling bills of exchange, a sophisticated form of IOU note, which were the foremost instruments of international trade finance. As the key players in international trade finance, with knowledge of both financial market conditions at home and the creditworthiness of overseas clients, the City merchant banks were uniquely positioned to act as intermediaries for bond issues by foreign governments and utility companies, the major borrowers in the international capital markets until after the Second World War.

Over the course of the nineteenth century, a handful of other houses joined Barings and Rothschilds as members of the elite group of merchant bankers, combining the activities of international trade finance and bond issuing. Many of the founders were foreign merchants: such as Schroders, Kleinworts and Hambros from Germany; Morgans, Seligmans and Browns from the US; and Lazards from France. There were also plenty of successful merchant banks founded by indigenous merchants, for instance Antony Gibbs, Cunliffe Brothers and Arbuthnot Latham, but they tended to fade or disappear as subsequent generations assimilated into the landed class. Contrary to popular myth, only a small minority of these families was Jewish – a mere four of the twenty-one leading firms in 1914 were Jewish houses. The successful merchant bankers became very rich. They bought country estates and large town houses. Some acquired titles, both British and foreign, the latter bestowed by governments of inferior creditworthiness grateful for assistance in raising loans.

But merchant banking could be a high-risk business and its history is littered with the corpses of long-forgotten firms. Each of the nineteenth century's many financial and commercial crises – 1825, 1836, 1847, 1857, 1866, 1890 – took its toll. In 1890 the illustrious house of Barings itself fell victim to a surfeit of Argentinian bonds, for which the market temporarily had no appetite. The firm survived thanks to a rescue put together by the Bank of England, fearful of the damage that Barings' failure would cause to the City and the whole international financial system.

The most serious crisis for the merchant banks as a group was the outbreak of the First World War. Many of them faced imminent bankruptcy because they were owed large sums by enemy firms, a substantial part of German trade being financed in the City. Amazingly, although the antagonism with Germany had been mounting for years, virtually no contingency planning for war had been done by either City firms or the authorities. With some improvised help from the Bank of England, which made special loans available to allow them to meet their obligations, most of them survived.

The 1920s saw a revival of the fortunes of the merchant banks, particularly during the years of Britain's return to the gold standard, 1925–31, that stimulated sterling trade finance and revived London's role as an international capital market. But the Central European financial crisis of summer 1931 was another disaster for many of the merchant banks. Firms that did business with Germany, the world's second largest economy, found themselves in dire straits when German external payments were suspended – in fact, they did not get their money back until two decades later. The 1930s, which saw the collapse of international trade and capital flows, were lean years for the merchant banks, and the outbreak of war in 1939 made matters even worse – leading to a loss of business called 'almost catastrophic' by the *Financial News* in July 1941.[4] The Luftwaffe, meanwhile, blitzed a third of the buildings in the Square Mile. By the end of the war, much of the City and its business activities were in ruins, both physically and metaphorically.

The Labour Party victory in the election of July 1945 was another bombshell: the news was greeted in the Square Mile, reported the *Economist*, with 'stunned surprise.'[5] The new government's first major measure was the nationalisation of the Bank of England, a gesture of revenge for the fall of the previous Labour administration during the financial crisis of 1931 that was blamed by the Left on a bankers' conspiracy. The Labour government of 1945–51 continued the wartime controls, allowing little scope for the resumption of the merchant banks' international activities. Moreover, after the war the dollar was the global currency and New York the world's leading international financial centre.

Exhausted by the effort of sheer survival and hobbled by official restrictions on lending and a weak pound, the merchant banks turned their attention to the domestic market. They focused on developing relationships with UK companies, particularly the manufacturing sector, for which they raised funds through equity and debt issues. But access to the capital market was strictly controlled by the authorities, and form-filling rather than entrepreneurship was the order of the day.

Amongst the merchant banks there was an unspoken 'gentleman's agreement' not to poach one another's corporate clients. This was fine for the incumbent firms, but it hardly suited newcomers trying to build a business. The challenge to the established order was led by Warburgs, the firm set up by refugee bankers Siegmund Warburg and Henry Grunfeld in 1946. The occasion was the deal struck by the directors of British Aluminium to sell the firm to ALCOA (Aluminium Corporation of America). Warburgs mounted a hostile takeover bid, a virtually unprecedented initiative, on behalf of a rival bidder. The Establishment firms came out in support of Hambros and Lazards, British Aluminium's advisers, and the firm's management. But the battle was won in the marketplace, where Warburgs' aggressive accumulation of shares made it victorious.

The 'Aluminium War' of winter 1958–9 put the City on the front pages and turned merchant bankers into celebrities. The acceleration of the restructuring of British industry, encouraged by Harold Wilson's Labour administration of 1964–70, provided them with plenty of work and kept them in the headlines. In the 1960s merchant bankers enjoyed a distinctly mystical status as fixers: the government even set up its own merchant bank, the Industrial Reorganisation Corporation, headed by a former Warburgs partner, Ronald Grierson, whose brief was to 'drag British industry kicking and screaming into the twentieth century'.[6] In fact, in these years, 'bring in a merchant banker' became a widespread panacea. How fitting then that after the election of 1970 it was a former merchant banker, Edward Heath, who became the new prime minister.

A tale of two cities

The revival of the City as an international financial centre, the basis of its importance today, was due to it becoming the principal location of the

Euromarkets – in *addition* to its traditional domestic activities. The rise of a market in offshore US dollars in Europe in the late 1950s was the outcome of a combination of economic and political factors. The most important was the recurrent US balance of payments deficits, resulting in a large pool of externally held dollars. These were augmented by dollars placed offshore by US corporations and investors, where they earned higher rates of interest than available at home owing to US banking regulations. Another source was the dollar balances of the Communist countries that were fearful of placing them on deposit in New York lest they should be taken hostage by the US government in a Cold War crisis.

The Euromarkets comprise a series of markets spanning the maturity spectrum: short-term, the Eurocurrency market; medium-term, syndicated loans and Euro notes; and long-term, the Eurobond market. Each has had a different pattern of development and presented varying opportunities for British banks and City firms.

The Eurocurrency market is a market for short-term loans and deposits, mostly between banks. It grew rapidly in the late 1950s and 1960s: in 1963 the overall market was estimated at $12 billion; by the end of the decade it was $65 billion, an annual compound rate of growth of 31 per cent. Some of the British overseas banks, notably Bank of London and South America, were important pioneers of the Eurocurrency market and the British clearing banks also played a significant part. But it was American money-centre commercial banks that really developed the market in London, soon being joined by European and Japanese banks: in 1960, seventy-seven foreign banks, mostly American, had a presence in London; by 1970 the number had more than doubled to 163.[7] Except in the early years, the merchant banks played only a minor part in the development of the Eurocurrency market, their balance sheets being too small for them to act as significant receivers of dollar deposits relative to the scale of the market.

The Eurobond market grew up to meet the requirements of governments and corporations for long-term finance. It was the creation of European banks and was developed as a means of competing with the US investment banks that dominated the international capital market in New York, where they got the lion's share of the fees and commissions. The Eurobond market was launched in July 1963 in London with a $15 million issue on behalf of Autostrade, the Italian national highways authority. Warburgs was the lead manager of the issue, with prominent German, Belgian and Dutch banks as co-managers. Within weeks of the opening of the

Eurobond market, President Kennedy announced the introduction of a tax on foreign borrowing in the US capital market to curb the outflow of dollars that was contributing to the gaping US balance of payments deficit. 'This is a day you will all remember forever,' Henry Alexander, president of US bank Morgan Guaranty, presciently told his colleagues on hearing the news. 'It will change the face of American banking and force all the business off to London.'[8]

The Eurobond market took off and the international capital market did indeed decamp to London, a remarkable stroke of serendipity for the City. Between 1963 and 1972 the volume of Eurobond new issues rose from $148 million to $5.5 billion. In the formative years from the mid-1960s to the mid-1970s, the merchant banks Warburgs, Hambros, Barings, Rothschilds and Samuel Montagu featured regularly in the league tables of Eurobond managers, as did Barclays, Lloyds and County Bank (NatWest's investment banking arm). But from the mid-1970s, the UK banks were sidelined in the Eurobond market by the leading Wall Street investment banks and the major European universal banks. In the 1980s only Warburgs made regular appearances in the top twenty, and by the end of the decade even Warburgs had fallen to near the bottom of the table.[9]

The quadrupling of the price of oil in 1973 gave a massive boost to the Euromarkets: over the years 1972–80, international commercial banks, mostly in London and New York, were recipients of $154 billion in short-term petrodollar deposits. While the oil exporters found themselves awash with oil revenues, other countries suffered balance of payments deficits that somehow had to be bridged and most governments took the view that borrowing was politically less painful than raising taxes or curtailing consumption. The foremost source of funding was by borrowing from international banks, which on-lent the petrodollars that they had on deposit from the oil producers.

The bulk of such so-called petrodollar recycling was arranged in London. It mostly took the form of large floating-rate loans with medium-term maturities, meaning three to ten years. Such loans to sovereign (government) borrowers and international agencies, or the borrowings of multinational corporations, were often so large that they were advanced by syndicates of banks, the risk exposure being too great for even the biggest international banks to be prepared to go it alone. The UK clearing banks and US and European banks were active as arrangers and participants in syndicated loans.

The merchant banks were unable to participate directly in the syndicated loan sector of the Euromarket because their balance sheets were too small. However, they did play a part in the market's early development in the late 1960s and early 1970s as participants in consortium banks. Consortium banks were specialist joint ventures formed by groups of international banks, mainly in London, to operate in the medium-term sector of the Euromarkets. Some merchant banks played active roles in the formation of consortium banks, and most of them became a participant in one or more. The UK merchant banks contributed their name, their knowledge of the London market, their contacts with the authorities and their expertise in syndication techniques, while the much bigger foreign commercial bank partners stumped up the capital.

This mutually advantageous state of affairs came to an end in 1974 when in the atmosphere of crisis following the failure of the German bank Herstatt, the Bank of England required formal undertakings from consortium bank participants guaranteeing the liabilities of their joint ventures. This demand drew attention to the scale of consortium participants' contingent liabilities, which were perilously large for the merchant banks. One after another, the merchant banks withdrew from the consortium banks, thereby severing their connections with the medium-term sector of the Euromarkets.

Hosting the Euromarkets, the world's fastest-growing and most innovative financial markets, *ought* to have provided a shot in the arm for the City's indigenous banks. It did, but only to a limited extent. Although the UK clearing banks were active in the Eurocurrency markets and in syndicated lending, domestic retail banking remained their core business. The fundamental problem was that their British corporate clients had only modest need of Euromarket finance, and when they did they could turn to a bank that specialised in it.

The merchant banks were unable to participate substantially in the Eurocurrency and medium-term loan markets because of the relatively small size of their balance sheets. Of course, they could have raised extra capital and taken on greater Euromarket deposits, but that would have diluted the control of the existing shareholders, in some cases still the founding families. The merchant banks and some of the clearing banks did make waves in the Eurobond market, but only at the beginning. One by one, they pulled out of the business or gradually slid down the league tables.

Why did the merchant banks lose out in the Eurobond market? Firstly, because the real focus of their energies was domestic corporate finance work, which was profitable and prestigious and did not require a large capital base. Secondly, because the lack of a large capital base became a problem with the introduction of issuing techniques such as the 'bought deal', an innovation of the late 1970s, that deployed the balance sheet as a competitive weapon. Thirdly, because by this time they lacked the client base of governments, international agencies and multinational corporations with which the large international banks had banking relationships. Fourthly, because even when they got a mandate to manage an issue, they had difficulty marketing the bonds. And finally, because after the heady years of the 1960s and early 1970s, competition became so intense that Eurobond primary market operations were scarcely profitable. In 1987 a strategic review of business conducted by Royal Bank of Canada's international investment banking operation, Orion Royal, revealed that its Eurobond activities had been unprofitable for years; even for Warburgs the Eurobond business seldom made any money.[10] The poor return on Eurobond business was less of a problem for the merchant banks' rivals, because they had deeper pockets and could cross-subsidise this prestigious, attention-winning activity from other earnings. Thus what initially appeared to be a golden opportunity for the merchant banks turned out to be distinctly tarnished.

The shortcomings in the merchant banks' Eurobond distribution capabilities were partly a reflection of a different failure of the domestic City to embrace the offshore City. This was the absence of integration between the domestic securities market and the offshore market. Eurobonds were neither listed nor traded on the London Stock Exchange, by-passing its firms of brokers and jobbers. Dealing was done over the telephone, and later on screen, between the banks' bond traders, and the securities were listed with the specialist clearing houses Euroclear in Brussels and Cedel in Luxembourg. This was why the merchant banks had difficulties in marketing Eurobonds, because they were unable to channel them via the Stock Exchange brokers through which they distributed their sterling securities issues.

A tale of one city

The cheap and efficient mechanisms of the Eurobond market called into question the Stock Exchange's anti-competitive and costly commission structure and its restrictions on membership. But so long as the sterling and offshore markets were kept separate by exchange controls there was no effective pressure for change.

Exchange controls, providing the authorities with control over capital movements by companies and investors, had been introduced in 1939 at the start of the war. They were retained afterwards to support the exchange rate. When sterling was floated in 1972 this purpose disappeared, but the controls remained. By then they had been around for so long that hardly anyone remembered working without them.

In the late 1970s the pound soared as North Sea oil turned sterling into a petrocurrency. In October 1979 the recently elected government led by Margaret Thatcher abolished exchange controls in the vain hope of curbing the rise of sterling to help the hard-pressed manufacturing sector. The move was also an opening salvo in the Thatcher administration's attack upon the post-war corporatist order. Remarkably, the move was made with little analysis of its impact on the City and not much more consultation with City interests, about which the Stock Exchange chairman, Nicholas Goodison, protested publicly and angrily at the time.[11]

Abolition took the City by surprise. 'I am sure we have planned for this,' declared a flustered clearing banker, 'but I have yet to find the man who did it.'[12] Most surprised of all were the 750 members of the Bank of England's Exchange Control Department, whose jobs disappeared overnight. But once the initial shock was over, the City began to take advantage of its new freedom: between 1978 and 1985 the overseas assets of UK institutional investors rose from £10.4 billion to £77.3 billion.

City fund management firms quickly developed international expertise, thus becoming well placed to service the international diversification of US pension funds that began in the 1980s. As a result, London emerged as a leading centre for international fund management. This, in turn, led to the growth of secondary market dealing in international equities and to the rapid rise in the number of foreign companies listed on the London Stock Exchange. The City became the centre for international equities trading, accounting for three-fifths of world volume. Moreover, abolition boosted London's position as an international capital market by allowing overseas borrowers to raise sterling loans – 'bulldog bonds' as they became known. It also led to a big surge in the sterling sector of the Eurobond market, which grew from being one of the smallest sectors of the market to fifth largest by the mid-1980s.

The removal of exchange controls exposed the insularity and uncompetitiveness of the UK's securities sector, which since the war had been domestically cocooned by exchange controls as a barrier to outward investment and by the weakness of sterling, making inward investment unattractive. The surge in the purchase of overseas securities by UK investors *should* have been a bonanza for UK stockbrokers, but in fact the bulk of the business was handled by foreign firms: according to one calculation, 95 per cent of the overseas investments made by the twenty leading British pension funds were handled by foreign brokerage firms.[13] This was one of the pieces of evidence that persuaded the Bank of England and ministers that the British securities industry was in need of a radical overhaul. The outcome was the deal arrived at in July 1983 between the Stock Exchange and the government, which led to the abolition of fixed commission rates and the end of the separation of the functions of broking and market making. At the same time, restrictions on the ownership of Stock Exchange firms were relaxed, allowing them to be purchased by banks for the first time. This package of changes that would transform the UK securities industry soon became known as the 'Big Bang'.

Between 1983 and October 1986, when the new trading arrangements became operational, all the leading securities firms, with the exceptions of Cazenove and Smith Brothers, were bought lock, stock and barrel by outside parties. In total seventy-seven Stock Exchange firms were acquired, turning more than 500 of their former partners into millionaires. Sixteen were purchased by merchant banks; twenty-seven by the clearing banks, and other UK financial firms; fourteen by US banks; and twenty by other foreign, mostly European, banks.[14]

The restructuring of the securities industry presented the UK merchant banks with a strategic dilemma. Should they stick with their established pattern of activities or should they diversify into securities business, following the 'integrated' model of the US investment banks? The current activities of the merchant banks – mergers and acquisitions, corporate fund-raising and fund management – were client-based, fee-paying, advisory activities. They were reasonably low-risk and required relatively modest amounts of capital. But how much longer would clients go on using them when they could get a full range of services, including in-house securities expertise, from an integrated rival?

The approach to business of the US investment banks was transaction-driven rather than relationship-based. That is, they bid aggressively for each mandate as a one-off piece of business, rather than as part of an ongoing client–adviser relationship. Moreover, the US investment banks derived substantial, but variable, revenues from speculative proprietary trading. This pattern of business was riskier and required more capital; but it could be highly profitable, especially in a bull market.

Most of the leading UK merchant banks – Barings, Hambros, Hill Samuel, Kleinworts, Morgan Grenfell and Warburgs – went for the integrated approach, based on the US model. So did Barclays, NatWest and Midland amongst the major clearing banks. The opposite strategy of sticking to their established pattern of business was adopted by Schroders, Lazards and Flemings amongst the merchant banks, and the stockbroker Cazenove. Rothschilds put a toe in the water by acquiring a minority interest in Smith Brothers, the other significant independent securities house, which became Smith New Court.

The UK merchant banks emerged from Big Bang ostensibly strengthened through diversification and expansion. In fact, at the end of the 1980s they appeared to be as formidable a presence in the City as in their original heyday a century earlier. There was – despite everything they had been through – remarkable continuity. No fewer than eight out of the top twelve firms in 1890 were still in the premier league a hundred years later, a much higher corporate survival rate than in most industries (see Table 6.1).[15]

Table 6.1 **Top merchant banks at the time of the Barings crisis of 1890 and in 1990 (£ million, partners' capital and shareholders' funds)**

1890	Capital	1990	Capital	Founded
Rothschilds	6.7	Warburgs	720	1946
Barings	2.9	Hambros	467	1839
JS Morgan	1.8	Kleinwort Benson	412	1830
Seligmans	1.5	Morgan Grenfell	354	1838
Lazards	1.2	Flemings	314	1873
Schroders	1.1	Schroders	310	1818
Hambros	1.0	Barings	193	1762
Brown Shipley	1.0	Samuel Montagu	179	1853
Kleinwort, Sons	0.8	Charterhouse	176	1925
Antony Gibbs	0.6	Singer & Friedlander	169	1916
Frederick Huth	0.6	Rothschilds	164	1809
Samuel Montagu	0.4	Lazards	126	1877

The great City sell-off

Already there were clouds on the horizon. The Big Bang process had led to massive over-capacity in the UK securities industry and margins and profits had fallen owing to keener price competition, although these developments had been hidden by the boom of 1985–6. Hill Samuel found itself in trouble almost immediately and was acquired by TSB in 1987, after which it quickly sank without trace. The stock market crash of October 1987 inflicted losses on the integrated firms. Morgan Grenfell suffered the double blow of big losses on its equity business and being caught up in the Guinness scandal. In 1989 the embattled management accepted an offer from Deutsche Bank, the first of the merchant banks to pass into foreign ownership

Deutsche Bank's acquisition of Morgan Grenfell was a strategic counter-move to the build-up of the presence of the Wall Street investment banks in London in the late 1980s. For instance, between 1986 and 1989 Merrill Lynch increased its staff in London from 760 to 1,600, Morgan Stanley from 608 to 950, and Goldman Sachs from 520 to 744.[16] Why this expansion? Essentially because the Wall Street firms had come to the conclusion that the process of European economic integration (with the single market due to be completed by 1992) would generate an investment banking bonanza. The advance of US investment banking operations in London was checked by the recession at the beginning of the 1990s, which led to a downturn in activity and profits. Business revived in 1992, and 1993 saw record profits on Wall Street. On the back of these earnings, the Wall Street firms launched a worldwide expansion drive, targeting London in particular as the bridgehead for Europe.

The expanding activity of the Wall Street investment banks, and soon Continental banks too, squeezed the UK merchant banks from two directions. First, competition for talent sent salaries soaring. Second, competition for business drove down fees and deprived them of mandates they would otherwise have expected to win. The US firms were in a position to bid aggressively for people and business because of the profits generated by their Wall Street operations, which enjoyed higher fee levels than were customary in London and were booming. Continental banks were also able to subsidise their London operations, thanks to the infinite patience of their shareholders. The outcome was that one by one, for one reason or another, almost all the UK merchant banks were sold to new overseas owners (see Table 6.2).

Table 6.2 **Sale of UK financial firms, 1989–2000**

Year	UK Firm	Purchaser	Price (£ million)
1989	Morgan Grenfell	Deutsche Bank	950
1995	Barings	ING	–
1995	Warburgs	Swiss Bank Corporation	860
1995	Kleinwort Benson	Dresdner Bank	1,000
1995	Smith New Court	Merrill Lynch	526
1997	BZW (Barclays) (part)	CSFB	100
1997	NatWest Markets (part)	Bankers Trust/Deutsche Bank	129
1997	Hambros	Société Générale/Investec	738
1997	Mercury Asset Management	Merrill Lynch	3,100
2000	Schroders (part)	Citigroup	1,350
2000	Flemings	Chase Manhattan	4,800

Warburgs had seized the opportunity of Big Bang to buy two leading firms of brokers and a top jobber, emerging without question as the foremost UK investment bank. 'It dominates the UK market,' commented *Euromoney* in August 1994. Nevertheless, by then even Warburgs was feeling the pinch from rising costs – and in an attempt to boost profitability it had decided in February 1994 to expand its proprietary bond trading activities, a significant source of profits at some US investment banks. But Warburgs' timing was disastrous, since the market plunged immediately and big losses were incurred. Warburgs' other weakness was the lack of a substantial presence on Wall Street.

By the time that the bond trading débâcle became public knowledge in autumn 1994, Warburgs had become involved in secret merger talks with Morgan Stanley, a tie-up which had the potential, in the words of a Harvard Business School study, 'to create the investment bank of the future, a global powerhouse with complementary operations in Europe, the United States and Asia'.[17] But when the parties were unable to reach agreement, Morgan Stanley publicly pulled out of the negotiations, leaving Warburgs dead in the water: it had failed to deliver either a satisfactory performance or a viable forward strategy. A drastic attack on costs, plus management defections, further depressed morale and reduced the firm to, as the *Independent* put it in February 1995, 'an apparently aimless and demoralised organisation'.[18] Three months later Warburgs was bought by Swiss Bank Corporation for the bargain price of £860 million, little more than its net asset value; in other words the Warburgs brand name, a year earlier the City's foremost franchise, had been rendered virtually valueless.

Barings also was in the doo-doo. The collapse of the City's oldest merchant bank, founded in 1762, was announced to an astounded public on 25 February 1995. Like Warburgs, Barings' management had been beguiled by the notion that trading was an easy way of making money and had effectively bet the bank to back the activities of its supposed star trader, Nick Leeson, in Singapore. In fact, Leeson had been making losses for years, but successfully covering them up while he reported profits to his bosses in London and took even bigger gambles in desperate attempts to recoup the money already lost. By the time the music stopped, he had run up losses of £830 million – just about wiping out the bank's capital. Unlike the Barings crisis of 1890, the Bank of England was unable to engineer a rescue by the other UK banks and refused to get involved itself. It argued that the failure of Barings did not pose a risk to the financial system as a whole; and that its direct intervention would not only undermine the discipline of 'moral hazard', but suggest to the City's many foreign banks that domestic firms were more equal than others, which would be damaging to London as an international financial centre. Although the Bank's final point was probably valid, it sent a signal to the other UK merchant banks that they could no longer count on special help from their protector of old, making the offers from Continental banks eager to get into investment banking in London even more difficult to resist. Barings, and its substantial liabilities, were bought by Dutch bank ING – for £1.

Unnerved by the fate of Barings and Warburgs, the management at Kleinwort Benson was receptive to an approach by Dresdner Bank. Arguing that the time had come to seek the support of a big commercial bank, they agreed to sell the business for £1 billion in June 1995. It was a fair but not spectacular price, amounting to a 20 per cent premium for the brand name, but a distinctly better deal for the owners than Warburgs or Barings managed. The following month, yet another significant City firm passed out of UK ownership. Wearied by, in the chairman's words, 'the same problems as before of trying to break into America and to build up corporate finance', the senior management at Smith New Court came to the conclusion that 'the Smith show was over' and accepted an offer from Merrill Lynch.[19]

The passing of Warburgs, Barings and Kleinworts into foreign ownership bestowed the mantle of UK national champion on to Barclays' investment banking arm, Barclays de Zoete Wedd (BZW). BZW – a Big Bang teaming of the firms of de Zoete & Bevan, a not quite top-notch broker, and Wedd Durlacher, a leading jobber, with Barclays Merchant Bank – had the advantage of its parent's substantial balance sheet. But somehow the business never quite came together to fulfil its potential. Internal wrangling compounded by cultural tensions with the parent took a heavy toll. As City commentator Christopher Fildes would put it: 'Asked who France's greatest poet was, André Gide replied: "Victor Hugo, *hélas*." That in its grudging way was the City's view of BZW.'[20]

In 1996 Barclays decided to commit further resources to BZW to give it the impetus to take on the US and European banks. A dynamic new chief executive was appointed, who started to hire new staff and restructure the business with the ambition of making BZW a global player. But if BZW was to take on the world, it would have to buy its way into Wall Street. This was not impossible for a bank of Barclays' size, but the senior management shied when faced by the cost and the risk. Even as BZW was being overhauled, the US investment banking industry was consolidating and the stakes were rising sharply. Barclays' chief executive, Martin Taylor, came to the conclusion that even the revamped BZW was 'sub-scale' in terms of the global game. And so Barclays pulled the plug and sold the equities and corporate finance business to Credit Suisse, though retaining the fixed-interest side which was renamed Barclays Capital.

But it was not quite time to carve RIP on the headstone of UK investment banking, for in theory there was still a candidate hoping to make the grade as a national champion – NatWest Markets. In fact, had the bid by NatWest Markets to buy Warburgs in 1995 been successful, it would have been a very plausible contender. However, the gentlemanly capitalists at Warburgs were horrified at the prospect of having to report to UK commercial bankers, whom they regarded as tradesmen, and turned to the Swiss for salvation from this dreadful fate. 'At a crucial moment for investment banking in the UK,' observes Philip Augar, chronicler of the decline of the merchant banks, 'class got in the way.'[21]

Building the business piecemeal in 1995 and 1996, NatWest Markets put in place the component parts of an effective operation and, in Augar's perhaps rose-tinted view, was becoming a formidable operation. In February 1997 it won the support of the NatWest main board for a big commitment to investment banking, one of the directors remarking to his colleagues that 'we are in serious danger of having a success on our hands'. But before the expansion plans could be implemented, the bank discovered a loss of £77 million in the books of NatWest Markets' derivatives business that had gone undetected for nearly three years. This embarrassment led to the departure of NatWest Markets' chief executive and a panic reaction at board level. Instead of being built up, NatWest Markets was dismembered: the treasury and foreign exchange functions were separated off and retained; European equities were sold to Bankers Trust; US and Asian derivatives to Deutsche Morgan Grenfell; Australian equities to Salomon Smith Barney; and the rest were closed down.

The retreats of Barclays and NatWest as players in the global investment banking game in 1997 have several common features. Traditional class and cultural tensions between commercial bankers and investment bankers played a part. So did wariness about the hazards of a costly acquisition in the US, where British banks had previously made some disastrous diversifications. Yet another factor undermining the resolution of both the Barclays and NatWest boards to persevere with investment banking was pressure from institutional investors who were sceptical about the quality of earnings from international investment banking. Instead, they applauded the conservative domestic strategy pursued by Lloyds Bank, which had focused its energies on UK retail banking – with spectacular returns for shareholders. 'The shareholders were starting to complain about our capital requirements and make unfavourable comparisons with Lloyds,' recalls Derek Wanless, NatWest group chief executive at the time. 'NatWest Markets became an issue at every meeting; it was a real pain in the neck. They said, even when it's going well, even if you do succeed, we won't value it so why bother to go through all the pain? If you fail, you've had it, and if you succeed we won't value it.'[22]

While Barclays and NatWest were retrenching, Hambros, founded in 1839, was falling apart. Hambros, the 'odd one out' amongst the merchant banks, had pursued an idiosyncratic development strategy, diversifying into insurance and estate agency business.[23] Its patchwork of activities produced poor results, not to mention a family feud and disgruntled outside shareholders. The final straw was its involvement in a disgraced takeover bid for the Co-op in spring 1997 that led to the resignation of key executives and the threat of legal action. Dismemberment took place in late 1997 and early 1998, against 'a mood of despondency across the entire firm, with heavy redundancies expected': the corporate finance arm was sold to French bank Société Générale for £300 million; the corporate loan business to the Belgian Générale de Banque for £10 million; and the 'rump' to South African investment bank Investec for £428 million.[24]

The sale of Schroders to Citigroup and of Flemings to Chase in the first half of 2000 was the final chapter (so far) of the story of the sell-off of the UK investment banks. Both firms had long protested their determination to remain independent, and with substantial shareholdings in the hands of the founding families there was scant likelihood of a hostile takeover bid. Uniquely amongst the UK investment banks, Schroders had a foothold in Wall Street, the medium-sized securities house Wertheim which it bought in 1986. But the US operation, difficult to manage and integrate with the rest of the group, proved more of a drain on management and resources than a contributor to the bottom line. Disagreements about the way forward on Wall Street caused friction amongst Schroders executives and led to resignations. Others began to depart because of uncertainty about the firm's future and the lure of big remuneration packages from rival firms.

'We were too small to be big, too big to be small,' was how Schroders' president, Sir George Mallinckrodt, would sum up the problem.[25] Expansion was one option. The purchase of Wasserstein Perella, a medium-sized Wall Street firm, was considered, as was a merger with Lehman Brothers. That would have brought Schroders up level with Credit Suisse First Boston, but still well behind Goldman Sachs, Morgan Stanley, Merrill Lynch and Salomon Smith Barney. So it was decided to sell the investment banking business, and to do so quickly before staff defections did further damage and while the bull market was still in full swing. Citigroup's investment bank Salomon Smith Barney was identified as the best match, since Schroders' UK and European operations filled a gap in its global network. Citigroup agreed and paid £1.35 billion for Schroders' investment banking activities employing 3,500 staff. At 1.7 times net asset value, it was a good price and there was admiration for the professionalism with which the 'inevitable' deal was done compared with other sales, such as Warburgs and BZW, not to mention Barings.[26] The asset management side of the business was not included in the sale and continues as an independent firm under the name Schroders.

A few months after the sale of Schroders' investment bank, Flemings accepted an offer from Chase Manhattan Bank for the whole firm. Since Big Bang, Flemings had successfully developed an integrated corporate advisory and capital markets capability and had built up a significant business in Europe and Asia. It was also a leading asset manager. But Flemings' management came to the same conclusion as Schroders about the viability of a middle-rank investment bank in the twenty-first century.

As the investment banking market became international, the UK players found themselves struggling because of the huge advantage enjoyed by the US firms, whose domestic market constitutes half the global market. Hence the imperative to establish a substantial presence on Wall Street, a challenge flunked by all the UK firms. As the larger European corporate clients began to shed medium-sized advisers in favour of the top US investment banks, the writing was on the wall for the middle-rank firms. 'The demise of the UK investment banks,' commented the *Financial Times* on the sale of Schroders, 'is a natural part of the process of international specialisation that results from globalisation.' [27]

But others blamed self-inflicted shortcomings rather than global processes. Philip Augar, a practitioner during the 1990s, ascribes considerable culpability to the amateurish 'gentlemanly capitalism' of particular firms, notably Barings, Warburgs, Hill Samuel and Hambros. As for the clearing banks, he blames pusillanimous senior management, class-based tribal warfare – and failure at the political level to defend a national interest. According to him, there were two key moments when a lead from the Bank of England or the government, as would surely have been forthcoming in France or Germany, might have made a difference and sustained a British bank amongst the global players: in 1995, when NatWest was in negotiation to acquire Warburgs; and in 1997, when Barclays was dithering about whether to commit major resources to BZW or to pull the plug. But such intervention was out of fashion in Britain and the sell-off proceeded.

Yet it would not be entirely perverse to argue that, far from being a national humiliation, the sell-off was a triumph of economic rationality. That the mass surrender of the UK merchant banks in the 1990s, and all those Stock Exchange firms in the 1980s, was in fact a rational exit at the top of the market from an industry which had been artificially cosseted by barriers to entry and cosy, cartel-like practices. It was an industry, furthermore, with highly cyclical and thus poor-quality earnings, in which UK banks would always be at a disadvantage relative to those with much larger domestic economies. In short, the argument runs, it was better – not just for the owners but also for the national interest – to get out while the going was good rather than suffer a lingering decline and attrition of value like the motor industry, which ended up in foreign hands anyway.

Hong Kong West

'I am sorry to announce the demise of the City of London,' wrote Christopher Fildes as yet another UK merchant bank threw in the towel. 'As from today, it is being re-launched as Hong Kong West. The City's genius has always been to reinvent itself. So Hong Kong West is just its latest invention. It is the first, though, in which its players have conceded that they cannot keep up with the game and must live by providing a playground for others.'[28]

Prior to the 1960s, employment in the City was almost entirely by British firms, but by the end of the decade the staff of the 163 foreign banks in London numbered 12,000. The foreign bank presence in London grew rapidly during the Euromarket boom of the 1970s, and by 1980 there were 453 foreign banks with 31,000 staff. By the end of the 1980s they had increased to 521 while their staffing had risen to 60,000. During the 1990s the number of foreign banks grew to 537, before declining to 481 in 2001 owing to amalgamations and economic difficulties in some emerging economies. About 50,000 people were added to their payrolls in the 1990s, making an overall total in 2001 of around 110,000 foreign bank staff in London.[29] By the beginning of the twenty-first century, two-thirds of those engaged in money-centre banking activities in London worked for foreign institutions.

The acquisition of UK merchant banks by overseas buyers made the headlines, yet in total the staff who found themselves with new paymasters from overseas numbered no more than 25,000, less than a quarter of total foreign bank staff in London in 2001. Of greater significance was the organic build-up of established foreign banks in London and the transfer of investment banking functions to London. Instances of the latter process were the shift by US bank Prudential-Bache International of its overseas headquarters from Luxembourg to London in March 1997 and the reallocation of responsibility for international operations from Tokyo to the City by Nikko Securities, Japan's third largest brokerage house, the following October.[30]

It was not just the UK merchant banks that passed into overseas ownership. Many of the major fund management firms have been bought by foreign owners: Phillips & Drew (by UBS), Morgan Grenfell Asset Management (by Deutsche Bank), Mercury Asset Management (by Merrill Lynch), Newton (by Mellon Bank), Flemings (by Chase), and Gartmore (by Nationwide Mutual).[31] Of the very large fund managers, only Barclays

Capital, Legal and General, and Schroders are now British-owned. Following the acquisition of Guardian Royal Exchange by Axa of France in 1999, a survey by the Fund Managers Association revealed that, for the first time, more than half of the workforce in the UK fund management industry worked for foreign firms.[32]

Amongst the UK insurance companies, eleven out of the top twenty firms conducting general insurance business (i.e. aviation, fire, marine, motor, personal accident and property) were foreign-owned by 2000, although the sector leaders CGNU and Royal & Sun Alliance were still British. Foreign ownership was less prevalent in the long-term insurance sector (i.e. life assurance, annuity and investment policies), where only six of the top twenty firms belonged to overseas owners and the leading five firms – Prudential, CGNU, Barclays Life, Standard Life and Lloyds TSB Life – were all British.[33]

Moreover, the two leading UK insurance companies harboured ambitions as international players. 'We will be creating a British champion,' commented chairman designate Pehr Gyllenhammer, announcing the £18 billion merger of CGU and Norwich Union in February 2000. 'Both companies were in the top league of European insurers, but do not have the critical mass for the consolidation that is ongoing.'[34] While CGNU focused on expansion in Europe, Prudential, which already had substantial US and Asian interests, was thinking globally. In March 2001 it announced a $21 billion agreed acquisition of the Texas-based US insurance company American General, the largest-ever transatlantic merger in the financial sector. American General was the biggest quoted US life insurance company and the newly combined group would be the world's sixth largest insurer. 'You can see a split between a select group of financial services and insurance companies that are going to be successful on a global scale while others will drift away,' said Jonathan Bloomer, Prudential's chief executive.[35] Much to his chagrin, the US insurance giant AIG launched a counter-bid and carried off the prize.

Bloomer's chagrin was matched only by that of Clara Furse, chief executive of the London Stock Exchange, which in October 2001 made a £570 million offer for London's derivative exchange, LIFFE, that most observers saw as a shoo-in. After all, it seemed the obvious 'London' solution, bringing together the City's foremost financial exchanges – and rightly or wrongly, few doubted that it was the Bank of England's preferred option. Yet LIFFE, unimpressed by the Stock Exchange's approach, chose instead to sell out to

Euronext (formed by the merger in 2000 of the Paris, Amsterdam and Brussels stock exchanges), even though the French bid was £15 million less. This surprise outcome was eloquent testimony to the genuine levelness of the London playing field and to the redundancy of 'national' solutions in an international financial centre; while a telling aspect of the new union was that Euronext would be switching its own derivatives operations to London and plugging them into the LIFFE Connect trading system.

International tie-ups have long been a feature of the leading City accountancy firms. Forerunners of KPMG and Deloitte Touche Tohumatsu operated as transatlantic businesses from the mid-1920s, and the latter now incorporates a leading Japanese firm. Arthur Andersen, which originated in Chicago, expanded into Europe in the 1950s and today has 85,000 staff with 390 offices in 84 countries. PricewaterhouseCoopers, the biggest of the City accountancy firms, has 135,000 staff with 850 offices in 150 countries. 'It is a global market,' commented Price Waterhouse chief executive Jim Schiro at the time of the mega-merger between that firm and Coopers & Lybrand in 1997. 'Ten years ago, we were operating in international markets. Today, you have globally integrated businesses.'[36]

The largest of the City law firms, Clifford Chance, has been the most vigorous in pursuing a global strategy. It became the world's biggest law firm in 2000 as a result of mergers with New York's Rogers & Wells and Germany's Pünder Volhard Weber & Axster. Freshfields, Lovells and Linklaters also merged with leading German firms to create pan-Europe businesses, a process taken furthest by Linklaters & Alliance that also absorbed leading firms from Belgium, Holland, Italy and Sweden and recruited a score of lawyers from the top Paris law firm. On the other hand, Wall Street law firms have mostly recoiled from mergers with London firms. Their preference for independence has been ascribed to incompatibilities between the US 'eat what you kill' pattern of partners' remuneration and the UK firms' 'lockstep' system that rewards seniority.[37] Instead, since the mid-1990s, Wall Street firms have been building up their own businesses in the City as a bridgehead from which to develop European networks. Their arrival with 'buckets of cash' to lure top British lawyers sent a frisson through the City firms, leading to further mergers and redoubled efforts to forge European alliances.

Looking at the picture as a whole at the start of the new millennium, a majority of City people work for foreign firms. In banking, the sole UK firm with global reach is HSBC, though it only appears towards the bottom end of investment banking league tables. In insurance, both CGNU and Prudential have substantial overseas interests, though the latter's first bid to become a global player did not come off. But a set of highly successful British-based accountancy and law firms are keeping the flag flying. However, their international reach has been achieved through mergers with foreign firms and most are well on their way to becoming cosmopolitan global confections.

The foreign ownership of much of the City has given rise to comparisons with the Wimbledon Tennis Championship: a tournament hosted by Britain but dominated by foreign players. Some, led by the Bank of England, take the view that this does not matter – that liberalised markets maximise economic efficiency and hence wealth creation. After all, Britain gets the benefits from hosting the event: the jobs; the taxes; the contributions to invisible earnings; and the profits from selling the strawberries and cream – in other words catering to the demands of the sector's highly paid workforce. 'Show me,' says the governor, Sir Edward George, 'a single statistic where the City is in decline.'[38]

What is the alternative? Intervention to support UK players would mean that the London market was no longer a level playing field and the UK authorities would forfeit their reputation as fair and dispassionate regulators. And why is it supposed that the authorities are able to judge better than the marketplace which firms, or how many firms, should compete in any market? Moreover, as globalisation proceeds apace, international banks are shedding national identities as they embrace staff, clients and shareholders from around the world – Citigroup's chairman Sandy Weill, with 230,000 employees worldwide, boasts of creating 'an unparalleled global footprint, being locally embedded in more than 100 countries and the leading nondomestic player in most'.[39]

Some are uneasy with a free-market stance. 'The fact remains that key decisions about the future of once British-owned merchant banks and securities houses will be made in Frankfurt or New York,' Hamish McRae wrote as early as 1995. 'It is hard to feel completely comfortable with this. There is the obvious fear that if the going gets tough, foreign owners are more likely to withdraw than home-based ones.'[40] In fact, just such a scenario appeared to be unfolding in spring 2000 as Deutsche Bank and Dresdner Bank toyed with a merger that might have led to the closure of Dresdner Kleinwort Benson with perhaps 6,000 redundancies in the City, though in fact the deal fell through.[41]

'Ownership brings influence,' argues Philip Augar, 'that's why branch offices always feel different to head offices.'[42] He contends that the domination of international investment banking by US firms casts New York in the role of the industry's global head office, with all other financial centres, including London, as subordinate satellites. He predicts that the brunt of the cutbacks resulting from future downturns will be borne by the satellite financial centres – notably London. 'What will emerge is a hub-and-spoke model run out of New York with a number of subsidiary centres on the rim. London will be just another city at the end of a spoke. It will be no worse off than Frankfurt, Paris or Zurich but as the current number two after New York, its relative status will be much diminished.'[43]

London's vulnerability in this scenario is partly a product of its lack of indigenous investment banks with a vested interest in its continued prosperity as a financial centre. 'Why should the heads of the foreign-owned, mega-conglomerates which dominate the City devote much time to its protection and enhancement?' asks Stanislas Yassukovich, one of the founding fathers of its international markets.[44] But then on the other hand, as the most cosmopolitan of all industries, the 'shock troops of global capitalism', as John Plender of the *Financial Times* calls them, they have no vested loyalty to any other financial centre, but will operate from wherever suits them best.[45]

So far there is no evidence of the fundamental reconfiguration of the relationship between New York and London suggested by Augar. If London is indeed now an investment banking 'branch office', it is a very big branch office where substantially more people work on the international side of the business than at 'head office'. Indeed, as a senior investment banker with a Wall Street firm puts it: 'When the downturn comes, it's New York that will take the brunt of the firings. Europe is where the action is and London is where that business is done.'[46]

An accident waiting to happen?

The leading players in the City today are a set of very large global investment banks that specialise in money-centre financial services, though some of them also undertake retail banking in their domestic markets. The same banks are also pre-eminent on Wall Street and have a major presence in other financial centres. The field is led by a trio of American firms, the

so-called 'bulge bracket', that regularly occupy top positions in the international investment banking league tables: Goldman Sachs, Merrill Lynch
and Morgan Stanley Dean Witter. Close on the heels of the bulge bracket,
and sometimes overtaking them in the league tables, are Credit Suisse First
Boston, Deutsche Bank, JP Morgan Chase, Schroder Salomon Smith
Barney and UBS Warburg.[47] Then there is a second rank of investment
banks with a substantial international presence, but which only occasionally make a place in the top ten, including ABN Amro, Bear Stearns, BNP
Paribas, Dresdner Kleinwort Wasserstein, Lehman Brothers, RBC Dominion Securities and Société Générale. And finally the niche players Cazenove, Lazards and Rothschilds, which, despite much smaller balance sheets,
are often to be found amongst the top twenty firms in the league tables.

The second rank may or may not include ING Barings, the investment
banking arm of Dutch insurance, banking and asset management group
ING, which got into investment banking in 1995 when it bought Barings
from the receivers in the wake of the Leeson débâcle. Subsequently it purchased Charterhouse Securities in London and a Wall Street boutique,
Furman Selz, for which it paid $600 million. Then it was rumoured to be
eyeing up one of the remaining US independent firms, Lehman Brothers
or Bear Stearns, to leap-frog into the top tier. Instead, in November 2000,
ING announced its withdrawal from New York and the scaling down of its
investment banking activities. Like Barclays and NatWest in 1997, the ING
board gazed into the Wall Street abyss and decided to beat a retreat rather
than bet the bank.

But other European banks have been more intrepid, or perhaps more
foolhardy. Credit Suisse took the Wall Street plunge back in the 1970s
through its tie-up with First Boston and more recently also acquired
Donaldson, Lufkin & Jenrette. Deutsche Bank bought Bankers Trust, Dresdner Bank purchased Wasserstein Perella, and UBS shelled out for Paine
Webber. The big US money-centre banks, notably Chase Manhattan, have
also been busy buying up Wall Street firms. Further consolidation, driven
by economies of scale and scope, is widely expected – particularly the
acquisition of the remaining independent middle-rank investment banks
by others trying to achieve critical mass. 'We are close to the end of the
third act of a five-act play,' is the way John Studzinski, head of European
investment banking at Morgan Stanley, puts it.[48]

The consolidation in the industry has meant that mergers and
acquisitions expertise, particularly on complex cross-border deals, is

concentrated in a few hands. This has resulted in conflicts of interest when banks find themselves on both sides of a deal. Goldman Sachs was confronted by just such a dilemma in 1999, when one client, Vodafone of the UK, launched a hostile bid for another, Mannesmann of Germany. A court injunction by Mannesmann forced the bank to step down as adviser to Vodafone. Handling such conflicts of interest is now 'item number one', says an investment banker. 'They can at least take comfort from one thing,' comments the *Financial Times*. 'The fact that there are so few of them is a source of strength as well as of reputational risk. As long as the top investment banks are needed to handle the biggest takeovers, the companies involved may have to accept the occasional appearance of conflict.'[49]

Competitive pressure to win corporate finance mandates to boost fee income, not to mention bonuses, has exerted a distorting effect on the candour and independence of the investment advice provided by in-house securities analysts. Fund managers are increasingly reluctant to take the research of the big US investment banks at face value because analysts have become puppets of the investment bankers. Empirical evidence is the 'death of the "sell" note': on Wall Street the ratio of analysts' 'buy' to 'sell' recommendations went from six to one in the early 1990s to 100 to one in 2000.[50] A snapshot in February 2001 revealed that the research departments of the ten largest banks had 57 'sell' recommendations to over 7,000 'buy' notices outstanding. Some firms have devised euphemisms such as 'underperform' or 'avoid' to circumvent the dreaded 'sell' word.

Bulge-bracket investment banks and aspiring bulge-bracket investment banks are costly operations. The foremost expense is their highly paid personnel, who are able to hold shareholders to ransom in the good years and extract a substantial part of the profits through salaries and bonuses. For many key staff, their bonus may be several times an already not inconsiderable salary. It is widely alleged that such performance-related payments encourage individual members of staff to take excessive risks because of the asymmetrical distribution of risks and returns: if the punt pays off he gets a big bonus; if it goes wrong, shareholders are lumbered with the losses. And even if he gets the sack, in a bull market he will probably walk straight into another job.

As a rule of thumb, an investment bank aims to operate on an 'expense ratio' – the proportion of revenues that go to pay the bills, mostly for staff – in the range of 50–60 per cent. Its ability to cover its expense cost base requires a substantial and constant deal-flow. But mergers and acquisitions, corporate fund-raising and securities trading are cyclical activities that vary markedly, being much more active and profitable in bull markets than in bear markets. And other sides of the business, such as privatisation work and project finance, are also only *intermittent* revenue generators. If the deal-flow falls off, expense ratios start to soar – in spring 2001, as business turned down, it was reported that they had risen to 80–90 per cent at some investment banks. It may be that there are reserves salted away from the good years or that there are other areas of activity with more regular earnings, such as fund management or retail banking, that can cross-subsidise the investment banking operations. But only in the short term. The fastest way of slashing costs to meet falling revenues is through redundancies – yet sackings not only vitiate all the painstaking and costly hard work of putting a star team together in the first place, but frighten and demoralise those who are left.

So when margins are squeezed, investment banks are tempted to look for ways of boosting revenues rather than cutting costs. As a general proposition, higher risks generate higher returns – so long as you avoid going bust. Proprietary trading is the fix to which investment banks tend to resort – with disastrous results for Barings, Warburgs and plenty of others down the years. But these days banks need not do it amateurishly themselves. There are professionals who specialise in sophisticated speculation for them – the hedge funds.

The hedge funds' capital is mostly subscribed by large investment and commercial banks that are circumscribed in speculating directly by banking regulations. Further funds are raised by borrowing, from shareholders and other lenders, some hedge funds having debt to equity ratios of 50:1. Successfully conducted, such geared-up speculation can provide much greater rates of return for shareholders than everyday banking business. In theory, with sophisticated mathematical models to take care of risk, they are veritable money machines.

New York based Long-Term Capital Management (LTCM) was one of the biggest and most prestigious hedge funds. Its directors included a former vice-president of the Federal Reserve, one of Wall Street's top traders and a winner of the Nobel Prize for economics – and it was backed *en masse* by the big investment banks. Nevertheless, it still went spectacularly belly-up in September 1998, owing to the Russian default and turbulence in the international financial markets. Its failure could have triggered the liquidation of positions estimated at $200 billion, causing mayhem in the financial markets. Likely losses to the banks from which LTCM had borrowed were put at $14 billion, a sufficient threat to the international banking system for the New York Federal Reserve to step in and arm-twist the shareholders to stump up $3.65 billion to re-capitalise the fund. The near-collapse of LTCM and the losses sustained by its backers were acute embarrassments for many of the world's biggest banks, including Goldman Sachs, Merrill Lynch, Deutsche Bank, Barclays and even the Italian central bank.

Investment banking is a risky business, and not just in the City. Relatively recent years have seen the fall of Drexel Burnham, Kidder Peabody and EF Hutton in New York and Yamaichi Securities in Tokyo. But they were just small fry. Surely today's consolidated, integrated, diversified mega-banks run by some of the brightest, or certainly best-paid, brains in town are too big and too smart to fail – aren't they? That is what they said about the *Titanic*.

Regulation provides an external constraint on the assumption of excessive risk by individual banks. But the big global US investment banks have no single regulator that assesses their activities in the round. It is a situation regarded by a senior figure at London's Financial Services Authority as 'the major threat to the international financial system at the moment'.[51] The US authorities agree; but hobbled by Congressional politics, they reply that reform will only be forthcoming 'after the next disaster'. If the fall out from LTCM's near-collapse was deemed potentially calamitous for the international financial system, what about the damage the meltdown of a bulge-bracket firm would inflict? Of course, it could not be allowed to happen – there would have to be some sort of rescue by the central banks. 'It is the world's taxpayers,' warns John Plender, 'who have most to fear from the investment banks.'[52]

7

The Mighty Markets

Kennedy assassinated, England winning the World Cup, Thatcher's fall, the death of Diana, 9/11 – almost anyone old enough remembers where he or she was. Only one British financial event is remotely a contender to join that pantheon: 'Black Wednesday' on 16 September 1992, when amidst humiliating scenes for the Major government Britain was compelled to leave the exchange rate mechanism (ERM) of the European monetary system, less than two years after joining it. As the dust began to settle that evening, the one thing everyone was agreed upon was that it was a date for the history books. Unusually for a spot verdict, it was spot on.

The sequence of events leading to this undignified exit had unfolded relentlessly. It began on 3 June when a referendum in Denmark rejected the recently signed Treaty of Maastricht. Next day Mitterrand committed France to a referendum (on 20 September). During the rest of June and into July the deutschmark strengthened on the back of dollar weakness, but sterling came under considerable pressure. In late July the government, desperate to achieve lower interest rates, contemplated altering the sterling–deutschmark parity off its own bat. But in John Major's retrospective words, 'the crucial judgement was made that a substantial devaluation, voluntarily made, would be likely to result in higher, not lower, interest rates, because the markets would lose confidence in sterling'.[1] From that point, whatever his misgivings, Major decided to stake his government's entire economic credibility on avoiding devaluation.

As early as 21 August the omens were poor, as the co-ordinated intervention that day of eighteen central banks proved unable to bolster the US dollar. 'It was the first big victory for the markets,' Major would note, 'and gave them a taste for blood that left them on the prowl, hunting ailing victims into which they could sink their fangs.'[2] On 1 September sterling went to its lowest level against the deutschmark since May 1990, but barely a week later Major publicly insisted that 'the soft option, the devaluer's option, the inflationary option, would be a betrayal of our future' and was therefore 'not the government's policy'.[3] Sterling was not the only European currency under pressure, and over the weekend of 12/13 September the Italian government decided to devalue the lira by 7 per cent against all other ERM currencies. Then, on Tuesday afternoon, came a development that genuinely shocked the British authorities: it emerged that Dr Helmut Schlesinger, President of the Bundesbank, had given an interview to a German newspaper stating that 'the tensions in the ERM are not over' and that 'further devaluations are not excluded'. Major did not exaggerate when he recalled that 'such views from one of the most influential central bankers in the world sent out only one message to the markets: "Sell sterling"'.[4]

Heavy selling of the pound (by both speculators such as George Soros and institutions such as banks and pension funds) duly began first thing on Wednesday morning, soon prompting massively expensive intervention by the Bank of England. At eleven o'clock there was a belated rise in interest rates, from 10 to 12 per cent. The chancellor, Norman Lamont, was watching the Reuters screen at the Treasury as the announcement was made: 'The pound did not move at all. From that moment I knew the game was up ... I felt like a TV surgeon in *Casualty* watching a heart monitor and realising that the patient was dead.'[5] With the Bank spending Britain's currency reserves at the alarming rate of £2 billion per hour, both he and the Bank's deputy governor, Eddie George, wanted British membership of the ERM to be suspended immediately. Major, however, decided on a final throw of the dice, and at 2.15 p.m. interest rates went up to 15 per cent. Again the move was viewed by the foreign exchange markets as a sign of weakness, not strength, and after sterling had staged a tiny, flickering rally the Bank was soon buying yet more pounds. 'That afternoon,' Soros recollected, 'it became a veritable avalanche of selling.'[6] Kenneth Clarke, one of the ministers close to Major, graphically evoked the sense of impotence at the other end of town: 'We had no power. The market and events had taken over. It became increasingly obvious as the day went on that we were merely flotsam and jetsam, being tossed about in what was happening ...'[7]

At about four o'clock, by which time the Bank had spent no less than £15 billion in support of sterling, it was agreed to let it go. Mark Clarke of the Bank of America remembered from a dealer's perspective that seminal moment:

> *Suddenly the Bank of England wasn't supporting pounds. Instead of a load of noise coming out of the voice boxes and everything, and around the dealing room, everyone sat in stunned silence for almost two seconds or three seconds. All of a sudden it erupted and sterling just free-fell. That sense of awe, that the markets could take on a central bank and actually win. I couldn't believe it ...*[8]

Three and a half hours later Lamont stood outside the Treasury and announced to the television cameras that, following 'an extremely difficult and turbulent day', UK membership had been suspended – a *de facto* devaluation.[9] Soros, meanwhile, had netted a cool $1 billion on his day's work.

The Major government would never regain its reputation for economic competence. How had the markets become so powerful? And what were the implications for politicians, central bankers and indeed citizens?

A walk out of the woods

It was back in the early 1970s that the new world monetary order (or disorder) began to emerge, with the messy, unpremeditated break-up of the system of pegged but adjustable exchange rates that had been laid down at the Bretton Woods conference of 1944. Many elements contributed to this break-up – including the unsustainable financial burden of the Vietnam War and the way in which the burgeoning Eurodollar market provided the financial ammunition for those speculating against the dollar – but whatever the precise causes, the cardinal fact was that by spring 1973 the era of floating exchange rates had begun. The demise of Bretton Woods, deregulation (in the British case, taking the form of the end of the clearing bank cartel in the early 1970s, the abolition of exchange controls in 1979 and the 'Big Bang' of 1986), rapid technological change (especially in the field of instant, low-cost communications) – together this was the broad context for the fundamental transformation of the international financial markets by the end of the 1980s. It was a transformation of immense complexity, but in its essentials had a fourfold character: size, globalisation, range of instruments and volatility.

1. *Billions and Trillions.* The figures have their own eloquence.[10] For example, whereas cross-border bond and bank lending in 1984 was $180 billion (of which $87 billion was in the form of Eurobond issuance), five years later the equivalent total was $440 billion ($224 billion in Eurobonds). In terms of the outstanding stock of international bond and bank lending, this had been less than $200 billion in 1973, but by 1989 soared to $3.6 trillion – equivalent to at least a quarter of the aggregate GNP of the industrialised countries. Not surprisingly, secondary market turnover was huge, for instance $6.3 trillion in the largely London-based Eurobond market in 1990, compared to $240 billion ten years earlier. The trend was similar at the short end of the international financial markets, typified most spectacularly by the world's foreign exchange markets (with London as the number one), where total daily volume rose from $10–20 billion in the early 1970s, to $60 billion in 1983, to $250 billion in 1986, to $620 billion in 1989, and to $880 billion by Black Wednesday. $880 billion a day ... it was, mind-blowingly enough, the equivalent of about $611 million a minute, or over $10 million a second.

2. *Stateless Money.* Fittingly, it was in 1992 itself that Richard O'Brien, chief economist at American Express Bank in London, produced a short, influential book on *Global Financial Integration* that had the striking sub-title *The End of Geography.*[11] Five years after the October 1987 crash had vividly demonstrated the futility of any one stock market attempting to erect a *cordon sanitaire* around itself, he persuasively argued that there now existed something not far short of a global financial market. The increasing seamlessness of securities (especially bond) markets, the ever-more insistent demand by investors for international diversification of their assets, the existence of a rapid-reaction, high-volume foreign exchange market round the clock – all were phenomena that pointed in the same, global direction. Bob Dylan may have once asked how it felt to be like a rolling stone, but for the largely anonymous owners of footloose capital hurtling round the world in search of the highest returns there was no great psychological problem.

3. *Plain Vanilla Not.* The twenty years after the break-up of Bretton Woods saw a profusion of new, often exotic financial instruments. The Euromarkets were a hive of ceaseless innovation, with recent developments by the mid-1980s including drop-lock bonds, flipflop perpetual notes and mismatch and minimax medium-term variable rate notes. Many of the new instruments were derivatives – notably futures and options – and at the start of the 1990s it was estimated that almost $7 trillion worth were outstanding worldwide.[12] These were instruments, often of considerable technical complexity and almost invariably little understood outside the markets in which they flourished, that were equally adept at fulfilling either a speculative or a hedging function: a very paradigm for a world that had lost its old fixed certainties.

Derivatives also included the new, complicated instruments – based on mathematical models – known as 'swaps', whether interest rate swaps or currency swaps. 'Suddenly,' Peter Montagnon wrote in the *Financial Times* in July 1985, 'borrowers are no longer restricted only to that particular market which offers the currency and type of debt they require. Instead they can pick and choose, launching issues in markets where they will get the best receptions or where funds are most readily available and then switching the debt into another currency, or from fixed to floating rate, or vice versa ...'[13] By the end of the 1980s the size of the interest rate and currency swap markets was about $2.5 trillion, and together they acted as an increasingly important bridge between the bond and the foreign exchange markets, thereby further contributing to the global seamlessness of the financial markets as a whole.[14]

4. *Moving Markets.* Shortly after Britain had been driven out of the ERM, the Bank for International Settlements noted that the current daily global foreign exchange turnover of some $880 billion 'must be many times the volume of purely trade-related transactions, and it therefore suggests that much exchange market business is now finance-driven'.[15] The phrase 'finance-driven' was not meant as a compliment, and without doubt there had developed in the financial markets generally since the early 1980s a whole new dealing culture: aggressive, simultaneously encouraging and feeding off instability, and essentially speculative. The highly leveraged 'hedge funds', such as George Soros's Quantum Fund, were starting to attract the most publicity, but probably the most influential exemplars, certainly in the bond markets, were the big and increasingly

global American investment banks like Salomon Brothers and Goldman Sachs. To read *Liar's Poker*, the marvellously entertaining 1989 memoir by Michael Lewis of Salomons, is to enter a world of naked greed, big swinging dicks, and the systematic, ruthlessly amoral pursuit of trading revenue.

The effect of such trading – much of which was proprietary trading, in other words done on the bank's own account – was at times seemingly to create a wide gap between the financial markets with their often spectacular, eye-catching gyrations, many of them provoked by big players with a vested interest in volatility, and the 'real' economy beyond those markets. The once iron connection between capital movements and trade had, the legendary management guru Peter Drucker reflected in 1987, 'become loose and, worse, unpredictable. We have no theory for an international economy that is fuelled by world investment rather than world trade. As a result, we do not understand the world economy and cannot predict its behaviour or anticipate its trends.' Ominously, he added: 'We also have no law for this new world economy. No country has thought through the rules.'[16]

Fractious and difficult to manage

In an obvious sense there was nothing new about the power of the financial markets imposing significant policy constraints upon British politicians and central bankers. Most famously, in the 1960s, Harold Wilson and George Brown bitterly condemned the 'gnomes of Zurich' for their reputedly malign influence on British economic well-being. Nevertheless, there was a clear sense in the 1970s, during and after the break-up of Bretton Woods, of the relationship changing. There was an emblematic episode during the currency turmoil of 1972, as Britain entered the so-called 'snake' (an attempt by EEC countries to stabilise their currencies against the dollar), only to have to leave it ignominiously five weeks later because of severe market pressures. In 1976 the protracted sterling crisis that led to Labour's explicit abandonment of Keynesian demand management and then the calling in of the IMF was almost wholly market-driven – especially accompanied as it was by a 'strike' in the gilt-edged market – and arguably unnecessary.

'It is no exaggeration to say that many politicians and officials associated with British economic policy now believe the financial markets to be the most important influences on policy,' the financial journalists William

Keegan and Rupert Pennant-Rea (a future deputy governor of the Bank of England) asserted three years later in their book *Who Runs the Economy?* 'The influence that concerns them is the power of the financial markets to vote with their feet, and wreck what the architects of policy naturally feel are good and well-designed policies. The things that ministers and officials sometimes say in private about the financial markets are virtually unprintable.'[17] Something of the flavour is recorded in Tony Benn's invaluable diaries. 'My experience with the City,' the prime minister and former chancellor Jim Callaghan told him in May 1978, 'is that if they've got you by the knackers they'll squeeze you ...'[18]

In accordance with its adherence to Friedmanite monetarism and general distaste for corporatist-style interventionism, the attitude of the Thatcher government to the exchange rate during the early 1980s was broadly one of 'benign neglect' (as the comfortable phrase went, whatever the ravages caused to manufacturing industry by a severely overvalued pound). By January 1985, however, the sharp rise of the dollar saw the value of a pound plummet to virtually that of a dollar, and from that point Thatcher's chancellor, Nigel Lawson, was no longer inclined to see the mighty markets – particularly the foreign exchange market – as necessarily his friends. Over the next few years he pushed hard for sterling to join the European Monetary System (created in 1978 as a zone of would-be monetary stability); engaged vigorously with other finance ministers in concerted joint interventions (as embodied in the Plaza Accord of September 1985 and the Louvre Accord of February 1987) that were aimed at reducing volatility on the exchanges; and from spring 1987 sought, in the most hands-on way possible, to 'shadow' the deutschmark.

This last initiative led to a bitter clash with his prime minister. Although Thatcher could be profoundly exasperated by the behaviour of financial markets ('Those whose eyes are glued to the screen and ears to the telephones of the world's exchanges have missed the point,' she angrily declared in February 1985 with sterling under the cosh), her gut instincts, in this area anyway, were non-interventionist.[19] She adamantly blocked entry to the ERM, publicly disavowed the notion of targets for sterling, and in November 1987 told interviewers that 'you cannot beat a speculator except over a short period'.[20] The difference between the two came to a head in March 1988 when, in the context of massive intervention by Lawson aimed at stopping sterling from rising too much, Thatcher flatly insisted on uncapping sterling and informed the Commons that, in a phrase that would echo down the years: 'There is no way in which you can buck the market.'[21]

The irony was that both she and Lawson had been enthusiastic advocates of financial liberalisation, whether in the form of exchange control abolition or the City's Big Bang. The question was how, as politicians and policy-makers, to cope with the practical consequences of that liberalisation. Later in 1988 they were at odds again, though this time behind the scenes. That November – more or less out of the blue, worried about the rising trend of inflation, and deeply frustrated by Thatcher's intransigence over ERM – Lawson sent her a memorandum proposing 'to give statutory independence to the Bank of England, charging it with the statutory duty to preserve the value of the currency, along the lines already in place and of proven effectiveness for the US Federal Reserve, the National Bank of Switzerland, and the Bundesbank'. Such a move, he argued, would 'enhance the market credibility of our anti-inflationary stance', help to 'depoliticise interest rate changes', and above all in the longer term 'lock a permanent anti-inflationary force into the system, as a counterweight to the strong inflationary pressures which are always lurking'.[22] Thatcher, as she would recall without undue compunction, was appalled:

> *My reaction was dismissive ... I did not believe, as Nigel argued,*
> *that it would boost the credibility of the fight against inflation ...*
> *In fact, as I minuted, 'It would be seen as an abdication by the*
> *Chancellor ...' I added that 'it would be an admission of a failure*
> *of resolve on our part'. I also doubted whether we had people of*
> *the right calibre to run such an institution.*[23]

Lawson was compelled to let his secret proposal rest. Less than a year later, however, his resignation speech of October 1989 gave him the opportunity to launch the proposal publicly. The genie was out of the bottle.

In one sense it was extraordinary that Lawson should have wanted to surrender control over monetary policy to the Bank of England. After all, it was not, as he stressed in his memoirs, that he was under any illusions that 'the Bank of England possesses any superior wisdom'.[24] Indeed, it had been a paradox of the 1980s that despite monetary policy being far more important than fiscal policy the stature of the central bank had significantly diminished. Among other factors, this owed something to Thatcher's deliberate appointment in 1983 of a rather weak governor

(Robin Leigh-Pemberton) and something to Lawson's own bruising self-confidence. Moreover, a series of episodes – including the Johnson Matthey affair in autumn 1984 and the BP flotation in autumn 1987 – had seen distinctly troubled relations between Lawson and the Old Lady. 'The traditional role of the Bank as a voice to advise and warn government has been reduced,' the *Financial Times* commented in January 1988 on the occasion of Leigh-Pemberton's reappointment, 'and its utterings now come more from the wings than from centre stage. The Bank's function has become limited to the more technical one of administering policy in the markets. Its ability to influence strategy has been further reduced by the personality of the Governor ...'[25] Yet later that year Lawson was seriously proposing independence for the Bank, which he intended to come into effect before the end of 1989. Why?

In large part the answer lay in his perception – shared by many – that the markets were, vis-à-vis the politicians, on the verge of becoming all-powerful. Quite apart from his own chequered grapplings with the foreign exchange dealers and speculators, there had been the seismic experience of the October 1987 crash of the world's stock markets, which in the British case had the effect of pushing Lawson into policies that rapidly turned successful, reputation-enhancing expansion into the disastrous, reputation-destroying 'Lawson boom'.

With a vision untroubled by doubt, leading American banker Walter Wriston formulated in 1987 what was to become the conventional wisdom:

> *The gold standard, replaced by the gold exchange standard, which was replaced by the Bretton Woods arrangements, has now been replaced by the information standard. Unlike the other standards the information standard is in place, operating, will never go away, and has substantially changed the world. What it means, very simply, is that bad monetary and fiscal policies anywhere in the world are reflected within minutes on the Reuters screens in the trading rooms of the world.*
>
> *Money only goes where it is wanted, and only stays where it's well treated, and once you tie the world together with telecommunications and information, the ball game is over ... You cannot renounce the information standard, and it is exerting a discipline on the countries of the world, which they all hate. For the first time in history, the politicians can't stop it. It's beyond*

the political control of the world ...

*In France, Mitterrand announced all those ridiculous moves,
and they lost a third of their foreign exchange in a week ...*

*At the end of the day, it's a new world and the concept of
sovereignty is going to change. Politically, the new world is an
integrated market in which nobody can get away with what they
used to. You can't control what your people hear, you can't control
the value of your currency, you can't control your capital flows.
The idea of fifteenth-century international law is gone. It hasn't
laid down yet, but it's dead. It's like the three-mile limit in a
world of Inter-Continental Ballistic Missiles.* [26]

For those (like Lawson) less sanguine about the financial markets juggernaut, there was comfort – and perhaps inspiration – to be found in the
example of the Federal Reserve Board, the US central bank. There, two
giants (one almost literally so) bestrode the scene during the 1980s. First
Paul Volcker almost single-handedly crushed inflation; then his successor,
Alan Greenspan, skilfully handled the 1987 crash by rapidly getting more
liquidity into the banking system. The Fed was also to the fore in managing the LDC (less developed countries) debt crisis from 1982 and in ensuring that the absurdly overvalued dollar achieved a reasonably soft landing
in 1986/7. In West Germany, meanwhile, the Bundesbank had been a
beacon of low-inflation, no-political-interference central banking for over
three decades.

Could the Bank of England raise its game and join the premier league?
Lawson may have had his doubts; but he knew that historically it had
always been close to the markets, which instinctively would tend to trust its
decisions rather than those of election-minded politicians. Either way, the
Bank itself applauded his initiative after it had been made public. 'Is there
something about the operation of monetary policy that makes it quite different from other elements of economic policy or indeed other elements of
government policy?' Leigh-Pemberton rhetorically asked in summer 1990,
tellingly enough in an interview with a new magazine called *Central Banking*. 'I think there is,' he answered. 'It's special to the extent to which a country, a democracy, the people at large, would regard the need to preserve the
value of their money and to pursue monetary stability as something which
is not one of the variables of everyday political or electoral policy.' [27] The
governor even claimed that if there had been an independent Bank in

1987/8 it would have been able to act more quickly to dampen down the Lawson boom – a boom that by this time had ended so catastrophically that it could not but strengthen the case for taking monetary policy out of the hands of politicians.

A few months later, on Friday 5 October 1990, the search for anti-inflationary market credibility took an apparently decisive different direction as Lawson's successor at No. 11, John Major, announced that Britain was at last entering the ERM, at a central rate of DM 2.95. 'Each morning I woke up between 4 and 5 a.m. and lay awake wondering how sterling would perform that day,' was how he recalled the months before that decision. 'Each hour I received market reports. The foreign exchange screen became a focal point of the day. A pfennig up or down influenced thinking far too much. I knew this could not go on.'[28] The markets also directly determined the timing, with the Bank warning Major in September not only that they were becoming increasingly 'fractious and difficult to manage', but also that this would 'worsen' in the approach to the EU summit in December.[29] Thatcher was finally talked round, though only with the carrot of a 1 per cent interest rate cut simultaneous with the announcement. Leigh-Pemberton, as keen as anyone to enter the ERM, reluctantly complied, but not without dispatching an admonishing letter to Thatcher, in effect saying that she should not take the reward before credibility had been won – a letter that in retrospect was an early glimmering of independence.

That weekend Britain's entry was almost universally acclaimed, with the main doubts coming from industrialists worried about 2.95 being too high a rate for export competitiveness. 'Fixed exchange rates are fashionable once more,' Martin Wolf noted in the *Financial Times*, arguing that the widespread perception in Britain was that almost two decades of floating exchange rates had brought an unattractive mixture of 'exchange rate instability', 'failures of domestic monetary control', and an 'apparent inability to obtain lower unemployment and higher output in return for more inflation'. Thus the allure of 'exchange rate discipline', with sterling now linked formally to the non-inflationary deutschmark, seen by everyone as the anchor of the ERM.[30] The markets might rage outside, but sterling, it seemed, had found a safe berth.

Britain's entry into the ERM was fully endorsed by the shadow chancellor, John Smith. By this time Labour's approach to the financial markets had, under the leadership of Neil Kinnock, moved a significant distance from the defiant socialism-in-one-country ambition on which it had so unsuccessfully fought the June 1983 election – itself soon after Mitterrand's abject U-turn in response to the unyielding disapproval of the markets had graphically revealed the futility of such an ambition in the late twentieth century. By the June 1987 election the commitment to re-impose exchange controls had been replaced by a rather vague capital repatriation scheme, seeking to use the tax system to encourage the return of institutional funds from overseas. Soon afterwards Lord Bernard Donoughue, a key figure in the Wilson and Callaghan kitchen cabinets who had subsequently become a high-profile stockbroker, sought to reinforce the message in an interview with *Marxism Today*'s David Goodhart:

> DONOUGHUE: *The City is one of the most rapidly expanding parts of our economy and, given the internationalisation of the markets, no future Labour government can control or direct the economy without the City's co-operation since national boundaries no longer exist for finance, and since a draconian siege economy is no longer conceivable.*

> GOODHART: *But this transfer of power from politicians to financial markets is precisely what many people find objectionable, especially as the markets usually dislike governments of the Left.*

> DONOUGHUE: *Look, it is just a reality, I'm not interested in whether it's a good or bad thing. One of the troubles with the Labour Party is that it spends too much time denouncing bad things and too little time understanding how things work. The City as a powerhouse of the international economy is an inescapable fact of modern life, and to the younger generation it's an attractive fact ...*

'In any case,' Donoughue added, 'there isn't really such a thing as a socialist approach to the City. It's like defence policy in that respect.'[31]

It was early in 1990 that Smith and Labour's City spokesperson, Mo Mowlam, launched the so-called 'prawn cocktail offensive', involving over the next eighteen months an intensive round of lunches in the City.[32] Essentially a drive to win credibility in the financial markets and thereby avoid the damaging prospect of a post-election flight of capital, it stressed membership of the ERM as the cornerstone of Labour's counter-inflationary policy and was adamant, as Smith told the *Financial Times* in May 1990, that Labour would 'relate its public expenditure programme to the realities of the economy'.[33] Given that Labour was clearly shaping to fight the next election on a mainstream social democratic platform – as opposed to something that could legitimately be called 'socialist' – it might have been expected to do the trick. In fact it did not. Although there was appreciation of the increasingly moderate tone of Labour's language, and few imagined that Labour any longer intended seriously to impede (let alone dismember) the economic functions of the City, a variety of major concerns, some rational and others less so, persisted. They included worries about devaluation, the minimum wage, higher borrowing, industrial interventionism, Kinnock's leadership qualities, and above all higher taxation, whether personal or corporate.

'The City holds its breath' was the title of the *Financial Times* leader on 4 April 1992, the Saturday before the election and at the end of a week in which equities, gilts and sterling had all taken a hammering. 'There is no glummer place in Britain than the City, as Labour apparently strengthens its position ...' The paper's explanation for this blue mood was pretty cynical but probably accurate: 'Taking the country as a whole, the impact of the proposed redistribution of taxes will be a matter of minuses and pluses. But in the south-east of England the losers will predominate, and nowhere will this be more true than in the City of London.'[34] The *Financial Times* itself surprised many on polling day by coming out for Labour, thereby not only backing the losing horse but for its pains receiving considerable criticism, even abuse, over the next few weeks from the City at large.

The cardinal lesson of April 1992 was that one of the two major political parties was still regarded by the financial markets – and, crucially, those who inhabited them – as less market-friendly than the other. Both Labour and the City may have changed (respectively, more moderate and less atavistic), but there lingered a critical absence of trust in their relationship. It would take Black Wednesday and two changes of party leadership for the City's ideal of full, unequivocal commitment to sound money, open markets, neo-liberal economics and internationally competitive rates of taxation to be consummated.

Beyond politics

By the mid-1990s it was the almost universally received wisdom that the financial markets called virtually all the shots that mattered. No one's thoughts attracted more attention than those of George Soros, while soon after Bill Clinton became US President in January 1993 his adviser, James Carville, made his celebrated assertion that if he had another life he would choose to come back as the bond market – and 'intimidate everybody'.[35] That summer, less than a year after Black Wednesday, the currency speculators blew the French franc out of the water, effectively signalling the demise of the ERM. Nation states – aware that the daily volume of global foreign exchange trading now greatly exceeded the total of their foreign currency reserves – increasingly lived in fear of where they would strike next. 'Recent events in Mexico are a reminder of the extreme fragility of financial market confidence and of the ability of foreign exchange markets to bury policymakers,' the Cambridge economist Willem Buiter noted in January 1995. 'The crisis happened despite the fact that the recent "change of government" was, following a 70-year-old Mexico tradition, no more than a cabinet reshuffle.'[36] Less dramatically, the daily judgement of the bond markets – 'the bond market vigilantes', as John Plender nicely called them that year – determined on a ruthless, unsentimental basis, in a multi-choice world of free capital flows, the price of a government's borrowing.[37] For finance ministers of almost any political persuasion, the question was how to get (and stay) in the good books of those inscrutable arbiters.

In what was arguably a massive failure of political will (as Thatcher had warned in the British context), the answer increasingly lay in transferring power to central banks. This was not entirely a market-driven process, in that Article 108 of the Maastricht Treaty required, as part of preparation for the eventual introduction of the single European currency, that member states align their national legislation with that for the projected – and independent – European Central Bank.[38] Nevertheless, the rapid movement during the first half of the 1990s towards independent central banks was far more than just a European phenomenon; while in terms of the momentum, it owed almost everything to a sense, to some extent supported by academic studies, that central bankers, precisely because they were above the electoral fray, could enjoy greater market credibility than politicians and therefore deliver low inflation, low borrowing and adequate growth.

Indeed, the enviable, much-publicised example of Greenspan effectively – and very successfully – running American economic policy during Clinton's first term even suggested that they might be able to deliver positively strong growth. *The Confidence Game: How Unelected Central Bankers Are Governing the Changed Global Economy* was the apt title of Steven Solomon's 1995 survey. 'Central bankers have come a long way,' Robert Pringle, editor of *Central Banking*, wryly reflected soon afterwards about this once shadowy sect. 'Thirty years ago they were regarded with some justification as boring, inward-looking and insufferably elitist. Not that they cared: they were guardians of the temples of high finance, necessarily inaccessible, unaccountable and secretive … What a change has taken place! As a breed, they are now all too anxious to please, to get across their messages, even – dare one say it? – to be loved.'[39]

Britain, as so often, lagged somewhat behind. Even so, faced by a glaring vacuum in economic policy in the immediate aftermath of sterling's enforced exit from the ERM, the Major government did take the first steps on a road that ultimately led to an independent Bank of England. Early in October 1992, following the recent examples of New Zealand and Canada, Lamont publicly committed the government to pursuing a formal inflation target-range; later that month he announced not only that the Bank would be publishing regular reports assessing how well the government was doing in meeting those targets, but also that the Treasury would be publishing a regular report elucidating his monthly meetings with the governor. Credibility and transparency – above all, in both cases, in the eyes of the markets – were now at the heart of the new economic policy framework, a shift that reputedly owed much to the urgings of the Bank's chief economist, Mervyn King.[40] Had enough been done? The *Financial Times* for one decidedly thought not. 'One cheer for the chancellor' was the title of its leader on Lamont's institutional reforms: 'What is needed is comprehensive reconsideration of the roles of the Treasury and the Bank of England. Mr Lamont wishes to persuade the world that the citadel on Great George Street still knows best. It does not, as the whole world now knows all too well.'[41]

Over the next eighteen months or so there was no shortage of voices supporting the *Financial Times*' view that it was really, after all, the citadel on Threadneedle Street that knew best – and should be given the chance to show it. In autumn 1993, for instance, there reported an independent panel chaired by Lord Eric Roll, president of Warburgs, and also comprising (among others) Sir Brian Corby of the Prudential, the renowned monetary economist Professor Charles Goodhart, the former Treasury mandarin (and now chairman of BZW) Sir Peter Middleton and the deputy chairman of Lloyds Bank, Sir David Walker. The City's great and good came down firmly in favour of an independent Bank (along the lines of the Reserve Bank of New Zealand) and had notably little truck with the loss of accountability that might involve: 'At present, so-called Parliamentary accountability for monetary policy connotes no more than the presence of the topic in a general and continuing Parliamentary debate about the government's economic performance, a debate whose real constitutional function is to furnish information relevant to quinquennial popular control by election.'[42]

Also in 1993, a mass of testimony given to the Treasury and Civil Service Committee, examining the independence question, was almost overwhelmingly in favour of setting the Bank free. One of the relatively few dissenters was a still robust former chancellor. After dubbing the fashion for an independent central bank as essentially a gimmick, Lord Healey declared: that 'the central problem is whether politicians have the guts to do what is necessary and the wit to recognise what is necessary'; that 'both of those are rare commodities, not just in politicians but in anybody'; and that there was the risk of what he called 'the German situation' (in which, 'because you have hived off inflation as the responsibility of an autonomous organisation, the government can go crazy on the fiscal side'). He finished with an uplifting defence of the need not to be enslaved by the markets, which 'we talk about as though they were God in heaven, but they are numerous men in red braces in dealing rooms who talk Cockney working for a lot of men in grey suits with red bow ties'.[43]

On the one side, then, a rolling bandwagon. On the other, the stubborn opposition of Thatcher, Healey and ... Major. The latter's memoirs unambiguously reveal that during his premiership he resisted the wishes of both Lamont and his successor Kenneth Clarke to grant independence. 'I disliked this proposal on democratic grounds, believing that the person responsible for monetary policy should be answerable for it in the House of Commons. I also feared that the culture of an independent Bank would ensure that interest rates went up rapidly but fell only slowly.'[44] Instead, what Clarke secured, in terms of further increasing the Bank's authority, was the retrospective publication from spring 1994 of the minutes of his monthly meetings with the governor, by now Eddie George.

It is a moot point how much over the next three years this change enhanced the credibility of monetary policy – indeed, right at the outset John Sheppard of Yamaichi International warned that 'the risk with this whole process is, if we do get to the situation where the Bank is pushing for a rate increase and the Treasury is resisting, sterling is going to be vulnerable because of the market's dislike of political interference'.[45] Something like that scenario occurred in the summer 1995 episodes of the '*Ken & Eddie Show*', as George argued during three successive meetings for a rise in interest rates, but was resisted by a chancellor conscious that the global economy was slowing down. The bond market duly punished Clarke, with ten-year gilt yields (the key indicator) going up. In the old behind-closed-doors days the central banker had often won the argument; now, with the new transparency but no shift of ultimate power, the finance minister had significant personal capital invested in the outcome. It was, from the point of view of the financial markets, perhaps the worst of both worlds.

Increasingly that was also the perspective of the shadow chancellor, Gordon Brown. The Labour politician of his generation with the keenest awareness of his party's history, he had no desire to enter No. 11 and find himself immediately plunged into the type of financial crisis that had scarred the chancellorships of Philip Snowden, Hugh Dalton, Stafford Cripps, Jim Callaghan and Denis Healey. No doubt, influenced by his adviser Ed Balls (who had written a pro-independence Fabian Society pamphlet back in December 1992), he believed sincerely in the broad economic arguments relating to an independent central bank; but above all he was desperate to avoid the miserable fate of his predecessors. In a word, he wanted the markets off his back.

It was a desire that found an entirely sympathetic ear from Tony Blair, Labour's leader from July 1994. At no point before the 1997 election did either man make an explicit commitment to outright independence – the manifesto itself merely affirmed that Labour would 'reform the Bank of England to ensure that decision-making on monetary policy is more effective, open, accountable and free from short-term political manipulation' – but in July 1996 the *Financial Times* revealed that 'the Bank of England is increasingly convinced that it would gain independent powers to set interest rates under a Labour government'.[46] Apparently this conviction owed much to talks between its officials and senior Labour representatives; and George recalled in 2000 how 'towards the end [i.e. of the Major government] I was of course having discussions with the then opposition leaders about the shape of a new system'. In fact, these talks were crucial. 'The composition of the members of the Monetary Policy Committee was discussed with Labour leaders when the original concept was being developed,' George also noted. 'Some people thought it should contain people from a wide variety of backgrounds. I insisted that we should have technical monetary policy experts.'[47] George duly got his way in 1996/7, presumably having explained that even the faintest whiff of corporatism would virtually destroy the MPC's credibility with the markets.

Of course, the independence decision was part of a wider recasting of Labour policy under Blair and Brown. In his Mais Lecture of May 1995, eight months after Brown had condemned 'the old Labour language' of 'tax, spend and borrow, nationalisation, state planning, isolationism' as 'inappropriate to the demands of the future', Blair spelled out how politics now operated within markets-ordained parameters:

> The first priority for a high-success economy is a tough and coherent macroeconomic framework for policy. We must recognise that the UK is situated in the middle of an active global market for capital – a market which is less subject to regulation today than for several decades. An expansionary fiscal or monetary policy that is at odds with other economies in Europe will not be sustainable for very long. To that extent the room for manoeuvre of any government in Britain is already heavily circumscribed.[48]

In April 1996 he took his message to Wall Street, where speaking to an audience of bankers and businessmen he reiterated his belief that 'errors in macroeconomic policy' by a future Labour government would be 'punished rapidly and without mercy' by the markets.[49] Up to that trip Blair had not quite convinced the doubters in the international financial community; but as a result of it, according to George Magnus (chief international economist at UBS) some three months later, 'international investors began to be persuaded that New Labour is nothing to fear'.[50] Interestingly, on the same trip, Blair was much struck by an article in the *Wall Street Journal* by Felix Rohatyn, a prominent Democrat as well as chairman of the investment bank Lazard Frères. Called 'Recipes for Growth', it argued that rapid wealth creation rather than redistribution was the key to social and economic progress; and on his return to Britain, Blair began to stress the virtues of the flexible labour market.[51] That summer the party's *Road to the Manifesto* appeared. 'The glossy pamphlet,' James Harding reported in the *Financial Times*, 'is framed with feelgood photographs – a policewoman hugging a pensioner, a father taking his young child on a carousel and bankers strolling through the City.'[52]

Shortly before the election there occurred the party's culminating surrender to the assumption that global financial markets must be obeyed.[53] Not only did Labour announce that it would not raise the levels of direct taxation bequeathed by the Tories, but it pledged to stick to Tory spending limits for its first two years. For democratic choice in macroeconomic policy it was a bleak moment; for the markets and those who manned them it was just the ticket. During the campaign, with the opinion polls unanimously pointing to a big Labour win, equities, gilts and sterling all appreciated. 'Labour's economic platform is a lot more market friendly than at any time in its history,' observed Keith Skeoch, chief economist at HSBC James Capel. 'There was always the fear factor in the market before, and that has gone.'[54] Nothing red was left except the dealers in red braces working for the men with red bow ties.

The modern world

Brown's landmark announcement on 6 May 1997 – that he was handing over responsibility to the Bank of England to set the interest rates that would seek to ensure the meeting of the government's inflation target – was probably the most impactful from the Treasury since Howe's abolition of exchange controls in 1979. The nine-member Monetary Policy Committee, charged with doing the business, was to comprise the governor and two deputy governors (all appointed by the government), four members ('recognised experts', in Brown's phrase) appointed by the government from outside the Bank, and two Bank nominees. 'Openness of decision-making will be ensured by the publication of minutes of proceedings and votes of the MPC,' Brown stated. 'There will be enhanced requirements for the Bank of England to report to the Treasury Select Committee of the House of Commons to explain and be questioned on their decisions.'[55]

On the whole Brown got a good press. 'Welcome to the modern world,' declared the *Independent*, while the *Daily Telegraph* gave the changes what it called 'a cautious welcome' – high praise from that quarter for a Labour government.[56] In the *Guardian*, Will Hutton was surprisingly relaxed. Whereas in *The State We're In* two years earlier he had asserted bluntly that 'to pass the control of interest rates to a quasi-private organisation run as an extension of one wing of the Conservative Party would be a disaster', he now looked ahead optimistically to 'a Bank of England that is more distant from the "gentlemanly capitalist" culture of the financial system than any we have so far experienced'. Such a Bank, as part of a modernised British state, would, he believed, finally lay to rest the ghost of Montagu Norman.[57] For Brown, though, the verdict that really mattered did not come from the broadsheets. The City's immediate reaction to the announcement was little short of exultant, with longer-dated gilts jumping by more than £4 – their biggest one-day rise in five years.[58] Despite Brown having sent his advance letter to George to the wrong address, the new government now enjoyed instant credibility in the financial markets.

In the event, it did not prove all honey for the inflation-busting MPC, especially during 1998 as it obstinately kept interest rates high despite the palpable damage being inflicted on the British economy by a strong pound. The consequence was to see the Bank uncomfortably exposed to forceful, at times even vicious, attacks – from both sides of industry, from columnists and cartoonists, even from trade union demonstrators gathered by the Duke of Wellington's statue outside the Royal Exchange. Nevertheless, after four years the broad consensus was that the MPC had done pretty well in this first phase of its life, certainly well enough to persuade the Conservative opposition to abandon its intention of returning control over monetary policy to the Treasury. Moreover, in terms of the potentially vexed question of accountability, the Bank's image benefited greatly from the obvious comparison with the considerably more opaque European Central Bank in Frankfurt.

Indeed, some even claimed that in this area there had been a positive upgrading since pre-1997 days. 'Because the responsibility is delegated but a quantitative objective is given or adopted, the whole process is much more accountable and much more transparent than it was when the minister of finance did it,' Charles Goodhart, one of the original members of the MPC, argued in early 2001. 'Ministers never specified what they were trying to do and so it was impossible to hold them accountable ... The whole process has become much more democratically accountable, even though an unelected body takes the decision.'[59]

More generally over these four years, Brown's watchword – and definitely soundbite word – was prudence. In February 2001 it was estimated that the Labour government's spending had risen at an average rate of only

1.2 per cent a year, less than half the growth rate of the economy and also less than half the 2.6 per cent of the Major years.[60] 'We should not begrudge Mr Brown his moment,' the *Financial Times*' Philip Stephens wrote a month later, shortly before the chancellor, sitting on an enviable fiscal surplus, delivered his final, widely applauded budget of Labour's first term. 'A centre-left government committed to low inflation, fiscal prudence and private enterprise is now a fixture in the nation's political landscape. In this case, familiarity should not breed contempt. Mr Brown has brought the Labour party further along the road to rigorous, market-based economics than anyone might have imagined even two or three years ago.'[61] The City – and international investors at large – agreed in spades. The year 1998 saw the largest-ever annual decline in British government bond yields; while over the four years as a whole the yield (in effect the risk premium) on long-term gilts fell from almost 7 per cent to about 4.5 per cent.[62] There was a revealing moment during the abrupt, unnerving September 2000 fuel crisis – a black cloud from an apparently cloudless sky – as Blair warned on the radio that the government must not take any action (i.e. to stave off the protesters) that might alarm the financial markets. In fact Prudence did have to raise her skirt a little, but not enough to upset anyone.

Yet it may well be that those outside the markets are now reaching the apogee of their intellectual deference. Not only are markets essentially reactive and herd-like in their behaviour, and thus capable of being shepherded or even led, but it is clear from empirical work done by the American political scientist Layna Mosley on the financial markets of London and Frankfurt that the constraints they impose allow, in her words, 'a significant amount of cross-national policy divergence among advanced industrial democracies'.[63] Specifically, she finds, as long as the sacrosanct macro-economic indicators are acceptable (above all, in the forms of low inflation and low deficits), then the markets are relatively unconcerned about how national governments achieve them, thereby tacitly extending considerable latitude in the conduct of micro-economic policy. The problem is that since Black Wednesday so few people in the British political-cum-economic establishment have questioned the 'Soros version' – the axiomatic assumption that the global financial marketplace is omnipotent and that nation states (whether in the form of elected politicians or unelected central bankers) cannot afford to challenge its assumptions.

What, however, if those assumptions prove demonstrably wrong? What, for example, if it turns out that the real challenge is not inflation but deflation? By spring 2001, with the world seemingly on the edge of a serious economic downturn, confidence was rapidly eroding in Greenspan and his confrères. 'Out of control' ran a stark headline in the *Financial Times*. 'Central banks have been invested with authority, trust and confidence. Now their ability to steer economies with a steady hand is being severely tested ...'[64] Indeed, shortly before, Goodhart had already pondered the durability of the present dispensation: 'Why have most central banks and most economies except Japan over the course of the last four or five years done so well? Is it purely an accident and good fortune, or good management? I would not be surprised if to a large extent it was down to good fortune. I don't think the present system has really been tried under adverse conditions.'[65]

The events of 11 September 2001, and the economic consequences flowing from them, dramatically provided such conditions. The world's central banks were rightly praised for their prompt and co-ordinated response, pumping massive amounts of liquidity into the global financial system, but by the end of the year it was clear that the deflationary threat had become real and dangerous – that, indeed, 'the Japanese disease' was all too likely to spread. 'We know what to do about inflation,' one leading City economist, HSBC's Stephen King, astutely commented. 'We know very little about how to cope with deflation.'[66] If the shit truly hits the fan, we may yet have a case – pleasing for the ironically minded – of the emperor's new clothes.

8

City 1 Industry 0

'**W**hat Is a Company For?' was the challenging title of a lecture given in December 1990 by the media's favourite management guru, Professor Charles Handy, at the Royal Society for the Encouragement of Arts, Manufactures and Commerce. Companies, he insisted, were 'communities not properties', while profits were 'a necessary but not sufficient condition of success'. During the discussion afterwards, he elaborated: 'We have to find a way of getting companies to understand that they are not just assets to trade on the stock market. The Japanese don't think like that. What impresses me about Japan is they have these statements about values and missions and they all believe them. We have them and nobody pays any attention.'[1]

Handy's lecture inspired a two-year inquiry under the auspices of the RSA. Called 'Tomorrow's Company – the Role of Business in a Changing World', it led eventually to a permanent body, the Centre for Tomorrow's Company. During the inquiry the RSA held half a dozen dinners in 1992 for top British industrialists (mainly chairmen and chief executives). The comments of about half those present reflected their disinclination to question existing, shareholder-oriented arrangements:

> *I challenge people around this table to tell me of a single hostile takeover of the last few years that hasn't been in the interests of the shareholder. The shareholders own the company. People who complain that the City doesn't understand them are not communicating with the City ...*

The shareholders to me are a necessary constraint. I am interested in growing the company and creating wealth for shareholders ...

We managed to cut our dividend because we felt that maintaining it would be wrong and the City accepted it ...

I haven't found short-termism so I don't see the need to change the systems within which we operate ...

The ultimate yardstick is the competition – the shareholder is merely the whistleblower who says that you haven't measured up to the competition ...

Too many people are trying to make excuses for poor performance. The clear message has to be that we are in business to maximise the returns for shareholders ...

By contrast other industrialists at the dinners expressed a high level of dissatisfaction with the City:

I think the City of London is not acting in the best interests of British industry today ...

The mutual protection system in Japan may have its critics, but it does allow concentration upon the longer term. I spend an enormous amount of my time worrying about how to improve the year-end performance and how it appears to shareholders instead of concentrating on making a better product ...

A third of our equity is held by institutions, the Pru and others. I have no complaint about them. I am worried about other investors who are advised by second-class analysts and fourth-class press. Most analysts can't read a balance sheet ...

I think it is quite significant that if you want to talk to Midland you go to them, and if you want to talk to Deutsche Bank they come to you ...

I spent the last two hours today talking to investors. I find it very difficult to relate to them. They are just analysts, barely any of the questions that they asked were in my view the important questions ...

Shareholders are only interested in their monetary return ...

Overall, these observations suggest a situation on the cusp. Would industry develop its critique of the City into a full-blown alternative to Anglo-Saxon, shareholder-driven capitalism? In retrospect, the most prescient words from round these 1992 dinner tables came from a sceptical industrialist who had also been a member of Thatcher's Cabinet: 'I suspect that we are looking at Germany and Japan as models. Much of their success is owed to what happened in 1946–47. Let's wait and see whether the next generation are so successful ...'[2]

The City under fire

Industry's quasi-disenchantment with the City by the early 1990s derived in large part from its experiences during the 1980s – a decade in which it simultaneously felt neglected by government (with a general sense emanating from Thatcher and her colleagues that Britain's economic future lay in services rather than metal-bashing) and exploited by the Square Mile. In the City two main trends were at work by the mid-1980s. Firstly, the leading investing institutions were no longer willing to put up with mediocre returns from British industry, especially in the context of the abolition of exchange controls making the world their oyster for City-based fund managers. In the eyes of much of British industry, this new impatience translated into one damning, all-purpose epithet: short-termism. Secondly, there was the emergence of a new breed of aggressive M&A (mergers and acquisitions) specialists in the corporate finance departments of merchant banks. Their approach to takeovers was intensely proactive and they were epitomised by the high-profile Roger Seelig and George Magan at Morgan Grenfell.

Fuelled by a rampant bull market, the value of acquisitions rose sharply: up from £2.3 billion in 1983 to £16.6 billion in 1986, the year of the titanic, controversial battles for Imperial and Distillers, acquired respectively by Hanson Trust and Guinness.[3] 'Rarely has the London Stock Market buzzed with so much takeover speculation,' the *Financial Times* declared as early as January 1985, warning that 'it is not a healthy phenomenon'.[4] Perhaps not, but over the next eighteen months it, like everyone else, could only watch as the hyperactive market for corporate control reshaped whole sectors of British industry and generated huge fees for incorrigibly fee-hungry corporate financiers, stockbrokers, accountants and lawyers.

Even after the takeover boom had peaked in 1986, three notable battles in the late 1980s helped further to confirm a widespread feeling that there was often something wrong about the outcome of these market-determined contests. In 1987 the Yorkshire supermarket chain Hillards fell to Tesco amidst claims by the defeated board of institutional irresponsibility. The next year another familiar part of the northern landscape, Rowntrees, failed to repel an invader, the Swiss food combine Nestlé, and again the air was heavy with recrimination. 'There is a great danger that we only value things we can measure precisely,' the CBI's director-general John Banham had observed soon after the Nestlé bid, noting the 'huge contribution' that Rowntrees made to the communities in which it operated. 'Whitehall is not the only place where it is easier to be precisely wrong than roughly right. The kind of exit P/Es [price/earnings ratios] that are widely regarded in the City as being "too good to resist" would look very modest on the Tokyo Stock Exchange.'[5] Finally, in autumn 1989, came the takeover of the Bristol-based Dickinson Robinson group, makers of Sellotape and Basildon Bond stationery. The successful predator was Pembridge Investments, the Bermuda-based vehicle of the opportunist financier Roland Franklin. 'It hardly reflects credit on the City,' commented even the *Financial Times'* staunchly unsentimental Lex column, adding that 'the speed with which shareholders deserted the group ought to re-open the old debate about short-termism among the institutions'.[6]

In fact, a hostile CBI report had already appeared in November 1988 about the financial institutions' focus on short-term profits and their lack of long-term commitment to British manufacturing industry; while in March 1989 the Trade and Industry Secretary, Lord Young, forthrightly attacked the City for failing to back 'some of Britain's brightest ideas', claiming that too little finance was available from banks and venture capitalists for high-risk, high-tech projects.[7]

Few industrialists felt more bitter about the City's shortcomings than Sir Hector Laing of United Biscuits, which in April 1986 had been pipped at the post for control of Imperial because of the belief of the key institutions that a victory for Lord Hanson would ensure a more effective 'sweating' of the assets. 'Fund managers are intent on doing their best for their funds and have no interest whatsoever in the businesses they invest in or the people who are producing the profits,' he asserted three years later.[8] In April 1990 he took the opportunity of his retirement to issue a crisp, imbued-with-paternalism pamphlet entitled *A Parting Shot*. 'United Biscuits' success,' he declared, 'has brought benefits to all its stakeholders, and I use that word advisedly. The word stakeholders reflects a more balanced view of the constituents of a company, and is one with which employees can identify.' What did he mean by 'stakeholders'? Laing explained that he had in mind not only shareholders, but also customers, employees, suppliers and the community at large.

He went on:

> While it is right to assert that a company must be run for performance rather than for the benefit of its management, it is wrong to define 'performance' in terms of a 'quick buck' for some shareholders. This subordinates all other constituencies to the immediate gratification of those whose only interest in the business is short-term payoffs. I cannot believe our society will tolerate this for very long ...
>
> The stock market is coming to be less a means of allocating capital to productive use, than an end unto itself – a computer game for those who compete in the 'Finance League'. But it is an eroding game, which undermines the true value of the counters with which it is being played – the national industrial and commercial base.

There followed the by now ritual nod to the East. 'It cannot be coincidental that the UK and the USA – the two countries with the freest market systems and the highest level of predatory activity – have the lowest level of re-investment as a percentage of total output over the last 20 years, at 12 per cent and 13 per cent respectively. Japan, not surprisingly, has the highest investment rate at 22 per cent.' Laing ended with an appeal to Britain's top fifty fund management groups, between them owning half the UK equity market: 'The destiny of this country's industrial base rests in their hands and those who exercise great power have a great responsibility to use their power wisely.'[9]

Accusations of City short-termism were very much in the air during 1990, especially as a new bout of recession deepened by the day, and in June the DTI organised a full-day conference to consider the question of whether this alleged failing had been responsible for a shortfall of industrial innovation. The two sides mainly talked at each other. 'You have my word,' Anthony Thatcher of the Dowty Group told the City's representatives, 'that the majority of my fellow industrialists are building at the same time as squeezing. We are driving for real shareholder value, but in a timescale that will not match the demands of some three-monthly-review fund managers, who see equities as merely trading counters.'[10] The other assorted industrialists who were present agreed, arguing that the City's concentration on short-run share prices had often made it impossible for them to undertake projects with long payback periods, since to do so would risk depressing the share price and even put the company 'into play', in other words make it vulnerable to a takeover bid.

It was an argument that those attending on the City's behalf refused to buy, countering that City scepticism about long-term investment had been a wholly rational reflection of the weaknesses of British management. So the debate went on, often circular and not always good-humoured, prompting one reporter to note that 'occasionally the two sides seemed close to dropping the normal niceties of conference debate and starting to kick one another hard in the shins'.[11] The only consensus that emerged was the unarguable one that there was a need for improved dialogue.

During the rest of 1990 the atmosphere continued to worsen. In September alone, Brent Walker's George Walker threw an angry right at City short-sightedness; the deputy chairman of ICI asserted forcibly that the stock market's volatility in recent years could not be reconciled with long-term development; and the about-to-retire Leslie Tolley, of Excelsior Industrial Holdings in Ashton-under-Lyne, Lancashire, complained to the *Financial Times* that industry was once again, as in the early 1980s, 'expected to carry the burdens of the attack on inflation (which should never have happened) through excessively high interest rates and artificially high exchange rates'. Looking back on his sixty-year career in manufacturing, he asked with undisguised bitterness: 'When will a Conservative government change the emphasis of its actions away from finance and the City of London towards manufacturing industry?'[12] The Thatcher/Major decision soon afterwards to enter the ERM at a punitively high rate presumably did not improve his mood.

It was in this antagonistic climate that Paul Marsh of the London Business School produced in November *Short-Termism on Trial* – an important, independent report, albeit commissioned by the Institutional Fund Managers Association (itself a sign of how heated and potentially embarrassing the City/industry debate was getting). Broadly speaking he gave a clean bill of health to the main investing institutions, not least on the basis of the fact that their average period of holding stock continued (as it had in a 1985 survey) to exceed five years, which as he justly remarked 'hardly seems highly speculative or a cause for serious concern'. Indeed, he even found that the stock markets of Germany and Japan had in recent years exhibited higher turnover rates than in the UK. As for the much-criticised market in corporate control, he noted that 'the language of acquisitions is highly emotive' before concluding on the basis of a wealth of empirical studies (in both the US and the UK) that 'the average picture which emerges is that the acquirer's shareholders gain significantly from acquisitions, and that the gains are greater in cases where the bid is opposed by management, or where there is a counter-bid'.

Overall, Marsh's assessment was blunt: 'Historically, the UK's lower level of investment can be attributed above all else to the relative dearth of profitable investment opportunities. This in turn mostly reflects supply-side factors – especially those related to the labour force, to productivity, and to the quality of management – and not shortcomings in the capital market.'[13]

Of course, Marsh's lucid if not necessarily definitive analysis was far from ending the debate – a debate that anyway, as he himself acknowledged, had a strongly emotional element to it. Indeed, it was only a few weeks after the publication of his study that Charles Handy delivered his agenda-setting lecture at the RSA. Furthermore, given the prevailing post-Thatcher reaction – even on the part of business leaders – against the sovereignty of naked market forces, it was hardly surprising that there should emerge a quest for a form of capitalism rather broader and more socially responsive than narrow shareholder capitalism. The big question was whether this would be one of those turning-points that, when it came to it, failed to turn.

All about EVA

In the event, the *deus ex machina* that arrived from foreign shores just in time to save the City's bacon was a small, unassuming, but immensely powerful phrase: 'shareholder value'. In fact, even though it was not until the 1990s that this essentially American concept conquered the world, it already had a history. In many ways it was a reaction, manifesting itself as early as the 1970s, against go-go, conglomerate-minded managers who seemingly prized growth and size for their own sakes rather than for what benefits they could deliver to the shareholders – the somewhat neglected owners of the companies that those managers were running.

Two figures stand out from the pioneering days. In a series of articles, Joel Stern of Chase Manhattan Bank pushed hard his notion of 'free cash flow', based in his homely retrospective words on 'the model of the corner grocery store, in which the surest indicator of success is a cigar box lid rising with net cash collections'.[14] And in 1979 an academic, Alfred Rappaport of Northwestern University's Business School, initiated the shareholder value revolution as such with his book *Information for Decision Making* – though it was not until 1986 that he published *Creating Shareholder Value*, which has been aptly described as becoming 'the bible for the shareholder value movement'.[15] Meanwhile, in American corporate life as a whole during the 1980s, the buzzwords increasingly were 'value', 'focus' and 'performance', with General Electric (under Jack Welch) and Coca-Cola (under Roberto Goizueta) leading the way in their emphasis on delivering the goods to the shareholders.

Inevitably, there emerged several different external measures of shareholder value. Probably the most influential by the early 1990s was that known as 'economic value added' (EVA), as propounded in the 1991 book *The Quest for Value* by Bennett Stewart, who nine years earlier had founded with Joel Stern the consultancy Stern Stewart & Co. Insisting in his first sentence that 'senior management's most important job must be to maximise its firm's current market value', and defining EVA as 'operating profits less the cost of all the capital employed to produce those earnings', Stewart declared that it would 'increase if operating profits can be made to grow without tying up any more capital, if new capital can be invested in projects that will earn more than the full cost of the capital and if capital can be diverted or liquidated from business activities that do not provide adequate returns'. Such an approach, Stewart argued in a key passage, would be keenly appreciated by the discerning arbiters of Wall Street:

> What truly determines stock prices, the evidence proves, is the
> cash, adjusted for time and risk, that investors can expect to get

back over the life of the business. What the market wants is not earnings now, but value now. The question is: How can discounted cash flow, which truly is at the heart of market valuation, become the driving and integrating force behind the financial management system?

The answer, naturally, was EVA, which Stewart in great detail demonstrated to be 'the right measure to use for setting goals, evaluating performance, determining bonuses, communicating with investors, and for capital budgeting and valuations of all sorts'.

A year after an influential article in the *Harvard Business Review* had maintained that the best way of stopping top executives from behaving like bureaucrats was not to reward them like bureaucrats, the chapter in Stewart's book called 'Making Managers into Owners' had an especially direct appeal for America's managers. It argued strongly in favour of a company selling its managers 'a very large number of in-the-money stock options with a rising exercise price'. That way, 'to come out ahead with the options, the managers must increase the firm's value faster than the cost of capital accrues, a result which depends upon increasing the EVA within the firm'.[16] Given that market value added (MVA), defined as the stock market value of a company less the capital invested, was deemed by Stewart to be the present value of all future EVA, it seemed – motivationally and financially – a virtuous circle indeed.

In not yet wholly converted Albion, the *Financial Times*' Barry Riley reviewed *The Quest for Value* in March 1991. Noting that Stern Stewart's 'elegant' approach had enabled that consultancy to 'present a new yardstick' for the performance of companies, with shareholder value supplanting growth in earnings per share or return on capital employed, he was distinctly sceptical about the book's universal applicability:

It pursues the characteristic Anglo-American theme that successful businesses should focus on top-down structure and corporate dealing rather than develop more basic bottom-up virtues such as refinement of employee relations or technological skills ... The Japanese and Germans must find all this rather strange ... The general approach appears to be to put constant short-term pressure on top managers, whereas many people believe that short-termism is the curse of American business ...

'Moreover,' Riley added, 'there is a crucial dependence on the validity of stock market valuations. If these are less reliable than Mr Stewart assumes, and the markets are sending misleading signals to company managers, the whole theoretical framework crumbles.'[17]

Happily for the shareholder value movement (exports division), there was already a British corporate hero singing the new approach's praises. This was Brian Pitman, who back in 1983 had become chief executive of Lloyds Bank, recently hit by the Latin American debt crisis and in the process of formulating its response to the imminent Big Bang. 'We had a big philosophical debate over two board meetings,' a board member would recall over a decade later, 'and switched from having multiple objectives to a single objective … Our single objective was creating increased shareholder value …We set a goal of doubling our shareholder value every three years …'[18]

Accordingly, Lloyds adopted a much more focused, retail-oriented Big Bang strategy than that of its principal rivals and over the rest of the 1980s and into the 1990s achieved such consistently excellent financial results that it was increasingly acknowledged as the most successful British clearing bank. Pitman himself (who would freely acknowledge his debt to American exemplars such as GE and Coca-Cola) made his first formal, public commitment in February 1986: 'Whatever the competition or economic environment, it is our task to manage our shareholders' funds as efficiently and imaginatively as possible to maximise long-term shareholder value.'[19] It was a blunt message delivered by a blunt man who almost single-handedly ended the paternalist/service/community/'Captain Mainwaring' tradition in British banking that, for better or worse, had endured for most of the twentieth century.

Elsewhere in the City, a significant early act of proselytisation was the *Shareholder Value Analysis Survey* produced by the accountants and management consultants Coopers & Lybrand at about the same time as Riley's review of Stewart. Based on extensive soundings, it found a significant divergence between chief executives and finance directors on the one hand and fund managers and investment analysts on the other:

> *In particular, top management make significantly less use of Shareholder Value Analysis than their investors expect. Additionally, the City believes top management should make greater use of SVA related measures for routine planning and*

management and for reporting to investors. Top management
believe that investors are mainly interested in short-term profit-
related measures, such as earnings per share, whereas the City
would like to see more attention paid to longer-term cashflow-
related measures.[20]

Some 70 per cent of UK companies, the report estimated, did not yet use a shareholder value approach either for routine planning and management or for investor reporting.

Why was Coopers itself so keen on SVA? Presumably there was a genuine belief, particularly relevant in the context of all the criticisms about City short-termism flying around at the time, that it offered a more forward-looking type of performance measurement than earnings per share. It also held out the promise of being relatively immune to accounting distortions – a hot issue in the immediate aftermath of the Polly Peck fiasco in September 1990, as its share price collapsed amidst accusations of fraud. Was there also a conscious realisation that the adoption of a shareholder value approach *throughout* companies could potentially be almost a licence to print money as far as management consultancies were concerned? Certainly, that was how it played out.

However, over the next few years – 1991 to 1994 – the larger debate was far from over. With downsizing, job insecurity and increasing globalisation all helping to create an apprehensive climate, even though the British economy *was* recovering by the end of 1992, by no means everyone was willing to sign up cheerfully to the brutal, unsentimental, Anglo-Saxon model of capitalism. In January 1993, coming out of its series of dinners the previous year, the RSA was able to gather together senior executives from twenty-five of Britain's top companies with a view to developing (under the leadership of Sir Anthony Cleaver, chairman of IBM United Kingdom) a shared vision of 'Tomorrow's Company'.

Soon afterwards came the publication of two important books that attracted considerable attention. *Foundations of Corporate Success* by John Kay placed great emphasis on what he called 'architecture', in other words, the links between a company and not just its shareholders but also its employees, customers and suppliers. Calling on companies to develop a network of stable relational contracts between these participants in the overall corporate endeavour, he praised Marks & Spencer as well as many

German and Japanese companies for having 'a strong sense of vision and mission' – but 'a sense of vision and mission which has arisen from within the company and from a recognition of its strengths, not one which has been imposed from outside or created by a corporate communications programme'.[21]

Meanwhile, the English translation of the thoughts of another guru, the French businessman Michel Albert, gave further ammunition for the disenchanted. 'With the collapse of communism, it is as if a veil has suddenly been lifted from our eyes,' declared his *Capitalism Against Capitalism*. 'Capitalism, we can now see, has two faces, two personalities. The neo-American model is based on individual success and short-term financial gain; the Rhine model, of German pedigree, emphasises collective success, consensus and long-term concerns.' Among the elements of the 'Rhine model' that Albert praised were the smaller role for the stock market, the less-frequent takeovers, the emphasis on investment from retained earnings and the lower dividend payouts to shareholders. Was this model economically competitive as well as socially desirable? Albert made a big claim: 'In the last decade or so, it is this Rhine model – unheralded, unsung and lacking even nominal identity papers – that has shown itself to be the more efficient of the two ...'[22] That might have been a plausible claim in 1991 when his book was originally published, but by the time of the English translation, the cruel reality was that the heavy economic cost (including soaring unemployment) of German reunification was starting to render absurd Germany's position as resplendent flagbearer of Rhenish capitalism.

The Anglo-Saxons anyway were biting back. 'Although I can understand some of the arguments of other groups,' Mike Sandland, chairman of the Institutional Shareholders Committee and chief investment manager of Norwich Union, grudgingly conceded in autumn 1992, 'I think that the degree of priority for shareholders should be so high that it is not possible for me to talk about other stakeholders in the same breath.'[23]

In 1993 – year of Kay and Albert – there were three telling straws in the wind. Under acute pressure from shareholders increasingly fed up with the enviable example of Lloyds, the Barclays board decided to recruit a chief executive (Martin Taylor) who came from outside the bank's charmed circle and was given the explicit remit of increasing shareholder value. The second straw was at ICI, which, two years after an unsuccessful assault on it by Hanson, took the decision to follow the advice of John Mayo, a corporate financier at Warburgs, and demerge its chemicals and drugs businesses – with Mayo himself leaving Warburgs and becoming finance director at the newly created Zeneca. The Hanson bid having exposed ICI to the charge of being an arthritic monolith offering indifferent shareholder value, this move not only seemed the best way of ensuring the long-run independence of both businesses, but heralded a rash of somewhat similar demergers in the mid-1990s. Thirdly, there was the start of UK Active Value, an active investor fund set up by an audacious duo, Julian Treger and Brian Myerson, with a policy of taking stakes in underperforming companies (such as Signet, Scholl and Kenwood) and then forcing through a restructuring in order to get the share price up. Employees, customers and suppliers did not feature big in their thinking.

Soon afterwards, in February 1994, the 'Tomorrow's Company' inquiry published an interim report. The *Economist*, never afraid to put the boot in, found it 'doubly useful: as a guide to what leading businessmen are thinking, and as a compendium of yesterday's platitudes'. Accordingly:

> *At the report's heart is the idea that British and American firms are too concerned with making profits for their shareholders. Obsessed with the stock market, they pay too little attention to the skills of their employees, the loyalty of their customers and the rightful claims of their fellow citizens. The report is more impressed by German and Japanese firms, with their emphasis on long-term, stable relationships among all their 'stakeholders'.*

Then came the magazine's predictable, perhaps unfair, but still powerful thrust:

> *The RSA's timing in damning the Anglo-American model now is unfortunate. In Japan, firms such as Toyota are questioning their commitments to their 'stakeholders', such as the guarantee of a job for life. Meanwhile, Germany's industrial giants are laying off workers and introducing performance related pay. Daimler-Benz has agreed to adopt American accounting standards in order to be listed on the New York Stock Exchange. And the near-collapse of Metallgesellschaft, another big German firm, has raised serious doubts about the effectiveness of German supervisory boards, which supposedly represent stakeholders.[24]*

Presumably much more to the *Economist*'s taste was *The Value Imperative*, an American treatise on value-based management (VBM) by James Taggart and others published the same year. It played an important part in imbuing the shareholder value movement with an increasingly narrow, dogmatic character – qualities that perhaps were attractive to a British corporate world feeling threatened by globalisation and always hot for certainties. 'The shareholders are not interested in what the company *per se* will look like in ten years,' Taggart and his fellow votaries of VBM proclaimed:

> They do not care how big its sales or assets will be, they do not
> care what business it will be in, whether it will be global or local,
> or even whether it will be an independent entity. Shareholders
> really want to know, or be able to forecast, one thing: How much
> wealth will the company create in the future? And that very
> simple, unadorned question must be the chief executive's focus as
> well.[25]

Moving from quest to imperative, from ought to must, the revolution was in no mood to yield to doubters. Least of all to an economics editor of the *Guardian*. Will Hutton was in his mid-forties in January 1995, when *The State We're In* not only became an instant best-seller but immediately established itself as a classic statement of the virtues of stakeholder capitalism – a form of capitalism that, in Hutton's eyes, was equally far removed from the corporatist stagnation of the 1970s and the Thatcherite excesses of the 1980s. In an earlier life, for six years in the 1970s, Hutton had been a stockbroker at Phillips & Drew. Despite broadly admiring the firm (much more meritocratic than most at that time), he had become increasingly disenchanted during those years with the City at large, which by the time he left he saw as an unwarrantably wealthy, selfish and opportunistic island, cut off from the rest of Britain and almost wholly indifferent to its fate. Perhaps inevitably, strong elements of that visceral distaste – hardly allayed by the events of the 1980s – permeated Hutton's book, a tract of huge energy and moral force. 'The City of London has become a byword for speculation, inefficiency and cheating,' he declared unequivocally in his first chapter.[26]

Even so, much of his analysis of the City's shortcomings was sober enough. The provision of unduly high-cost capital, the imposition of unnecessarily short payback periods, an inherent bias towards takeovers giving short-term stock market rewards at the expense of long-term investment – all were part of Hutton's formidable charge sheet. Altogether it drew an unflattering picture of a financial centre that any seriously reformist new government would want as a high priority to tackle at a deep institutional level, from the Bank of England downwards. 'The great challenge,' Hutton wrote, 'is to create a new financial architecture in which private decisions produce a less degenerate capitalism. The triple requirement is to broaden the area of stakeholding in companies and institutions, so creating a greater bias towards long-term commitment from owners; to extend the supply of cheap, long-term debt; and to decentralise decision-making.' In short, 'the financial system needs to be comprehensively republicanised'.[27]

Naturally, the City did not make a formal response. There was (sadly) no *ex cathedra* utterance from Eddie George. Instead, the *Financial Times* – in some sense the voice of the City – delegated its review of Hutton's book to Martin Taylor, by now ensconced for over a year as chief executive at Barclays. *He* in an earlier incarnation had been a journalist on the paper's Lex column, and the fact that their careers had followed reverse paths gave an added piquancy to the encounter – as did the fact that Taylor's piece did not appear until March, by which time Hutton's book had become a *cause célèbre*.

Much of the review sought to expose the author's technical ignorance. Hutton's attack on the short-termism of pension funds was vitiated by the way he 'skates over the point that their maturity profiles make these funds, taken as a whole, the longest-term investors of all'; his sweeping condemnation of the Bank of England as short-termist, on the grounds of its activities in the overnight money markets, was undermined by the fact that 'he has somehow forgotten that it also operates in the long-dated bond market'; while as for his failure to recognise that 'monetary instability and high nominal interest rates compel investors to favour immediate cashflows', this was explained by the loftiest of payoff lines, 'I think he simply does not understand this'. In similar vein, Taylor also accused Hutton of being 'shockingly naïve' about 'the more controlled environments of Germany and Japan' in which he 'seeks inspiration'. The olive branch came near the end: 'In one central, awkward, area, Hutton is completely right. British capitalism's rejection of social values and reaction against earlier collective excesses has gone too far. Too much individualism is bad for too many individuals.'[28]

It was not enough. 'The "shocking naivety" is not my description of Germany,' Hutton declared in his riposte the following week, 'but Martin Taylor's apparent view that while British capitalism has gone too far in rejecting social values the financial system has played no part in this development nor should play any part in changing it. This won't wash – and beyond the City it doesn't.'[29]

Such was the enormous impact of Hutton's book that inevitably his spirit was hovering in the background when just over nine months later, on 8 January 1996, Tony Blair made his celebrated speech to the Singapore business community, during which he set out his vision of 'a Stakeholder Economy':

> We cannot by legislation guarantee that a company will behave
> in a way conducive to trust and long-term commitment. But it is
> surely time to assess how we shift the emphasis in corporate ethos
> from the company being a mere vehicle for the capital market to
> be traded, bought and sold as a commodity, towards a vision of
> the company as a community or partnership in which each
> employee has a stake, and where a company's responsibilities are
> more clearly delineated.[30]

Blair was careful to avoid any anti-City rhetoric, but his apparent ideal hardly sat comfortably with the traditional stock market orientation of the Anglo-Saxon model. His speech received considerable publicity (helped by an otherwise rather barren few days for news), and a week later the historian and political economist David Marquand, one of the most thoughtful cheerleaders for a post-Thatcherite way forward, enthusiastically proclaimed that it marked an irreversible step-change in Labour's thinking – that, in short, it was the long-awaited Big Idea.

'A stake through a heart of old simplicities' was the memorable title of his lengthy piece in the *Independent*. Declaring that 'the neo-liberal triumphalists of the early Nineties, who confused the economic victory of capitalism with the end of history, were premature,' he claimed that Blair, 'in nailing his colours to the stakeholder mast', was 'opening the door to a left-of-centre project for government, more radical than anything attempted in this country in modern times'. Marquand stressed, however, that 'the notion of a stakeholder economy ... must imply a profound break with the assumptions and practices that have been central to Britain's shareholder capitalism for nearly 300 years'. And he issued a solemn warning:

> It is easy to say you want a stakeholder economy. It is much more difficult to face down the massive nexus of vested interests – international as well as domestic – which stands in the way.
>
> Moving towards a stakeholder form of capitalism would imply, at the very least, radical changes in company law, radical changes in the financial system, radical changes in industrial relations and radical changes in the relationship between central and local government. The role and status of a company would have to be redefined, so that managers had a duty to stakeholders as well as to shareholders. The insistent pressure of the stock market would have to be blunted. Capital would have to accept organised labour as a social partner ...
>
> Stakeholder capitalisms are more competitive in the global marketplace, and more popular with the world's currency markets, than shareholder ones. The short-termism, asset-sweating under-investment and disdain for human capital that were endemic in the Anglo-American version of shareholder capitalism may be good for property owners in the short term, but they are sure sources of relative economic decline and currency depreciation in the long term.
>
> Unfortunately, it does not follow that the world's financial markets will look with favour on a switch from the shareholder to the stakeholder model in the early stages, before the new policies have had time to work. Without measures to de-couple the domestic economy from increasingly feverish global markets, no such switch can be made.

Marquand concluded with a rallying call to his new champion: 'Mr Blair has gone too far to turn back. His only choice is to charge on. When battle starts – as start it will – he will need all the help he can get.'[31]

The only game in town

Sadly for the prospects of moving from a shareholder to a stakeholder version of capitalism, most other commentators were negative in the immediate aftermath of Blair's Singapore *démarche*. Two heavyweights were particularly influential. 'The snares of stakeholding' was the title on 1 February of Samuel Brittan's weekly *Financial Times* column. After a nod to Adam Smith's famous remark about how one did not depend upon the benevolence of the baker for one's daily bread, the long-standing champion of economic liberalism went on: 'Motivation apart, businessmen do not have the *knowledge* to advance the public interest directly and will serve their fellows best if they concentrate on maximising their shareholders' equity rather than promoting exports, combating global warming or solving political problems.' According to Brittan, the stakeholding approach would lead to 'a general mushiness', in which 'everyone is supposed to promote the interests of everyone else and no one is really accountable for anything'. And after noting in passing that 'there are too many romantic notions about how businesses are run in the German-speaking countries', he stressed that the great advantage of the traditional company structure was that – certainly as far as managers were concerned – it went with the psychological grain: 'People function best if they have specific responsibilities for which they are held accountable by means which are transparent, verifiable and respect the realities of human nature.'[32]

It was from a quite different direction that a few weeks later the economist Meghnad Desai (who sat on the Labour benches in the House of Lords) launched a memorable attack on Hutton and, by implication, stakeholding. 'Debating the British Disease: The Centrality of Profit' was a brilliantly written fourteen-page review of *The State We're In* that advanced three main propositions. Firstly, that Hutton had chosen to ignore that the big problem of recent British economic history had been the dramatic collapse of manufacturing profitability in the 1970s, a problem that the Thatcherite medicine had adequately if brutally treated. Secondly, that Hutton had simultaneously overestimated the financial importance of the City in relation to British industry (which according to Desai relied on new equity for barely 10 per cent of new investment) and underestimated how the City had changed in character (more international, more meritocratic), in the process becoming one of the great British success stories. And thirdly, that Hutton's Keynesian sympathies had blinded him to the fact that since the abolition of exchange controls in 1979 there was, as far as Britain was concerned, only one game in town, essentially that of infinitely mobile, profit-seeking international capitalism, no longer bounded by the nation state. 'The issue is not state versus market, or neo-classical versus Keynesian economics,' Desai concluded. 'It is whether to work with the grain of the system based on profitability (no other system being any longer on offer) and follow policies which enhance rather than impede profitability, or go under.'[33] A month before Blair made what was to be an epochal visit to Wall Street, the 'Tina' (there is no alternative) message could hardly have been spelled out more clearly.

Blair himself was already starting to retreat from his vision of a stakeholding economy. Straight after the Singapore speech the Tories had accused him of merely offering a reheated form of old-style corporatism; his shadow chancellor, Gordon Brown, evinced little enthusiasm for the new tack; and, most damagingly of all, the notion of 'stakeholding' played badly with the focus groups. Moreover, although stakeholding may have had a pleasing ring to it in soundbite terms – with all its attractive connotations of social harmony and inclusivity – the realisation soon sank in that if the notion was to be taken seriously, at the level of reshaping the capitalist system, it would mean not only upsetting some powerful interests (including the City), but going against the larger global flow.

Writing in the *Financial Times* a week after the speech, Barry Riley conceded that there was an understandable environment for the stakeholder approach ('Recent years have been notable for restructuring, unacceptable employment levels, and sometimes provocative promotion of shareholder value'), but insisted that 'Mr Blair has not chosen his moment well', in that 'the two biggest stakeholder economies, Japan and Germany, are in trouble'. He then gave comparisons that spoke for themselves: 'Shareholders have benefited in the US and UK during the 1990s. Stock market indices in these countries, measured in dollars, have shown average annual growth of 10 per cent and 6½ per cent respectively. Japan has been slightly negative, and Germany and France have recorded 5 per cent or less.'[34] Blair also had the problem of Hutton, given that stakeholding was so closely identified in the popular mind with the scourge of the City and the last thing that Blair wanted to do was to provoke the financial markets. For others of a stakeholding disposition, conscious that the long Tory years were about to end, it was a vexing situation.

Accordingly, during the early months of 1996, Blair declined in subsequent speeches to put any further significant flesh on his stakeholder vision. Instead, he took refuge in semi-meaningless platitudes. 'The stakeholder economy is about making us One Nation again.' And: 'A stakeholder economy is not about tying companies up in red tape. But it is about changing the culture of our industry, so that we can compete on the basis of quality and not only cost; on the long term as well as the short term; on trust, not simply a quick buck.'[35] By late March, pondering these and other effusions, even Marquand was pessimistic: 'I'm extremely doubtful that all that is required is a change in corporate attitudes, and I'm left wondering whether it is possible to turn in this direction, given the globalisation of the financial markets.'[36]

His pessimism was justified. 'Now you see it, now you don't' was the somewhat acid title of a piece by John Lloyd (a journalist with a particularly sure grasp of what was going on inside New Labour) in the *New Statesman* in July. Asserting that the prevailing perception in the Labour leadership was that once stakeholding 'goes beyond warm words to cold policies, votes could be lost', he also claimed that the leadership's increasing conviction was that attempting to shape an alternative version of capitalism was 'a fighting of yesterday's battles, an attempt to make a trade-off between the markets and the state, or the market and society, in ways the real world will not allow'.[37] By March 1997, weeks away from a general election, stakeholding was apparently dead in the water. 'After a brief flirtation with the term, Labour leaders now seem embarrassed to mention it,' Gavin Kelly and Andrew Gamble (proponents of stakeholding) regretfully noted. 'They are more concerned to explain what they do *not* mean by stakeholding than to say what they *do*.'[38] After a nasty fright the horses were resting easy in their stables, Augean or not according to taste.

Blair's retreat accurately mirrored prevailing attitudes in the British corporate world. As early as June 1995 the RSA's *Tomorrow's Company* report came down in favour of a voluntary approach to stakeholding – though that Hutton-tainted word was for the most part avoided, with instead the emphasis being on developing 'an *inclusive* approach as a route to sustainable success, supported by investors, educators and policy makers'.[39] Fourteen months later it was all-out war as the Institute of Directors published a report (pointedly enough called *Short-Termism and the State We're In*) specifically refuting Hutton's claim that fund managers exerted excessive pressure for high short-term returns.[40]

By 1997, against the background of a sustained bull market and ceaseless takeover activity, shareholder value was entrenched as an almost unassailable mantra. In March, two months after running an article called 'EVA fever' about Stern Stewart's roll-call of clients having expanded eightfold in the past three years, the magazine *Management Today* unveiled its first comparative survey of Total Shareholder Returns (TSR) – essentially a combination of share price performance and dividend payments, by this time the main basis for calculating directors' bonuses in the case of over half the FTSE 100 companies.[41] Soon afterwards the management consultancy PA Consulting Group issued the results of a survey of the chairmen, chief executives and finance directors of the FTSE 500. Asked to respond to the statement 'We believe that the key objective of our senior management is to manage for shareholder value', their collective reaction was striking. Strongly agree: 55 per cent; agree: 41 per cent; neutral: 3 per cent; don't know: 1 per cent.[42] It was no wonder that Mick Newmarch, the former Prudential chief executive who had become a consultant to Price Waterhouse's shareholder value division, remarked in October that 'there's no doubt in my mind that the advance of shareholder value is inevitable'. However, as his colleague Philip Wright stressed at the same time, there was still work to be done in propagating the gospel: 'If you talk to people on the audit side of our business, they'll say they've never heard of it. That's because they deal with corporate controllers. The talk about shareholder value is still at board level.'[43]

Perhaps, but it was crystal clear which way things were going. 'Investment banks hold frequent conferences on the subject,' Tony Jackson observed rather wearily in the *Financial Times* in December 1997, 'where executives from companies as diverse as Pirelli, Lloyds Bank and Boots troop to the microphone to tell how shareholder value has changed their lives.' As for the once-resilient Continent, he added that 'a senior Brussels bureaucrat remarks privately that Italian and German company bosses who five years ago could not have told you their share prices now talk of little else'.[44] Two months later another *Financial Times* writer, Peter Martin, agreed that something fundamental was happening. In the wake of the recent wave of demutualisations in the English-speaking world, he argued in his Global Investor column that the 'underlying shift of mood that this rupture with the past represents' was 'a more ruthless "what have you done for me lately?" view of the purpose of collective economic activity'. He went on:

> *This is widely shared, among shareholder-owned companies as
> well as in mutuals. It is, indeed, the* reductio ad absurdum *of the
> principle of shareholder value, to which it is now fashionable for
> companies to subscribe regardless of their place of origin and
> historical traditions. Companies that were founded as expressions
> of technical or national pride increasingly see themselves as
> vehicles for maximising the net present value in shareholders'
> hands.*[45]

It was, as Martin did not need to add, a notably mono-dimensional view of
the world.

Of course, for any new chairman or chief executive looking for a flag to
fly and wanting credibility in the City, the language of shareholder value –
an American concept in an increasingly Americanised world – had obvious appeal. The story of Cadbury Schweppes is instructive. In the early to
mid-1990s it was (largely under the influence of the chairman Dominic
Cadbury) broadly in the stakeholding camp, befitting its strong Quaker-
cum-paternalist traditions. That changed after September 1996, when John
Sunderland became group chief executive and soon looked to make his
mark. 'Cadbury Schweppes' governing objective is growth in *shareholder
value*,' proclaimed the mission statement that applied from April 1997. 'We
will deliver this by competing in growth *markets*, with strong *brands*,
focused *innovation* and value enhancing *acquisitions*. Our organisation is
increasingly energised to manage for value.' There were, according to the
letter to their shareholders that Cadbury (still chairman) and Sunderland
sent with the 1997 annual report, five key elements to 'Managing for Value':

- raising the bar of financial performance;
- applying the principles and techniques of Value Based Management
  to the development of strategy throughout the Group;
- sharpening our culture through greater accountability,
  aggressiveness and adaptability;
- developing an outstanding management team with the required
  qualities of leadership;
- aligning the financial rewards of the management team with those
  of our shareholders.[46]

Few 'non-aligned' readers of this stuff would have quarrelled with Tony

Jackson's remark in May 1998 that 'value-based management has become something of a cliché'.[47]

At about the same time, the *Financial Times* published the results of a survey of top executives in FTSE 100 companies. The responses suggested that they were a happy breed. 'How often do your major investors try to use muscle behind the scenes to make you change your strategy, financial targets or corporate governance?' Rarely: 51 per cent; never: 41 per cent. 'How well do your major investors understand your business?' Well: 56 per cent; quite well: 28 per cent. 'Do you feel hampered in taking the correct long-term strategy?' No: 89 per cent. 'Do you feel major investors are long-term investors?' Yes: 98 per cent.[48] Clearly that once bitter City/industry debate was a thing of the past, replaced by smiles all round.

What had happened? The most persuasive analysis – doubly so for coming, unusually, from the inside – is that of Tony Golding, who until his retirement in 1998 was first a fund manager and then an investment banker. 'Industrialists no longer make speeches about "short-termism" because the rules of the game have changed,' he argues in his recent book about the City. 'The 1990s saw the emergence of a New Industrial Compact between senior management and institutional investors. Today's CEOs [chief executive officers] and FDs [finance directors] accept the process of regular dialogue, the mantra of shareholder value, target setting and performance appraisal as a fact of life.' Chief executives also took on the chin what had become a dramatically short life expectancy – a 1999 study found that the average tenure of those in the FTSE 100 hot seats was barely four years. But if short, also sweet, often very sweet. Golding again:

> In the financial arrangement implicit in the New Industrial Compact the rewards for success are extremely high, mostly in the form of incentive bonuses and, more especially, options. During the second half of the 1990s, stock options came to account for up to half of the total remuneration of the board directors of larger quoted companies. Stock options link the opportunity to generate a very substantial capital sum directly to the performance of the share price ... The modern CEO has every interest in maximising the share price for his owners because that is the mechanism through which he receives his real reward.

The price of failure was not too offputting either, with the investing institutions usually being willing to countenance payoffs in the region of £400,000 to those chief executives whom it deemed to have underperformed.[49] Granted that no sector of society talked more in the 1990s than top businessmen about the implacably tough, competitive world in which we now all lived, it was in every sense a bit rich.

Golding's 'New Industrial Compact' perhaps understated the reality. Arguably, it was more like an unholy alliance. Industrialists, given an unprecedented opportunity to dip their hands into all the lovely honey of a heady bull market, learned during the 1990s to do things the City's way. It was no longer a relationship of equals. Instead, the fund managers, investment analysts and corporate financiers called the tune, while the once proud captains of industry threw away their battle honours and danced all the way to the bank.

The City victorious

'Delivering shareholder value is one of the key corporate aims if, in fact, it is not the one and only *raison d'être*,' was how the March 2000 issue of *Management Accounting* began its synopsis of a new book called *Delivering Shareholder Value Through Integrated Performance Management*.[50] If proof was needed of that assertion, one only had to turn to the British clearing bank sector, where during the previous winter one of the Big Four, National Westminster, had come under siege (from the Bank of Scotland and the Royal Bank of Scotland) and, almost unthinkable at the outset, lost its independence – essentially because over the years it had failed to create sufficient shareholder value and during the takeover battle had been unable to persuade shareholders that it was going to do much better in the future. It was a lesson not lost on Barclays, where in spring 2000 the new chief executive, Matthew Barrett, courted hugely unfavourable publicity by his policy of closing down whole swathes of his branch network. His justification, however, was that he (in the words of one press report) 'went down a storm when he appeared for the first time in front of a City audience to present the bank's annual results'.[51] The rationale was similar that autumn when the venture capital company 3i – once a very *pro bono publico* organisation – closed its Cardiff office because there were not enough entrepreneurs in Wales. 'We are here to serve our shareholders, we have to do what we think will be profitable,' explained a director.[52] In November 2000 Will Hutton, almost six years after the publication of *The State We're*

In, conceded how far away his version of capitalism still was from winning through: 'Companies that want to be predators in the current record-breaking round of mergers and acquisitions must support their share price by delivering ever higher short-term profits. Chief executive officers know that, while they talk the language of corporate social responsibility, the real game is keeping up their share price.'[53]

For any who were unsure how to play that game, the answer was to spend a residential week at what was no longer the home of lost causes. 'The Oxford Senior Executive Finance Programme focuses on the drivers of financial performance,' promised Templeton College's advertisement in February 2001. 'Value is the currency of financial performance; but what does shareholder value mean for business? Risk is inevitable; but how do you manage it? What are the financial implications of competing in the global arena? The programme equips senior executives with a critical understanding of those elements of the business which create value ...'[54]

Value, value, value – and not only in the Anglo-Saxon world. 'The first edition of *In Search of Shareholder Value* has been translated into nine languages,' Andrew Black and Philip Wright (both of PricewaterhouseCoopers) proudly declared in 2001 in their foreword to the second edition, reviewing progress since the book's original publication in 1997. 'In Europe, the first contested takeovers in Germany (Vodafone–Mannesmann) and in Italy (Olivetti–Telecom Italia) were fought around arguments on value, as was the bank merger in France of Paribas and BNP. In each case the spread of global institutional investors had a heavy influence on the outcome. All over the world, there has been a recognition that managers pursuing strategies divorced from shareholder value are not creating the same amount of wealth as those whose strategies are linked to shareholder value.'[55] Things were changing even in Switzerland, where, not long before his death in October 1998, a former president, Pascal Delamuraz, had felt compelled to warn that the country's motto had always been 'one for all and all for one', not 'shareholder value'.[56]

The case of Germany was particularly important and, for obvious reasons, symbolic. A moment laden with implications occurred in November 2000 when Heinrich von Pierer of Siemens chose to emphasise 'shareholder value' in an address to 3,000 employees in Munich. 'This is a new term for Mr von Pierer,' noted one British paper: 'In the past Siemens' long-standing chief executive has been careful to talk about "value creation" when addressing the workforce. By contrast "shareholder value" evokes slash-and-burn Anglo-Saxon capitalism. If you are a lifelong member of the Siemens family, it is not a reassuring turn of phrase.'[57] Barely two months later the announcement by Bertelsmann (the huge, privately owned media group) that it was committed to at least partial public ownership was a significant step in the recasting of the German corporate landscape. So too was the agreed takeover in April 2001 by Allianz (Germany's biggest insurer) of Dresdner Bank, seen as likely to trigger a wider restructuring of the country's financial services sector.[58] In Germany as elsewhere, politicians, trade union leaders and others may have grumbled, but business itself now increasingly knew it had to play by the Anglo-Saxon rules.

Those rules were pretty competitive, especially with the rising force of shareholder activism. A key landmark was the ousting in January 1999 of Mirror Group's David Montgomery, after its shares had underperformed the market by 34 per cent over the past five years.[59] Here the leading roles were played by the fund managers Hermes and Phillips & Drew (the latter no longer a stockbroking firm), though over the next two years the active investors that attracted the most publicity were Treger and Myerson at UK Active Value. Ongoing targets by 2001 included the mini-conglomerate Novar and the glassmaker Pilkington. 'Our role is to highlight problems we see in management – being actively involved produces a better performance,' was how Myerson justified UK Active's interventions, while in less nobly disinterested terms Treger added that 'you can take it as read that our fund advisory activities would not have grown as much as they have unless investors were happy with our returns'.[60]

Taking institutional investors as a whole, though, one must not exaggerate the frequency of their interference in management decision-making. 'The resources and time required are considerable,' was how a fund manager put it in June 2000. 'People only get really exercised in the event of a real disaster.'[61] Nevertheless, all the cumulative evidence would strongly suggest that by 2001 the major British companies were under far more intensive day-to-day shareholder scrutiny – scrutiny that was *liable* to turn to intervention – than had been the case even as recently as ten years earlier.

Such was certainly the uncomfortable experience of three British giants: BT, Kingfisher and Marks & Spencer. 'When I took over the City weren't talking about splitting BT up but making it bigger,' Sir Peter Bonfield remarked with evident exasperation in July 2000, as he found himself becoming a victim of rapidly changing nostrums amongst investment analysts.[62] That self-important community also played it every which way over the question of third-generation mobile phone licences: at the height of the mobile phone craze successfully urging BT to take a huge punt (in the event, £10 billion in Britain and Germany alone), but then castigating Bonfield and the chairman Sir Iain Vallance when it became clear that BT had horribly overpaid.[63] By March 2001, with BT shares at a three-year low, institutional shareholders were almost openly calling for one or both of the knights to fall on the sword – and Vallance duly obliged the following month.

At Kingfisher (the retail conglomerate owning Woolworths), Sir Geoff Mulcahy had had over the years a fluctuating, often difficult relationship with his shareholders. In January 2001 it was approaching a new nadir, as an apparently upbeat trading statement turned out to be a veiled profits warning, prompting one disgruntled analyst to assert that 'what happened amounted to insider dealing'.[64] By March he was under fire from investors unhappy about prospects for a previously announced demerger. For his part he insisted that 'we have to do what we think is right for the businesses and what we think is best for shareholders – hopefully those will coincide'.[65] Best described as a defiant apologia, the tone said much about the relationship.

Things were even worse at M&S, the much tarnished jewel in the British retailing crown. A study by the performance monitoring consultant Oak Administration found that no other company in the FTSE 350 had destroyed more shareholder value (67 per cent, as measured by TSR) in the three years from December 1997 – a dreadful start to what already promised to be a turbulent year.[66] Luc Vandevelde had been recruited in 2000 to try to restore M&S's tattered City reputation, but it was clear that it would be a painfully slow road to full recovery. It seemed a long time since, back in early 1997, the financial writer John Plender had applauded M&S as a company that pursued wider social values 'without having any problems keeping shareholders happy'.[67] Now another pro-stakeholder, John Kay, entered the fray, claiming that M&S's spectacular fall from grace had resulted from its being put under unnecessary pressure by 'the stock markets of the racy 1990s' to improve profits above an already what-should-have-been-acceptable 5 per cent or so annual growth. Not so, according to a shareholder, Howard D. Biederman (managing director of New York-based Projects Unlimited), who fired off a letter to the *Financial*

Times attributing M&S's decline to decades of unwarranted arrogance, including its stubborn belief that 'a store's primary function is not profit but to satisfy the customer – and from that will evolve profit'.[68] John Lennon once defined communism in Britain as shopping at Marks & Spencer; some thirty years on, capitalism (shareholder-value-style) in Britain had become *not* shopping there.

During the summer and early autumn of 2001, however, the varying fortunes of these three companies paled into insignificance beside the trauma of the British telecoms giant Marconi, in an earlier incarnation the solid, much-respected GEC. Between March and September that year its underlying position changed spectacularly: from a net worth of £4.5 billion to a deficiency of assets against liabilities of £805 million. Inevitably the once-lauded two key figures – Lord Simpson and John Mayo – took most of the flak, departing Marconi in some ignominy. Yet as the details of this high-profile debacle (involving large-scale redundancies) became known, so the City's role was the subject of considerable critical scrutiny. The *FT*'s City editor, Martin Dickson, candidly shared out the blame:

> It rests with the boosterish analysts who failed to question the perpetual high growth Marconi (and its rivals) saw in telecoms; the corporate financiers who facilitated its absurdly expensive cash acquisitions (in common with deeper-pocketed rivals); the bankers who extended loan facilities without asking the right questions; institutional shareholders, who demand managers create 'shareholder value' yet measure that by short-term share price performance; and the financial press, with our shallow need to create heroes ... [69]

Early in 2002 an only semi-repentant Mayo (who perhaps wished he had never left Warburgs) published a lengthy exercise in self-justification, stressing that the new regime had taken over in 1997 against a background of 'the prevailing view of investors that GEC was a business that had increasingly failed to deliver shareholder value', and that therefore the fundamental priority was to reverse that perception. Plender for one was unimpressed. 'Throughout his articles Mr Mayo harps constantly on the theme of shareholder value,' he noted, before pointing out that yardsticks like TSR took no account of risk – and that, whatever Mayo's temporary achievement in keeping his shareholders happy, Marconi was now technically insolvent. In short, 'Phooey to total shareholder return when Marconi lives on a knife edge'.[70]

Taken as a whole, by the twenty-first century the City/industry relationship no longer retained even a semblance of equality. 'Sir Fred has had a frustrating Christmas season,' Dickson reported at the start of 2001 about Sir Fred Holliday, who as chairman of Go-Ahead Group and Northumbrian Water had been trying to persuade other business leaders outside the Square Mile that something needed to be done about the increasingly flagrant way in which investment banks advising on takeovers not only charged outrageously high fees (Blue Circle, for instance, had recently spent £27 million on advisers while defending itself against Lafarge), but almost invariably declined to itemise their costs, let alone demonstrate their value added. 'He tells me,' Dickson explained, 'that at party after party senior business figures agreed with him, but none was prepared to put his head above the parapet. Companies seem scared of offending banks, lest they find it hard to get an adviser if they find themselves on the receiving end of a takeover.'[71]

Indeed, Dickson might have added that, given the way in which investment analysts and corporate financiers at the same investment bank were in a mutually profitable alliance to keep up the flow of M&A activity, the best bet for a company not wanting to be put 'in play' was to keep as low a profile as possible. Outspoken industrialists like Sir Hector Laing and Sir John Harvey-Jones seemed a distant memory. Nevertheless, it was far from a simple, black-and-white case of bad guys and good guys. As Kay had pointed out as far back as 1990 (at the DTI's now long-forgotten conference on short-termism), the awkward truth was that there existed 'a deal-driven culture among both management and large parts of the City of London, and each of these sustains the other', in that 'on the one hand we see fee-hungry advisers and, on the other, we see managers who find expansion by acquisition a great deal easier than expanding through selling in the marketplace'.[72] Nothing had happened in the intervening years to weaken that culture.

Occasionally, quite apart from the Marconi saga, there was an unwelcome glare of publicity on the dominant, City-imposed norms. One such moment occurred on 1 February 2001: in an almost insouciant response to the news that the Anglo-Dutch steel giant Corus was cutting over 6,000 jobs (mainly in Wales), the stock market traded energetically in the shares, which rose almost 10 per cent, the second best performance that day in the FTSE 250.[73] Government ministers fulminated, but the company's dry-eyed chairman, Sir Brian Moffat, had delivered the savage restructuring plan that his shareholders had been impatiently calling for. Amidst much anti-Corus and some anti-City rhetoric flying around elsewhere, David Aaronovitch in the *Independent* drew the only rational conclusion: 'Annoy Rhodri Morgan [first minister of Wales] and the worst that can happen to you is a nasty stare. Annoy your shareholders …'[74]

Soon afterwards Hutton, by now chief executive of the Industrial Society, published a plan by which companies would be put under regulatory and fiscal pressure 'to report on their approach to corporate social responsibility, community investment, ethical practice and sustainable growth'. Anthony Hilton, the *Evening Standard*'s City editor, was scathing: 'It is almost as if he had never heard of globalisation – the phenomenon that means goods and services can be supplied any time, anywhere. This has brought excess capacity in almost all product lines and ferocious competition in every sector, the likes of which business has never seen before.' Hilton was especially scornful of the way in which Hutton upbraided business for concentrating only on financial targets: 'He fails to accept that companies that do not focus all their efforts on the bottom line will be swept aside by their less squeamish, better focused, more single-minded competitors. Of course, it would be "nice" if Vauxhall kept Luton open or Corus the Llanwern steel plant in defiance of economic gravity …'[75]

The rules of the global corporate game were apparently set in stone – almost as unyielding as those of the Eton wall game. The umpires were the world's equity markets, with the London market as dominant as ever in the European time zone. Not even the recent internet bubble – involving a serious misallocation of financial resources and a temporary dimming of the lustre of the investment analysis profession – had affected their ultimate authority. It required a massive leap of the imagination to envisage a different set of arbiters emerging. Six and a half decades after Keynes had condemned the stock market for its short-sighted encouragement of casino-style capitalism, there were no signs of such a leap being taken.

9

Public Places, Private Finance

At Cazenove's – since the inter-war period the City's leading firm of corporate stockbrokers – there was by the 1980s an invaluable, if seldom articulated, rule of thumb: never have anything to do with a businessman who was connected with a football club. Rugby union and cricket were the City's games, certainly at board or partnership level, not soccer, which still had a largely working-class following and for twenty years had been blighted by rising levels of hooliganism. Nor anyway, in strictly financial terms, was there much for bankers, brokers and others to get their teeth into: of the big football clubs only Tottenham Hotspur was floated on the stock market; the Football Association sought to prevent directors from enriching themselves; and amongst supporters there persisted a strong if largely emotional sense that football clubs were part of their local communities and had a purpose that transcended the merely commercial. 'Generations had supported their clubs, standing on terraces, loyalty an article of faith, and the clubs, for all their faults, had never thought to overcharge them, the shareholders still, even in the late 1980s, not mostly in it to make money,' David Conn has eloquently written in *The Football Business*. 'The clubs were companies in structure, but clubs in style, and football was a game, not a means of making money.'[1]

All this changed in the 1990s, as more or less simultaneously two things happened. The first was the astonishingly rapid commercialisation of top-flight soccer in the wake of the formation in 1992 of the breakaway Premier League and its lucrative deal that same year with Sky television. Income (from a mixture of TV fees, steeply increased ticket prices and systematic merchandising) soared, while the gap between the rich clubs and the rest became an unbridgeable chasm. If that was an unconstrained expression of market forces, the other development was in its way part of the post-Thatcher reaction: namely, the way in which the middle class (sharing Gazza's tears, reading Nick Hornby's *Fever Pitch*, chorusing 'football's coming home' during Euro 96) suddenly found in soccer a source of identity, even community, that went beyond the naked acquisitive individualism that in the 1980s had seemed all-sufficient. It was a mood that Blair in opposition astutely tapped into (witness his celebrated heading session with Kevin Keegan), and during the 1997 election itself he and his party made much of how Britain was at last 'coming home' with Labour.

The City did not realise immediately that something significant was afoot, but by the 1996/7 season it was deeply involved in the football business. Manchester United as well as Spurs had already been floated on the stock market, and they were now joined by Chelsea, Newcastle United, Aston Villa, Leicester City and Sunderland. 'Newcastle United is one of the UK's leading football businesses,' declared a typical prospectus. 'It generates high-quality revenue streams by selling viewing rights to its football matches and by selling a range of branded products.' Among the company's 'key strengths' were 'the size and loyalty of its supporter base which ensures large audiences'.[2] At the Newcastle end the flotation was masterminded by Mark Corbridge, recruited from NatWest Markets to be joint chief executive at St James's Park – a route out of the Square Mile never before trodden. The City's bullish mood (deriving no doubt in part from fashion, but predicated above all on a belief that the coming of pay-per-view would be an unbeatable cash-cow) was exemplified in a report published in March 1997 by the investment bank UBS. Its very title, *UK Football plc: The Winners Take It All*, could hardly have been more graphic, with few if any tears being shed for the losers who took nothing. As for the future, market forces (and the M&A departments of investment banks) would decide: 'We expect more corporate activity in the sector as media and possibly leisure companies grow to understand the value of the rights and franchises possessed by the top clubs.'[3]

Four years on, the City is no longer quite so bullish. Players' wages are taking up an unwarrantable slice of what would otherwise be profits, the pay-per-view revolution has temporarily stalled, and there are signs that the middle-class love affair with soccer may have peaked. Nevertheless, financial power has continued to concentrate in the hands of the big clubs, and the shareholders – led by the City institutions – are now unequivocally the masters of a club's destiny, not the supporters. 'If the teams fail to take value creation seriously,' Erik Stern of management consultants Stern Stewart (apostles of shareholder value) warned in December 2000, 'they will eventually go out of business or fall to those who do.'[4]

The so far sorry, bungled story of the attempt to build a new national stadium at Wembley epitomises the City's stranglehold over what used to be known (wholly unironically) as 'the people's game'. Unable to attract sufficient support from the debt markets for the planned £660m redevelopment, the Football Association was compelled by the end of 2000 to go back to the drawing board and try to produce a cheaper design, preferably with higher revenue projections. By 2002, two years since the last Cup Final in the old stadium, little visible progress had been made and the FA was apparently rethinking its whole policy. Memories of the twin towers – let alone the policeman on the white horse – already seemed to come from a distant, less bottom-line fixated world.

Everything has a price

The football story is merely part of a much larger story: in essence, how the market over the last twenty years has penetrated whole areas of British life previously either ring-fenced from market forces, or at the least operating by not wholly market criteria. This process of 'marketisation' has not always directly involved the City as such, but invariably there have been powerful financial pressures at work – pressures entirely compatible with what one might call City values, which in turn (as we have seen) have been increasingly widely disseminated, to the point where they are now part and parcel of the psychic and linguistic landscape. The upshot has been not only a radical shifting of the boundaries between the public and the private in terms of provision, but also a cumulative assault on the very fabric of civil society, traditionally occupying a position between the state on the one hand and the market on the other. Football clubs (originally nonprofit making organisations) had once been part of that civil society – until, like the City itself, they became clubs no more.

Arguably, a decision taken even before Thatcher came to power was crucial in the unfolding of this larger story. This was the willingness of the Wilson government, in its search for cross-party support, to include contracting-out rules as it framed the state earnings-related pensions scheme, or SERPS, that eventually came into being in 1975. These rules involved, Nicholas Timmins has written in his authoritative history of the welfare state, 'an absolute acceptance in principle by Labour of the importance of occupational schemes, and thus of the private sector'.[5] During the Thatcher era itself, as part of the explosion in individual financial provision, people were increasingly encouraged (especially through legislation in 1988) to opt out of SERPS and into their own personal schemes – inducements so persuasive that by 1993 some 5 million people had done so.[6] The scandalous mis-selling of pensions by the life insurance companies meant that it was not all roses for those who took this step, but the broad shift was incontrovertible and probably irreversible.

So too elsewhere. The privatisation programme of the 1980s has now become such a familiar historical fact that it is easy to forget just how revolutionary it seemed at the time – especially on the eve of the first really big privatisation, British Telecom in late 1984. By the end of the decade, with British Aerospace, Cable & Wireless, Britoil, Jaguar, BT, British Gas, British Airways, Rolls-Royce, British Airports Authority, British Petroleum, National Bus Company, Rover Group, British Steel and the water industry all completely or substantially sold off, the everyday face of the British economy had been transformed.

It was a programme that produced handsome profits for many City banks, brokers, lawyers, accountants and others – profits that were particularly undeserved in that the City during the critical early stages had been far from sharing Thatcher's messianic zeal for denationalisation. The February 1981 flotation of British Aerospace was managed by Kleinwort Benson in conjunction with a distinctly apprehensive Bank of England; while among Kleinworts' co-underwriters, Schroders and Morgan Grenfell were reluctant participants, with little or no faith in privatisation as such. Nor was there much more bullishness as the almost £4 billion BT issue approached. At a dinner party attended by Nigel Lawson (like Thatcher, a believer) but mainly comprising top industrialists and leading merchant bankers, the chancellor was struck by how, with the notable exception of Martin Jacomb of Kleinworts, 'each and every one of them roundly declared that the privatisation was impossible: the capital market simply was not large enough to absorb it'.[7] Of course, it did not take long for history to be rewritten, and within a few years the impression would be created that privatisation had been one of the great City inventions, now ready to be exported to the rest of the world. But as with that other equally cardinal, equally mythic development, the abolition of exchange controls, the truth was that the City had followed rather than led.

During the second half of the 1980s, with the privatisation programme more or less an established success, the Thatcher government began to look elsewhere in its mission to introduce the discipline of the market. Three key targets stood out: broadcasting, the education system and the National Health Service – three central elements of British civil society. By the mid-1980s the BBC was an institution under siege, not only on account of its alleged left-wing bias, but because it was viewed as complacent, inefficient and profoundly non-entrepreneurial. 'British broadcasting should move towards a sophisticated system based on consumer sovereignty', was the uncomfortable conclusion reached by the Peacock Committee in July 1986, and within a year a programme-maker, Alasdair Milne, had been replaced as director-general by an accountant, Michael Checkland.[8] In 1989 the management consultants Price Waterhouse produced a report for government examining privatisation options – a report that led directly to the privatising of the Independent Broadcasting Authority's transmission operations, with Price Waterhouse as sole financial advisers to the Home Office – and in 1990 a new Broadcasting Act required Channel Four to compete with ITV companies in the selling of airtime.

In education, meanwhile, the great Thatcherite upheaval was under way from autumn 1987 with the publication of Kenneth Baker's Great Education Reform Bill ('GERBIL'). It was, as Timmins comments, a mixed bag. 'While the curriculum was plainly being nationalised, and grant maintained schools would be centrally funded, other measures were decentralising, handing more powers to governors and parents in something that was a long way short of a real market, but was recognisably more market-like than the set-up it replaced.'[9] Baker also introduced testing, as well as ending academic tenure in universities. As for the NHS, another high-profile battleground, changes (always billed as 'reforms') introduced in the late 1980s sought to improve financial controls and to introduce an internal market. Thatcher was always acutely aware of the electoral importance of the NHS, which enjoyed widespread sentimental attachment, and here she moved somewhat circumspectly.

Taken as a whole, though, her legacy was momentous – in these areas quite as much as elsewhere. Above all she changed the terms of the debate, as she preached relentlessly that there was no such thing as a free lunch, that the days of a guaranteed job for life were over, and other uplifting nostrums of the unfettered market. It was a way of looking at the world that gradually seeped into the national psyche, destroying as it did so the ability of Britain's leading institutions to offer more than token resistance. The universities, for example, were quite unable in 1988 to prevent Baker from replacing the academic-dominated University Grants Committee (UGC) by the University Funding Council (UFC), the latter body stuffed with representatives of commerce and industry intent on shifting resources to subjects likely to benefit the GNP. In effect Thatcher, helped by her more trusted ministers and a largely supportive press, was softening up civil society. The City, and other exploiters of market possibilities, would be able to step into the ring when the opponent was already groggy.

Jam tomorrow

The Major years were less didactic, more consensual in tone, but the underlying reality was continuing marketisation. Although the NHS remained funded by the taxpayer, the provision of services within it became increasingly diverse (involving the private sector at many points), while NHS trusts and GP fundholders operated under ever-stricter budgetary controls. In the Prison Service, the UK's first privately run (by Group 4) remand prison opened in 1992 at the Wolds, Humberside. At the BBC the introduction in 1993 of Producer Choice, essentially a mechanism seeking to apply market pressures to the BBC's in-house activities, was possible only through the good offices of no fewer than three City consultants – Coopers & Lybrand, Price Waterhouse and Ernst & Young.[10] Three years later a further market mechanism was created at the BBC with the arrival of the internal purchaser–provider split between BBC Broadcast and BBC Production.

Perhaps the most dramatic changes were in education, where league tables – hitherto almost confined to sport and the Eurobond market – became mandatory. Short-term contracts proliferated in higher education, business schools mushroomed (approaching a hundred by 1997, having been only a handful in 1979), and a series of government initiatives (such as the establishment in 1994 of so-called 'Foresight Panels') enforced a new intimacy between research councils and university scientists on the one hand, industry and business on the other. Moreover, with the government ensuring that funds to higher education institutions were increasingly dependent on their ability to attract students, the uncomfortable fact by the mid-1990s was that universities (including the former polytechnics) were essentially in a real (not simulated) market situation, with those failing to garner enough applications likely to face a bleak future.

Nor was that all. Privatisation may have been running out of steam by the early 1990s, but in November 1992 Norman Lamont took up the slack by announcing the Private Finance Initiative (PFI). It did not come entirely out of the blue. Back in the Heath era there had been a strong political desire to use private capital in the public sector, but this had fallen foul of the argument that it would have the effect of 'crowding out' necessary resources for the private sector. A more immediate antecedent was legislation in 1990 that had the effect of making NHS capital expenditure the responsibility not of the government but of the NHS trusts. In November 1992 itself there was a strong element of financial expediency – in effect, getting capital expenditure off the government's bloated balance sheet – but if Lamont did not have any sense of the latent implications, it is quite possible that Major (the prime mover) did.

What exactly was the PFI? Some five and a half years, and much ensuing confusion, after Lamont had launched it, the *Investors Chronicle* offered from a broadly sympathetic standpoint ('Investing today for jam tomorrow') a useful encapsulation:

> *The private finance initiative enables goverments to get the private sector to build and run otherwise unaffordable infrastructure projects. But it would be risky for one company to put up, say, £200m to build a road. A typical project involves several companies bidding together to put up some of the total project cost. The rest of the money comes from bank loans.*
>
> *The consortium that wins the bid has the right to run the project over a period of, say, 25 years, after which time that project reverts to state ownership. During this time it gets payments from the government to cover both the cost of building the project – including the cost of loan repayments – and maintaining it. The consortium is also entitled to a return on its equity, normally in the range of 12 to 20 per cent, to reflect the risks involved in designing, building and running a project.*
>
> *The tricky part of PFI is agreeing who is responsible for which risks ...[11]*

Perhaps inevitably, the first three or so years of PFI were predominantly occupied by legal and bureaucratic wrangling, with little concrete being achieved and the City displaying fairly tepid enthusiasm for the whole idea. This was despite the best efforts of Lamont's successor, Kenneth Clarke, who in November 1993, after noting that progress had been 'disappointingly slow', set up a Private Finance Panel.[12] Its first chairman was Eurotunnel's Sir Alastair Morton, who would confidently assert that the PFI had the potential to be 'the Heineken of privatisation – taking the private sector to the parts of the government machine not reached by previous privatisations'.[13] By the end of 1994 the chancellor was talking with equal blitheness about almost 700 PFI projects being in the pipeline amounting to a value of no less than £21 billion; but as Francis Terry, editor of the journal *Public Money & Management*, observed at the start of 1996, 'there is still considerable doubt especially among the construction industry and some City institutions – wondering where the £21 billion of funding will come from – as to how much the PFI will eventually achieve beyond a few eye-catching projects' such as the Channel Tunnel Rail Link or the Second Severn Crossing.[14]

In fact, it was during 1996 that the PFI achieved some sort of lift-off. Not only was the government able to claim by the autumn that it had agreed contracts (almost all in the past year) worth £6 billion, but the provision of finance was significantly widened as the long-term capital markets began to be used on a regular basis.[15] Landmark transactions included the issue by First Hydro Finance of £400 million of twenty-five-year bonds to finance the acquisition of the pumped storage electricity generating assets formerly owned by the National Grid and the Road Management Group's similar recourse to the UK debt capital market (for £165 million) in order to fund the Swindon–Gloucester road and A1(M) 'design-build-finance-operate' upgrade projects.[16]

By this time the Private Finance Panel was being chaired by a leading City fund manager, Alastair Ross Goobey, who publicly declared in October 1996 that 'in property, IT, roads, prisons and the Ministry of Defence it is all going well'. He was interviewed as part of the *Financial Times*' ten-page PFI survey, which included large advertisements for Charterhouse ('The PFI bank'), Price Waterhouse (helping to negotiate PFI deals for eight new hospitals), CIBC Wood Gundy (boasting a dedicated PFI and infrastructure equity fund of up to £125 million) and KPMG ('From Stonehenge to satellites, via 28 NHS Trusts, a dozen defence projects, pathfinder education schemes, the Channel Tunnel Rail Link and the Millennium Exhibition, the PFI is a major business for KPMG').[17] But if the City, or at least part of it, was waking up, these were still early days. An anonymous foreign banker based in London put it well early in 1997: 'PFI is effectively a new industry. Inevitably, there has had to be a massive education process on both sides.'[18]

The PFI did not go unchallenged. Hutton in the 1996 paperback edition of *The State We're In* referred to 'the malign impact of the Private Finance Initiative on public provision'.[19] Even a much more pro-markets commentator, the *Financial Times*' Martin Wolf, was sceptical. 'A clever spending wheeze' was the title of his piece that summer about PFI, in which he expressed concern about the lack of 'adequate control of the public spending implications' and concluded: 'The PFI could turn out to be a more effective way of providing public services. But it could also be a bit of a swindle.'[20] There was no such ambiguity in Skye, where the recently opened bridge connecting the island and the mainland had been financed by a consortium of two construction companies (who built it) and the Bank of America. High tolls had led to sustained protests by the islanders – or, in the *Financial Times*' measured words in October 1996, 'the Skye bridge does little for the public image of PFI in Scotland'.[21]

There was also serious anxiety about the implications of PFI in terms of the NHS, where (as even Ross Goobey conceded) progress had been poor. 'The initiative will not bring new money to the NHS,' declared an article in the *BMJ* that August. 'The services provided by privately financed capital projects will have to be paid for out of the cash limited, tax financed budget of the NHS.'[22] The following spring, a week before the general election, the same journal published the findings of three case studies of the use of private capital to fund NHS hospital developments, based on the plans produced for schemes (in Lothian, Calderdale and Bromley) that had reached an advanced stage. The bleak conclusion was that 'rather than being "a tremendous opportunity for the modernisation of the NHS", the private finance initiative is likely to lead to a shrunken NHS that will not be able to provide a comprehensive range of health services to all sections of the community'.[23] Séan Boyle, of the independent King's Fund, agreed: 'Making private capital available for health service facilities is a commercial decision, not necessarily linked to benefit in terms of the overall system of healthcare delivery.'[24]

Labour in opposition did not have a serious problem with PFI, or indeed the general concept of the public–private partnership (PPP). This was especially so once it had shifted by 1996 from its earlier position of wanting to exclude PFI from health entirely, on the grounds that it was privatisation by the back door. No doubt it helped that most of the electorate regarded the whole subject of PFI as a deadly combination of dull and incomprehensible. Instead, the warm noises were made about matters that pressed the right emotional buttons. The skies (aka the air-traffic controllers) were not for sale. It was wrong for people to profit out of incarceration. The railways (recently privatised by the Tories, on the premise that they needed a huge injection of City money) would be returned to public control. Anyone voting Labour in May 1997 might have had a reasonable expectation of seeing the inexorable eighteen-year process of marketisation checked and, to an extent, reversed.

Jam today

For a new government desperate to keep a tight lid on public borrowing and direct taxation, and a new prime minister with little or no ideological commitment to the superior virtues of the public sector ('What matters is what works'), PFI (or PPP) had an obvious appeal.[25] Some leading City figures played a major role in ensuring that the flow of deals quickened appreciably under Labour. For example, Malcolm Bates (chairman of the Pearl Group) conducted a crucial review of PFI soon after the election that not only led to the ultimate resolution of the vital if arcane question of PFI accounting standards, but more immediately persuaded the government that PFI should come under more central control through a new Private Finance Taskforce. The Taskforce's first chief executive was Adrian Montague, previously co-head of global project finance at Dresdner Kleinwort Benson. 'Do you think there is a danger that the private sector is taking on too much project risk?' he was asked in an early interview. 'No,' he replied. 'There should be no limit for equity investors and debt providers.' And again: 'Are there any sectors which you do not think are suitable to be tackled by the PFI?' 'No. I think it is possible to structure a deal in any sector ...'[26]

Two PFI deals had a special piquancy during Labour's first term. The first was as early as December 1997, when Partnership Property Management (PPM) signed the so-called Prime Contract. 'This is more than just a sale and leaseback of 700 properties to an international real estate investment consortium,' noted *Project Finance*. 'PPM will also provide property management services to the Department of Social Security over the 20-year life of the agreement.' And who had a majority shareholding in PPM? The answer was Whitehall Street Real Estate Limited Partnership VII – a £15 billion investment fund owned by partners and clients of Goldman Sachs. Or in the magazine's apt words about a scenario that would once have seemed inconceivable, 'unemployed citizens will queue to collect their dole cheques in offices largely owned by Goldman Sachs and its wealthy institutional and private clients'.[27]

The other deal was for the Birmingham Northern Relief Road (BNRR), reaching financial closure in September 2000 – over ten years after the notion of this being Britain's first major toll road had originally been proposed. The intervening years had witnessed much controversy: Friends of the Earth and the Birmingham Chamber of Commerce at daggers drawn, the longest-ever public inquiry into a UK road scheme, and Labour in opposition apparently vowing to prevent it before, in office, changing its mind.[28] The financial arrangements were made by Bank of America and Abbey National, between them responsible for underwriting the entire £685 million senior debt. Dresdner Kleinwort Benson acted as financial advisers to the consortium awarded the concession (Midlands Expressway Limited), and soon after financial closure its head of project finance, Jim Barry, reassured potentially nervous investors by highlighting the unusually long concession period (fifty-three years) and the fact that MEL had total power to control toll rates.[29]

'Now, at long last, the private sector's complaints about the difficulty of the process have diminished,' noted Timmins in November 2000 in the *Financial Times*' annual PFI survey. A total of over £16 billion worth of PFI deals had been signed, another £16 billion worth of deals were in procurement, and PFI itself was 'becoming a sub-set of a much wider involvement of private finance in public sector projects, with the whole now travelling under the umbrella of public-private partnerships'. The latest Treasury estimate was that some £25 billion worth of PPPs would be signed over the next three years. An accompanying list of the project names of the biggest UK PFI deals already signed in 2000 gave some flavour of their range: MoD Whitehall Building; GCHQ Buildings; Connect Communications Cable Network; University College of London Hospital; Nottingham Express Transit Line OneSystem; A13 Thames Gateway; and Premier Prison Services Refinancing.[30]

A glance at the pages of the March/April 2001 issue of *Private Finance Initiative Journal* suggested a world buzzing with optimism. The former merchant banker Adrian Montague, now deputy chairman of Partnerships UK (PUK – the former projects arm of the Treasury's PFI Taskforce and a PPP in its own right), had taken up a part-time position advising John Prescott and Lord MacDonald on the use of private finance in transport. Rumours were 'rife' that the Highways Agency, responsible for managing trunk roads and motorways, was going to initiate a number of PPPs. And declaring that 'implementing modern, smarter procurement of goods and services is a challenge for virtually every public sector organisation, and should be,' Beverley Hughes, parliamentary under-secretary of state at the DETR, wrote enthusiastically of the latest wave of PPPs. 'It is clear,' she concluded, 'that partnership approaches to procurement offer us many exciting opportunities to improve public service delivery.'[31]

Even so, there were in spring 2001 still some dissenting voices. 'The increasing influence of the private sector in the criminal justice system means shareholders' interests come first,' argued Stephen Nathan (editor of *Prison Privatisation Report International*), in the context of a steadily increasing number of PFI prisons – financed, designed, built and operated by the private sector – coming on stream. 'Who shapes criminal justice policy? Is it professionals, politicians and the public? Or is it Group 4 share-holders?'[32] That was debatable, but incontestable was the series of embarrassing failures in the application of the PFI to information technology: in Timmins' words, 'as the débâcles such as the swipe card for the Benefits Agency and the Passport Agency computer show, in IT it has significantly failed to deliver its promise of trouble-free risk transfer to the private sector'.[33] As for health, there was little conclusive evidence by this time that the PFI had brought major benefits. A report in April by Jon Sussex, on behalf of the Office of Health Economics (the pharmaceutical industry think-tank), found that the balance of benefits and costs when comparing PFI hospitals with conventionally purchased ones was 'a fine one'.[34]

In none of these areas, though, was the government's attachment to the PFI/PPP approach under serious political pressure. The air traffic control and London Underground sagas were very different, with both issues making waves disturbingly close (from Labour's point of view) to the June 2001 election. Although the government did manage to push through Parliament the partial privatisation of National Air Traffic Services (NATS), along PPP lines, such was the widespread concern about safety standards being compromised that it was forced to choose a consortium – to run the system – that was explicitly pledged to operate on a 'not-for-commercial-return' basis.[35] Safety was also at the heart of the increasingly acrimonious conflict about who would run the London tube lines. Under the government's PPP plans, several consortiums (one of them, Link, chaired by Michael Cassidy, a former big hitter with the City Corporation) were bidding for the contracts: but in the eyes of the mayor Ken Livingstone and his American adviser Bob Kiley, the lack of a unified management structure under the PPP approach threatened safety.

As negotiations between the two sides foundered during the spring, public opinion was largely against the government, enabling the press to indulge in the demonisation of Shriti Vadera – an unyielding Treasury adviser to Gordon Brown who had spent most of her career at Warburgs. 'Shriti and that top echelon of advisers are sticking to their guns because they think it is the only way to get more efficiency into the Tube,' a City source told the *Evening Standard* in March. 'It is very much the merchant banking view of the world: that only people experienced in the harsh world of the private sector can possibly understand what it takes to get things done.'[36] Soon afterwards, a letter to the same paper from a disgruntled Bucks commuter reflected the general frustration: 'I find it incredible that Shriti Vadera – for all her "real-world" business and management experience after 14 years in the heady, private-sector world of concrete, glass and marble towers of a leading City investment banking house – should be in a position to exercise such influence on the issue.'[37]

Ultimately, whatever the twists and turns ahead (including a sharp dip in City/government relations following the controversial October 2001 decision to force the privatised Railtrack into administration), none of this seemed likely to deflect Labour from its approach – certainly in terms of PFI/PPP as a whole. The justified expectation, moreover, was that the comprehensive, government-initiated report on the subject expected soon after the election – with Hutton's old friend Martin Taylor chairing the commission – would endorse overall an expansion of the programme. Belatedly, it was starting to dawn on observers that something of potentially fundamental importance was under way. 'Twenty years ago, private sector involvement in public sector capital projects in health and education would have been politically impossible,' Graeme Leach, chief economist at the firmly free-market Institute of Directors, observed in April 2001. 'Twenty years on it is possible to envisage a future with private sector involvement in all aspects of current and capital provision. The PPP may ultimately change our concept of what is and isn't the government's responsibility.'[38]

Leach's reference to education was apposite. There, the process of marketisation – and subordination to what either explicitly or implicitly were bottom-line City values – accelerated with disconcerting rapidity during Labour's first term. By spring 2001 some twenty local education authorities (LEAs) were receiving all or part of their education services (excluding actual teachers in the classroom) from the private sector. Business sponsorship of specialist schools and schools that were part of education action zones was expanding. And the February 2001 green paper, in effect promising to dismantle the comprehensive system in secondary education, signalled for the first time as a practical political possibility the widespread privatisation of 'failing' state schools.[39]

For the City, not renowned previously for its interest in state education, these were all welcome and positive developments. Soon after the green paper, looking back on his years as chief inspector of schools, Chris Woodhead referred somewhat sardonically to how what post-ideological New Labour had really come to want was 'pragmatic education policies, implemented with crisp Arthur Andersen efficiency'; though he added that 'Arthur Andersen and other consultancies – brought in at huge expense to advise the education department – have not always been able to find workable solutions acceptable to the various vested interests, such as local education authorities and unions'.[40] Even so, the clear buzz by this time was that education 'support' was a growth sector – a buzz typified by the increasingly high City profile of Nord Anglia, the Cheshire education services specialist whose chairman (Kevin McNeany) at the start of 2001 sold £510,000 worth of shares to Merrill Lynch.[41] As for sponsorship, HSBC (already generally active in backing specialist language or technology schools) made headlines in April 2001 when it agreed to pay £800,000 to Shropshire's pioneering Thomas Telford School (itself already backed by a City livery company, the Mercers) to enable it to devise an online mathematics course.[42]

As it happened, a particularly eloquent story in this new, utilitarian century came from the private sector. 'A group of male governors, who are mainly City board-room types, had met for lunch the week before and seem to have decided that she had to go,' was how a dissenting governor of Woldingham School in Surrey explained to the press in September 2000 the abrupt departure of the headmistress. Claiming that a 'macho' management style was invading independent education, he added that 'a school doesn't run like a City company – I found the whole thing quite grotesque'.[43] It was just the sort of story to provoke Michael Prowse, the resident counter-culture irritant in the Saturday *Financial Times*. 'The notion that business provides an ideal role model for schools suffuses the whole of Labour's educational strategy,' he argued some months later in a full-frontal attack. 'The emphasis on league-tables, on performance-related pay, on head teachers as macho "chief executives", on competition as the only spur to achievement, and on management mumbo-jumbo, are all derived from a belief that schools can succeed only if "taken to market" …'[44]

Inevitably, the trends were similar in higher education, where the controversial introduction of tuition fees opened the way for the top universities to move, perhaps in Labour's second term, to an overall charging policy based on supply and demand. 'Over everything hangs the shadow of monetarism,' lamented one (non-economist) academic in 1999. 'Not much in universities is valued these days apart from what can readily be translated into financial currency. The old currency of scholarship has virtually passed away.' Ann Oakley, a professor at the University of London's Institute of Education, added that 'the apex of the devotion to money as the measure of all things is the financial management review, in which a team of external profit-making consultants is raked in to carry out some form of cost–benefit analysis of a particular department or type of activity'.[45]

During 2000 there were three notable moments. David Blunkett, then education secretary, made a keynote speech at the University of Greenwich insisting with deliberate emphasis that higher education must not shirk its responsibility to make a critical contribution to the UK's economic success.[46] The Committee of Vice-Chancellors and Principals changed its name, apparently without consultation, to the much more corporate UK Universities.[47] And when Blair decided to show the visiting Bill Clinton a British university, he chose (out of over a hundred candidates) the very entrepreneurial Warwick, which enjoyed a reputation for working with industry, had developed corporate citizenship into a key area of research, and with more than seventy businesses coming under its Earned Income Group was generating almost two-thirds of its own income.[48] Back in the late 1960s the left-wing historian E. P. Thompson had lambasted 'Warwick

University Ltd' (where he taught), but in truth he and his confrères had not seen anything yet.

Increasingly, it behoved universities to develop contact with the financial markets and those close to them. Edinburgh University, faced like many other universities with a sharp reduction in funding per student at the same time as a doubling in student numbers, announced in November 2000 that – in a ground-breaking deal – it was raising £40 million in cash through an unsecured loan from the Prudential. 'It's a new approach – to borrow to restructure the university,' remarked the finance administrator at another university.[49] Of course, PFI/PPP schemes were already well established in universities by this time, often involving the private sector building and maintaining student accommodation in return for guaranteed rental income. One of the key players in this burgeoning market was Jarvis's University Partnerships Programme (UPP), which by early 2001 had secured prospective funding of £500 million from Abbey National and Barclays.[50]

The deal that really spoke volumes, though, had nothing to do with student rent. This was the arrangement, announced in November 2000, by which the recently quoted investment bank Beeson Gregory agreed to put up a third of the £60 million cost of Oxford University's projected new, state-of-the-art chemistry building in return for half the university's share in any spin-off businesses coming out of the building during its first fifteen years. Understood in the agreement was that Beeson Gregory, specialists in advising high-technology and biotechnology companies, would work closely with the university in spotting potential 'spin-out' candidates at work in the building.[51] Once upon a time the dreaming spires and the Square Mile had seemed utterly different worlds: no longer. Symbolically enough, a few months later, the retiring senior partner (Giles Henderson) at one of the City's leading law firms, Slaughter and May, was named as the new master of Pembroke College.[52] The news would hardly have pleased one alumnus, Dr Johnson, who always took a pretty dim view of 'the cits'.

The great man's scepticism was surely justified. City people, City markets, City institutions – all have their legitimate places in a healthy, well-ordered capitalist economy. But in the end, for all its occasional flurries of 'animal spirits' (such as during the internet boom), the City is a mechanistic, two-dimensional place, by definition concerned ultimately with rather narrow matters of profit and loss. The money calculus, in other words, dominates – and indeed, it would make no sense if it did not.

There are, however, other things in life, including other values, other criteria, other purposes. An eloquent defender of the world beyond the market was a rather different Oxford master, David Marquand of Mansfield College. Reflecting in November 2000 that there had been through the 1980s and 1990s 'a relentless Kulturkampf' – mainly from the new Right, but insufficiently repudiated by New Labour – 'designed to root out the values of the public domain, accompanied by an equally relentless attack on the institutions in which they were embedded', he sought to assess the damage done to civil society by this 'incessant marketisation', the assumption that 'there are no citizens, there are only customers':

> The growing interpenetration of politics and business; the sleaze that has accompanied it; the dumbing down of the BBC and the broadsheet press; the culture of sponsorship which has invaded virtually every form of public entertainment, from opera to football; the diversion of academic energies from the pursuit of knowledge and the education of the young to a desperate scrabbling for advantages in mindless assessment exercises – all tell the same story. They show that the dykes our Victorian ancestors built to protect the public domain from invasion by the market domain have been breached at point after point. Even more damagingly, so does the virtual disappearance of the notion of the public interest from public discourse ...[53]

Unwittingly, the City had been somewhere near the forefront of this invigorating but also destructive trail of marketisation. That will only change if those with a bigger picture of society than the City has ever had summon up the resolve to begin to reverse the process.

10

Global Portal

For many years the distinctively salmon-pink *Financial Times* (established 1888) was the City's village newspaper. It monitored market movements, published lengthy price lists, and related the odd judicious morsel of unsensational gossip. After the Second World War it extended its coverage to embrace British industry, and then from the 1960s it began to reinvent itself as an *international* financial and business newspaper. By the 1970s its foreign news pages were unrivalled in the British press and in 1979 it started printing a European edition in Frankfurt. Over the next twenty years the *Financial Times*, printing around the world, successfully took on the *Wall Street Journal* – and even made a significant impact in the North American market. In April 1998 it became the first-ever daily newspaper to sell more copies outside its country of origination than inside. And by 2001 its worldwide sale was over 500,000, almost double that of five years earlier.[1] Written and edited in offices looking across the Thames to the City, it was a remarkable achievement – and equally, graphic testimony to London's unrivalled global reach.

London – global city

More than any other city in Europe, more than any other city in the world, London is a *global city* – a focal point for contacts all over the world, a cosmopolitan cocktail of people and activities with an outward-looking orientation. The only comparable place is New York. The City (like Wall Street in relation to New York) has played and plays a crucial part in promoting and sustaining London as a global city. After all: 'The "things" a global city makes,' according to Saskia Sassen, author of *The Global City: New York, London, Tokyo*, 'are services and financial goods.' [2]

London has one of the world's most international workforces. It includes 47,000 Americans, 36,000 Germans, 35,000 Italians, 30,000 French, 25,000 Japanese, 24,000 Spaniards and 12,000 Koreans.[3] A substantial proportion of them work in the City – in banks, securities houses, law firms and insurance companies. Amongst the Americans, a quarter work in banking and finance and the law. The City is host to a fifth of the Japanese firms in London and half the Korean corporations.

'Take a walk to Broadgate on a cool summer's day,' urges financial journalist Margareta Pagano. 'Milling around in cafés and bookshops you will find Italian derivative traders, American corporate financiers, Lebanese arbitrageurs, Dutch brokers, Moroccan rocket scientists, German bond salesmen, Swiss equity market makers, Japanese swappers and even the stray Essex forex boy. There is no other financial centre in the world with a talent pool to match that of the City.'[4]

Since the 1990s the City has seen a veritable invasion of European workers – such as Daniela. Often they enter the City labour market through a posting to the London office of a bank from their home country. Some return, but many move on to new jobs with other firms, landing some of the best-paid positions. A survey by head hunters Napier Scott in summer 2001 revealed that continental European applicants for City jobs were better educated and had superior mathematical and linguistic skills than their British counterparts. It showed that the best-paid and most intellectually demanding posts in sales, marketing and analysis were four times more likely to be filled by foreigners, though home-grown talent continued to dominate on the trading side. 'There is a total misconception in the rest of the country that jobs in the City of London have all been taken by a privileged elite from the South East of England,' reflected chief executive Shaun Springer. 'This is far from the truth – the top jobs have mostly been taken by non-UK citizens from Europe, and the country should be thankful as it allows London to maintain its predominance as a financial centre.'[5]

International communications are a crucial underpinning of this cosmopolitan cast. Heathrow has more international passengers than any other airport in the world and Gatwick is the eighth busiest. Traffic from Stansted and Luton is expanding rapidly. Then there is the City Airport, near Canary Wharf, which is handy for short-haul flights to European cities. Together, London's five airports handle more than 100 million international passengers a year.

Some 250 destinations are served by a direct flight scheduled at least once a week. London is the hub of the two most heavily used international route systems: London–New York, the busiest long-haul route with thirty-four flights daily to New York and Newark, NJ; and London–Paris, the busiest short-haul route with forty-one flights a day. Daily, there are 141 flights to the US, including thirty to the West Coast and eleven to Chicago; twenty-four to Frankfurt; twenty to Milan; and fourteen to Madrid. There are thirty-nine flights a week to Tokyo. Paris and Brussels are also accessible by frequent and rapid Eurostar rail services via the Channel Tunnel.

Telecoms are another form of communication. As the first European country to deregulate and privatise its telecoms industry, the UK provides a more extensive and cheaper range of telephone services than on the Continent. Ranked by European business executives in terms of quality of telecommunications, London scored 1.43 compared with 0.87 for Paris and 0.83 for Frankfurt.[6] Some 230 countries can be direct-dialled from London, more than from anywhere else. Low costs have stimulated London's emergence as Europe's telecoms hub, the centre through which European and multinational corporations route their communications. Driven by the City's demand for state-of-the-art information technology, a cluster of internet and financial software firms has grown up along the Square Mile's northern fringe – comprising the most dynamic concentration of new-technology businesses in Europe.

English – the global language – is an unreplicatable communications asset. One in five of the world's population speak English with some degree of competence. It is the main language of books, newspapers, international business, diplomacy, academic conferences, airports and air traffic control, science, technology – and the internet. Four-fifths of all electronically stored information is in English.

It is also the language of international finance; the common tongue was one of the reasons why in the 1960s most US banks decided to establish their Euromarket operations in London, rather than in Paris or Luxembourg or elsewhere. English law is much used in commercial contracts. Disputes are resolved principally in English courts or through arbitrations and mediations conducted in London in a wide range of areas, including banking and insurance, maritime and aviation, commodities and construction, and oil and gas.

The resolution of international commercial disputes has been a rapidly growing activity in London since the mid-1990s. Up to 5,000 international arbitrations and mediations take place there every year with millions of pounds at stake. The fifty or so organisations that provide dispute resolution services include trade associations, specialist arbitration and mediator organisations, exchanges and professional institutes. Foremost amongst them are the Centre for Dispute Resolution, headquartered in London, the London Court of International Arbitration and the London Maritime Arbitrators Association. To accommodate the burgeoning dispute resolution industry, a new purpose-built International Dispute Resolution Centre is being established.

A unique trajectory

London's standing as a global city has roots way back in history. It began with its emergence as the world's busiest maritime port by the end of the sixteenth century. As the major European entrepôt on the transatlantic and Asian trade routes it became the most important centre for trading cargoes and commodities, attracting colonies of merchants from all over Europe as well as Muscovy and Asia Minor. The development of the British Empire in the seventeenth and eighteenth centuries expanded its outward orientation, notably towards North America and India. In the nineteenth century it emerged as a great imperial city, the heart of the most extensive empire the world has ever seen. Queen Victoria's reign also saw the forging of strong financial and commercial links with Australasia, Africa and Latin America.

A cornerstone of Britain's outward orientation has been its 'special relationship' with the United States. The independence of the American colonies from 1783 made little difference to Anglo-American trade or business ties. The United States was the UK's largest trading partner prior to 1914 and British investment was important for the development of the US railroad system. More broadly, British capital exports over the century prior to 1914 also played a fundamental role in the development of the global economy by financing railways, urbanisation and primary goods production in Australia, New Zealand, South Africa, Canada, Latin America and Asia. The outward flow of funds was reversed during the First World War, as Britain, alone amongst the allies, raised a series of massive loans in New York, tapping the savings of US citizens to assist its war effort.

The Anglo-American economic entente continued in the twentieth century. In the 1920s, while politicians bickered and procrastinated, the governors of the Bank of England, Montagu Norman, and the Federal Reserve Bank of New York, Benjamin Strong, worked together to restore the functioning of the shattered international financial system. A subsequent Anglo-American duo – John Maynard Keynes, who spent much of the Second World War in Washington representing the UK Treasury, and Harry Dexter White of the US Treasury – were the architects in 1944 of the Bretton Woods system of fixed exchange rates, under which the world prospered in the 1950s and 1960s. It was in these decades that many major US corporations spread their wings internationally. More often than not, an early step in their development as multinational corporations was to establish a presence in the UK. Today there are more corporate headquarters in London than any other European city. Amongst the *Fortune* 'Global 500' companies over 65 per cent are represented in London – streets ahead of Paris (9 per cent) and Frankfurt (a nugatory 3 per cent).

The City–Wall Street financial axis was reinvigorated in the 1960s and 1970s with the expansion of US banks in London, and there was some movement in the other direction too. The 1980s and 1990s saw a further strengthening of the relationship, in the sense that US banks became the pre-eminent players in both financial centres. These last two decades also saw a massive build-up of UK direct investment in the US following the abolition of exchange controls in 1979. North America is much the most important area for UK direct investment, with 29 per cent of the total – 7 per cent more than to all the countries of the European Union put together. The US is much the biggest direct investor in Britain. Moreover, the US remains Britain's largest single trading partner, well ahead of Germany or France (though not of the EU as a whole).

Britain's trade with the non-EU world is the highest of any EU country as a percentage of the total. Despite almost three decades of EU membership and much-vaunted pronouncements about convergence by Labour ministers, the UK economic cycle remains closer to that of the US than to that of Germany, reflecting the substantial and long-standing trading, financial and investment links between the two English-speaking nations.

Historically, the comparison is striking between Britain's international outlook and the parochialism of other European countries. In the nineteenth century, in contrast to Britain's ever-growing transatlantic and global ties, the continental powers were much more focused on antagonisms in their own continent or their own internal affairs. France, Holland, Spain and Portugal lost most of their overseas colonies during the French wars of 1793–1815 or soon after, circumscribing their world perspectives. Austria, Russia and Turkey remained imperial powers, but regional in extent and preoccupations. Germany and Italy became particularly inward-looking during the decades they were going through the throes of establishing themselves as nation states. The 'scramble for Africa' towards the end of the nineteenth century was more an expression of their European rivalries than a new interest in the outside world.

In financial matters, London was a significant source of trade finance for continental merchants in the nineteenth century, but long-term capital raising by European borrowers was undertaken mainly in Paris or Berlin or other continental bourses. For most of the twentieth century too, the City's interface with Europe was minimal, although there were exceptions at the level of individual firms such as Schroders, Lazards and Warburgs. European banks and borrowers were active early in the Eurobond market in the 1960s, but soon they were simply participants in the new international capital market along with everybody else.

The rise of the Euromarkets in London, which had the effect of returning the City and the UK to the heart of the global economy, coincided with the arrival of the question of 'Europe' as an issue in British politics. The 1960s saw two failed attempts to join the Common Market before the UK was finally admitted to the club in 1973. Simultaneously, in other words, the UK was being pulled in two diametrically different directions: on the one hand towards an inward-looking regional trading bloc (and embryonic political federation); on the other hand towards an outward-looking global marketplace. Four decades on from the 1960s, it remains unclear how that deep contradiction in Britain's long-term destiny is going to be resolved.

London and the pretenders

The US banks that flooded into London to participate in the Euromarkets in the 1960s were perceived as a threat by leading continental bankers – *Le défi américain* (the American challenge), to cite the title of the bestselling tract by French politician Jean-Jacques Sevan-Schreiber published in 1968. Many continental banks and some of the UK clearing banks joined informal 'banking clubs' to promote co-operation in the face of this common enemy.[7] Five such entities were formed, though they made little difference in practical terms.

From the 1960s, most of the leading Western European banks also established a presence in London, more than 160 of them by the mid-1980s. Big Bang then provided an opportunity to buy into the London securities market that was taken by half a dozen major continental banks. Between 1989 and 1997, Deutsche Bank bought Morgan Grenfell, ING acquired Barings, SBC got Warburgs, Dresdner Bank purchased Kleinwort Benson and Société Générale took over Hambros. Others, such as Commerzbank and ABN Amro, increased their presence through hirings. By raising their commitment in London, they were able to enter the global marketplace and to compete with the American banks without having to establish a presence on Wall Street, though a few did this too.

In the 1990s London emerged more and more as Europe's leading financial and business city. Throughout the decade it consistently topped the annual survey of European cities as business locations conducted by commercial real-estate consultants Healey & Baker.[8] Their evidence was collected by a systematic sample of senior executives from Europe's 15,000 largest industrial, trading and service companies. The most important factors in London's favour were: all forms of international communication (but *not* internal transportation); the availability of suitable staff and office space; and foreign languages spoken (i.e. English, the host tongue).

Access to markets is the most important single factor influencing location decisions, being identified as such by almost two-thirds of senior executives. London scores highly on account of being rated by them as having the best external transport links, the best telecommunications and as the most important European centre for internet-related business. As regards qualified staff, the second most important location factor, the scale and scope of London's labour market give it a long lead; it is the calibre of the workforce, not the cost of labour, that is decisive. Interestingly, and perhaps surprisingly, the 'quality of life' and freedom from pollution are the least significant factors, being cited by just one in ten senior managers.

Paris and Frankfurt rate overall second and third amongst European cities as business locations in the Healey & Baker survey. They occupy these positions in relation to access to markets, availability of qualified staff and quality of telecommunications. Paris is top city for internal public transport and for international rail and road links, but lags considerably behind London and Frankfurt for international air links. Frankfurt scores highest for staff productivity, but poorly for the quality of life of employees (ranked 22 out of 30) and the cost of staff (ranked 25).

In the 1990s both Paris and Frankfurt took steps to mount a challenge to London and to win a greater share of Europe's international money-centre business. In Paris a high-powered promotional body, Paris Europlace, was formed with the brief of winning foreign business for the Paris markets. It is backed by the Banque de France, the Paris city council, the bourse, the big banks and more than 100 financial institutions, French and foreign. And the French government lends political support. The campaign has enjoyed some success in enticing foreign banks and investors to become active in the French markets, though it was unable to persuade participants in the new euro-denominated bond market to adopt French rather than German govenment bonds as the benchmark.

Orchestrated by the urbane Frenchman Jean-Francois Théodore, the Paris, Amsterdam and Brussels bourses merged to form Euronext in September 2000. At first commentators dismissed it as an also-ran, but they changed their tune when in October 2001, in the face of counter-offers from the London Stock Exchange and Deutsche Börse's Eurex derivatives division, LIFFE opted for a £555 million merger with Euronext. Subsequently the Lisbon and Warsaw exchanges decided to join. Moreover, speculation was rife that the London Stock Exchange, jilted in its wooing of LIFFE and strategically adrift, would sooner or later merge with Euronext, a dazzling piece of footwork on Théodore's part.

Frankfurt, the original home of the Rothschilds, has been an important European financial centre for centuries. After the Second World War it became host to Germany's central bank, the three largest commercial banks and the country's largest stock exchange. The dominant centre for domestic financial services, it also developed significant international activities: 243 foreign banks have a presence there. Some 75–80,000 people work in banking and insurance in Frankfurt, though many of them are in retail services rather than money-centre activities.[9]

The formation of *Finanzplatz Deutschland* in 1996 – in the wake of winning the European Central Bank in 1994 and with the launch of the euro on the horizon in 1999 – marked a determined drive to develop Frankfurt into a global financial centre, contesting London's pre-eminence in the European time zone. Backed by the three big banks and the Deutsche Börse, the body was charged with the promotion of Frankfurt as an international financial centre by identifying and remedying structural weaknesses and by pushing its case to all levels of government. A challenge to London was mounted in the market for financial derivatives based on the bund, the German government bond. In the mid-1990s LIFFE, London's larger and longer-established derivatives exchange, had the lion's share of the bund market, the biggest European derivatives product, much to the irritation of Eurex, Frankfurt's derivatives exchange. At LIFFE the contracts were traded on the floor of the exchange by the traditional and colourful method of open outcry, but at Eurex dealing was screen-based and office-bound. As it became clear from autumn 1997 that electronic trading was cheaper and more efficient than open outcry, the volume of contracts traded in Frankfurt began to surge upwards and soon virtually all bund-based derivatives trading switched to Eurex.

Eurex's triumph in the 'battle of the bund' was hailed as a turning-point and that the writing was on the wall for the City. It certainly put the cat among the pigeons at LIFFE, which promptly adopted screen trading. But London continued to be where the international banks and their traders wanted to operate from; they simply routed their orders through the Eurex computer in Frankfurt. While Eurex got the transaction fees, Germany did not capture the other benefits, the broking commissions and the tax take.

The promotion of *Finanzplatz Deutschland* was directed by Werner Seifert, the abrasive Deutsche Börse chief executive. His strategy was the development of a Frankfurt-based 'trading silo', a vertically integrated entity undertaking everything from tracking of stocks, commodities and financial derivatives to a comprehensive clearing and settlement system. But others jibbed at this vision, fearing that it would Balkanise Europe's financial markets by forcing the creation of competing 'silos' in London and Paris and was at odds with the EU's goal of creating a pan-European financial network. Deutsche Börse's attempts to merge with the London Stock Exchange in 2000 and to purchase LIFFE in 2001 were both rebuffed. However, in 2002 Seifert took full control of the Luxembourg-based securities settlement business Clearstream, the last building block of his stock-to-derivatives trading silo.

But this achievement was overshadowed by the defection in protest of major clients UBS and JP Morgan Chase to rival clearing system Euroclear, viewing the acquisition by Deutsche Börse as anti-competitive. And there were other clouds on the horizon. There was the challenge from Euronext. There was disillusion with the performance of the Neuer Market, the stock market for high-growth companies, where prices had crashed and new offerings had dried-up. There were troubles too at Frankfurt's big three commercial banks, whose tall towers dominate the city's skyline, earning it the nickname 'Mainhattan'. Weakened by bad debts and intense competition in Germany's fragmented banking system, Dresdner Bank had been acquired by insurer Allianz in 2001, shifting control to Munich. Commerzbank, in which Munich Re was a significant shareholder, seemed poised for the same fate.

But most alarming of all for Frankfurt's *Finanzplatz Deutschland* project were developments at Deutsche Bank, the leading German bank. Since the late 1980s, Deutsche Bank had pursued a corporate strategy of focusing on international investment banking activities and for a moment had even contemplated pulling out of German retail banking altogether. Headline-making milestones in this strategy had been the acquisition of UK merchant bank Morgan Grenfell in 1989, US investment bank Bankers Trust in 1998, and US fund manager Scudder in 2001, but there had been substantial organic growth too. By 2002 more than half the bank's 98,000 employees lived and worked outside Germany, 11,000 of them in London. Moreover, almost two-thirds of earnings came from the investment banking operations based in London and New York. Thus rumours in autumn 2001 that Deutsche Bank was planning to move its headquarters to London were all too plausible. Relief in Frankfurt was almost palpable when Deutsche Bank denied the speculation. 'It would have been a devastating psychological blow,' comments Thomas Schmengler, head of German markets at real estate firm Jones Long LaSalle.[10]

Yet there was no doubt that the balance of power within the bank was shifting away from Frankfurt. 'The product expertise is disappearing abroad to London and to the US, while what we are left with in Frankfurt are the follow-on functions that diminish Frankfurt's appeal as an international financial centre,' says Jürgen Felsmann, a financial analyst in the city.[11]

'Frankfurt's main handicap is, quite simply, Frankfurt,' is the disarmingly caustic view, from a London vantage-point, of Stanislas Yassukovich. 'The expatriate community that populates an international financial centre has cultural and lifestyle expectations which Frankfurt cannot meet. Germany has moved its international financial business to London for the simple reason that London is where the people to operate it can be found.' Yassukovich adds of Frankfurt's political masters that 'any government that would sponsor a tax designed to drive the Eurobond market outside the EU (the withholding tax directive) can hardly be interested in financial services as a core national interest'.[12] Martin Roth, a journalist on the influential *Frankfurter Allgemeine Zeitung*, is almost Prussian in his gloom: 'Attempts so far to create a German financial-services entity of European or even global cut have done little except foster the impression that boys have been sent out to do men's work'.[13]

Just another currency

Since 1994 Frankfurt has been home to the new European Central Bank (ECB), identifying it with the euro more closely than any other financial centre. Proximity to the institution that sets euroland's interest rate confers advantages to banks with a presence in Frankfurt, argues Breuer: 'We in Frankfurt have decided to play on that – in a friendly competitive manner. We will try to establish close connections with the decision-makers in the ECB and thus cultivate a better market feeling for the decisions to be made.'[14] But even with the launch of euro notes and coins in 2002, there were no signs that the ECB was proving the magnet to the world's financial institutions that German bankers had hoped for.

The UK's position of staying out of European monetary union – launched in January 1999 – created some anxiety in the City. In July 2000 – a few months after Cassandra-like noises from the then Lord Mayor, Lord Levene – the European senior executives in the Healey & Baker survey were asked what effect they thought this policy would have on London's position as a financial centre over the next five years. Almost three-quarters predicted a significantly negative impact.

Yet in 2001 a comparative study of London and Frankfurt by the Anglo-German Foundation found that 'the new currency has had no wholesale effects on changing business relations between the two cities ... London remains the main European financial centre.'[15] Much of London's financial business is conducted in euros: more than 40 per cent of foreign exchange trading; more than 60 per cent of transactions at LIFFE; and almost half of the OTC derivatives business.

A Bank of England survey of key European market participants, undertaken almost two years after the introduction of the euro, revealed that for most such firms their euro foreign exchange dealing and their treasury and risk management functions are concentrated in one centre, most often London.[16] London is also the principal location of their international bond and equity trading and research, their non-government euro-denominated bond and equity issuance and their mergers and acquisition advisory businesses. It is estimated that 70,000 City jobs, equivalent to almost the whole of Frankfurt's wholesale financial services sector, are dependent in some way on activity originating from clients based in other EU member states. About one-third of this activity is international banking, but corporate finance, equities, derivatives and foreign exchange also have an above-average proportion of customers from continental Europe.

None of this should be surprising. The strength and depth of London's financial markets creates the liquidity that stimulates competitive pricing for transactions of all sizes and for non-standard products. The unrivalled concentration of skills and experience allows banks operating there to achieve substantial external economies of scale. Moreover, they benefit significantly from economies of scope generated by the presence of the full range of financial service operations in a single location.

The City's output of money-centre services constitutes 53 per cent of total EU output of wholesale financial services of £73 billion (€120 billion). This concentration of activity results in significant economies of scale and scope that are estimated to reduce the cost of the provision of wholesale financial services for EU customers by about 17 per cent.

London's efficiency and cost advantage attracts use of its services by both EU and non-EU clients, particularly multinational corporations that account for a disproportionately large share of usage, that otherwise might well seek such services in New York or Tokyo or some other non-EU international financial centre. Likewise private individuals, who might otherwise turn to Switzerland as a provider of their investment requirements.

Quantitative measurements of the efficiency of the City and its contribution to the EU economy have been attempted by the Centre for Economic and Business Research, an economic consultancy. This has been done by comparing the actual situation in the year 2001 and a hypothetical model – on the basis of some 'heroic assumptions' and bold estimates – in which money-centre services are spread evenly across the countries of the EU proportionate to their respective Gross Domestic Products: the 'fragmented market hypothesis'. [17]

The fragmented market hypothesis model estimates that the even dispersion of wholesale financial services around the EU would lead to a fall in the scale of the City's output from €63.5 billion to €15.3 billion, less than a quarter of its current size. About two-thirds of City employment would disappear, some 203,000 jobs. The increased costs deriving from the loss of economies of scale would lead many customers to seek services outside the EU. The study suggests that only €14 billion of the business lost by the City would go elsewhere in the EU. Of the remainder, €20 billion would migrate to financial centres outside the EU, notably New York or Switzerland, while €14 billion of business would simply disappear, made uneconomic by the higher costs without the efficiencies of the large market in London. The outcome would be that the EU's GDP would be €28 billion lower (0.3 per cent) with a net loss of 192,000 jobs across the region. The UK would bear the brunt of adjustment, its GDP falling by €33 billion, but Luxembourg, Netherlands, Germany, France, Belgium and Italy would suffer too.

A twenty-first-century choice

Recovering from many years in the doldrums, Britain ended the twentieth century as the world's fourth-largest economy, having recently overtaken both France and Italy. Much of that last-minute spurt was down to the big-number, value-added performance of the newly deregulated City of London – indeed, no other country in the world is now so economically dependent on its financial services industry.[18] That industry in turn relies heavily on operating in an open environment with intimate links to all parts of the developed – and developing – world. The European dimension *does* matter to the City, especially in the short to medium term with the already started shake-up of the European financial system; but in the long term, not least for demographic reasons, the global dimension matters even more. If the euroland project came to mean a reorientation of the City from an outward global perspective into an inward-looking regional bloc, it would not only run counter to the huge accumulated thrust of the City's history, but prevent it from making a full contribution to its host country's future prosperity. Even if the euro was a more securely based project than it is, there would still be no rational case for seeking to dismantle Britain's unique global portal.

11

A Triumphal Note?

City State offers a reading of Britain present and Britain past that places the City foursquare in the centre of the frame. As recently as twenty years ago, there still seemed a rough parity between the manufacturing and service sectors of the British economy; now, after two decades of relentless de-industrialisation, it is transparently obvious that manufacturing will in the future never be other than the junior, subordinate partner to Britain's flourishing services – of which none is more flourishing, at the start of the twenty-first century, than financial services. Back in the mid-1980s there was much breast-beating when the *Financial Times* failed to devote an editorial to a House of Lords report on Britain's manufacturing future. These days, governments do not even bother to commission such reports.

Looked at in the long sweep of history, this should hardly be regarded as an abnormal state of affairs. A schematic (if crude) breakdown is suggestive:

- Sixteenth and seventeenth centuries: England starting to take off as an international power, based largely on commercial strength.
- Eighteenth century: the rise as a great power gathering momentum, now based on finance as well as commerce, but manufacturing making an appearance late in the century, as Britain pioneers the ˙eventually worldwide Industrial Revolution.
- Nineteenth century: all systems go, for the only time, as Britain dominates the world in commercial, financial *and* manufacturing

terms almost throughout the century, though by the end Britain's industrial supremacy is under threat from Germany and the US, whereas commerce and finance are still full steam ahead.
- Twentieth century: problems on all three fronts after 1914, but from the 1960s finance – and finance alone – bucks the trend.

For so long a predominantly commercial centre, then both a commercial and financial centre, and now almost exclusively a financial centre, the City has been at the heart of this story. By contrast, even when Britain was the industrial 'workshop of the world' in the 1850s, the commercial and financial sectors were just as important to national prosperity – so much so, indeed, that even then it was already thirty years since Britain had last enjoyed a trading surplus on manufactured goods. So, manufacturing as merely a blip on the historical radar? Not quite, but it is a salutary counter-perspective to still-entrenched assumptions (and images) about the over-riding importance of Britain's smokestack heritage – a heritage that has wrongly overshadowed the crucial commercial-cum-financial dimension.

In the last thirty years the City has enjoyed its second golden age and most indicators suggest strongly that, notwithstanding short-term fluctuations, this long-term growth and prosperity will continue for the foreseeable future. It is a moot point, nevertheless, whether the City's mood should be *unambiguously* triumphalist. Of course, such is the astonishing range and depth of London's critical mass as an international financial centre that it is hard to see a genuinely threatening challenge coming from Frankfurt, Paris or anywhere else in the European time zone. Nor do we believe that the now largely foreign ownership (or 'Wimbledonisation') of the City is a likely cause of diminished international standing, though Philip Augar's eminently reasonable view that we will only know either way when there is a deep and sustained bear market (which, according to him, will lead to a massive transfer of financial power from London to New York) remains to be tested. Of course, in theory, modern technology allows financial firms to operate from anywhere in cyberspace, but in reality there is as yet no evidence that international financial centres are an endangered species.

The lesson of history is that – once established – leading international financial centres retain their primacy until toppled by an external shock that profoundly dislocates business. War has been the most common form of shock – the Spanish conquest of Antwerp in 1585, the French occupation of Amsterdam in 1795, the Franco-Prussian War of 1870 that throttled the aspirations of Paris, the First World War that led to the migration of the international capital market from London to New York, or the Lebanese Civil War of 1975 that put paid to Beirut as the Middle East's leading financial centre. The damage done to New York by new government taxes and restrictions in the 1960s was a different sort of shock, but equally disabling.

Could the euro be another such shock? If Britain were to 'sign up', this would, as we argue, run diametrically counter to the City's uniquely *global* historical trajectory – a trajectory intimately linked to questions of mindset and orientation. Such a move would also, in a more immediately tangible sense, have unfortunate regulatory implications, potentially eroding one of London's key competitive advantages – namely, a traditionally light but assured hand on the regulatory tiller. Even so, few in the City, however personally Eurosceptic, seriously believe that Britain joining the single currency would *decisively* impact upon the City in a negative way. The Bank of England might not relish the prospect of becoming a branch of the European Central Bank, but that is another matter.

We are inclined to agree with the Eurobond market veteran, Stanislas Yassukovich, that *if* there is a real long-term threat to the City, it is of a quite different nature. 'Complacency, loss of distinct corporate culture, fragmented leadership, excessive bureaucracy, poor service, lower ethical and quality standards, lack of collective motivation,' he wrote in gloomy, itemising fashion in 1999. 'All of these diseases sap the strength of the once-healthy enterprise, and even an apparently overwhelming competitive advantage collapses. In one form or another these illnesses are all evident in the City ...' Yassukovich elaborated: electronic delivery of financial products and services was diminishing the importance of location; the decline in syndication of large transactions was turning investment banks into huge, 'transactionally self-sufficient' financial supermarkets with less and less need to share deals with close neighbours; and both these trends were contributing to the 'loss of a City style and standard of dealing', thereby diluting its 'brand image' and competitive advantage. He was also concerned about the tendency towards increasingly inflexible regulation; about a lack of leadership from the Bank of England, suffering a loss of authority after the stripping of its banking supervisory function; and about the way in which the spread of an unhealthy bonus culture had 'undermined corporate loyalty and diminished collective responsibility for standards'.[1] Altogether this intriguing analysis provokes as an obvious analogy the fall of the Roman Empire – in other words, decline from within. But the only antidote to the harmful trends identified by Yassukovich would be a reversion along club-like lines; and a club is what the City no longer is.

Foremost amongst the transactionally autonomous financial supermarkets are the 'bulge-bracket' investment banks – these latter-day merchant princes that bestride the developed world and owe allegiance to no sovereign authority. How much would it matter if one of them – Morgan Stanley, say, or Credit Suisse First Boston – went belly up? Naturally it would be a disconcerting turn of events, presumably for New York even more than for London, but one could argue that in at least four ways the effects might be beneficial. The Americans would start thinking more urgently about the regulatory aspect of global investment banking; the endemic risk-taking, bonus-seeking culture would sustain a heavy blow; there would be enhanced pressure to clarify the seriously blurred demarcation lines at these investment banks between corporate financiers and investment analysts; and finally, such an apparently cataclysmic occurrence would do much to undermine the current, absurd state of affairs in which legions of far from irreplaceable financiers, traders and analysts are remunerated as if they had the unique franchise of a Tiger Woods or a Robert de Niro or were risking their own capital like a real entrepreneur. A handful or two – the so-called 'rainmakers' – no doubt are equivalents, but the great majority are not.

This line of thought raises the question whether the continuing existence of the last workers' republic (admittedly a republic without copper-bottomed job security) might at some point become a significant political issue. 'The Left is largely silent,' the *Independent*'s Hamish McRae noted during the 2001 election campaign, about the fact that 'the disparity between City earnings and those of the rest of the country is wider than ever'. His explanation for the Left's reticence about this disparity focused persuasively on society as a whole: 'However uncomfortable many people may feel, the open jealousy of the Eighties seems less evident.'[2] The notion of an entrenched psychic shift was also on the mind of Libby Purves, as at about the same time she reflected in *The Times* on 'the increasing tendency to measure success not by achievement but by money':

> *Captains of industry demand vast bonuses which cannot possibly make their lives any more comfortable, outsourcing makes every*

deal a financial one, mediocre books make news because of record advances, actors are described in terms of film rates, and no suburban crime report is complete without a reference to the victim's '£500,000 house'.

The unhealthy, ultimately frustrating fascination with the rich has infected New Labour as much as any Tories. They adore millionaires ...

The result is that nurses, doctors, police, soldiers, teachers, university lecturers, firemen and other useful people feel permanently at a disadvantage when they look at media-folk, bankers, cappuccino barons, dot-com superstars, It girls, and other not particularly useful people who happen to earn more.[3]

Is this new materialistic, money-oriented value system a permanent fact of life in our increasingly Americanised society? Back in 1989 an angry young Scottish politician called Gordon Brown fulminated against Thatcherism in a book-length tract called *Where There Is Greed* ... By the fifth year of a Labour government, with this son of the Manse as chancellor throughout, the American Jerry Springer was launching in May 2001 the latest British television gameshow – succinctly called *Greed* – with every hope that its catchphrase 'Let's get greedy!' would become part of the national argot. On the face of it, the City's fat cats will continue to sleep easily.

Certainly that fits in with the prevailing conventional wisdom: Britain cannot afford to jeopardise her international economic competitiveness by being seen as a high-tax country – with all the unfortunate echoes of the 1970s – and the City is integral to that competitiveness. After all, overtaxed international bankers can always walk away and take their skills elsewhere. Nevertheless, it was potentially of considerable significance that by the 2001 election the British political agenda had shifted away from taxation (with Labour again specifically promising not to raise income tax) and towards the issue of public sector services – in human terms, less an election about accountants, more one about nurses. Crucially, the centrepiece of Labour's manifesto was an explicit commitment to the widest possible use of private resources in order to deliver those services. The City, as we have seen, has had a vital role to play in the still-evolving world of PFI and PPP – a role that, given the widespread assumption amongst New Labour thinkers that the judicious application of the private sector represents the last chance to save something that can still legitimately be called the welfare state, is certain to increase over the next few years. Public opinion, however, remains sceptical: an opinion poll the week after the manifesto's launch found that less than one-fifth of voters believed that private companies should run NHS hospitals, even with the NHS paying all the costs of the care.[4] There followed, in the election itself, the astonishing triumph in Wyre Forest of Richard Taylor, a retired rheumatologist standing as an independent and running on the single policy of saving Kidderminster Hospital from PFI-driven closure. In short, the stakes are high, and the City's already somewhat tarnished reputation is likely to suffer if it is generally viewed as cynically ripping off a beleaguered public sector.

The 2001 election campaign itself was conducted, as almost every commentator noted, amidst an atmosphere of unprecedented apathy – and, more than that, alienation, culminating in a historically low turnout. For all the huffing and puffing by the parties, the macroeconomic choice presented to the electorate was only really a choice at the margins; while the politicians themselves seemed to be reduced to little more than managers, relatively powerless figures in the by now well-established age of global financial flows, global companies and global economic forces generally. Is there any realistic chance of the seemingly irresistible tide of globalisation starting to ebb? Amongst other places, Seattle, Prague and Davos, even the City of London in June 1999, have in recent years all seen well-publicised demonstrations by a vigorous if often directionless protest movement. But in the end, it is difficult to disagree with the commonsensical proposition that globalisation will be with us so long as it continues to deliver the economic goods to most of the population of the developed world. Whatever the short-term future of the American economy and thus the world economy, there is little realistic sign of that delivery system – one in which the financial markets play an ever-greater part – seizing up. Whatever society's discontents, in other words, it is not yet time to start dusting off the once so pervasive phrase 'the crisis of capitalism'.

That is a far cry, however, from passively accepting Francis Fukuyama's well-publicised view that the collapse of communism and accompanying triumph of liberal capitalism somehow spelled 'The End of History'. The appalling events of 11 September 2001, when the gleaming Twin Towers of New York's financial district were transformed in barely an hour into Ground Zero, were alone enough to render that concept absurd. Nevertheless, what is striking from the perspective of February 2002, as the twenty-first century begins to unfold, is that the near-apocalyptic economic scenarios so widely bandied about in the immediate wake of 9/11 have broadly *not* been fulfilled – and that instead the real dangers to the global financial machine have appeared from *inside* the system. Put another way, the time-honoured virtues of greed, deception and incompetence, as practised within the citadels, ultimately pose a far graver threat than anything coming from the caves of Afghanistan.

Incompetence was undoubtedly the issue when Unilever took Merrill Lynch Investment Managers to court, claiming that in its former guise as Mercury Asset Management (MAM) it had seriously mismanaged a major slice of Unilever's pension fund. After a case lasting twenty-eight acrimonious days, Merrill decided in December 2001 to settle out of court, paying Unilever an estimated £75 million. The outcome was especially humiliating for Carol Galley – the so-called 'Ice Maiden' who had done so much to build up MAM – while the ensuing *schadenfreude* was predictably widespread. 'For years, Carol Galley and other City high-flyers specialising in stock picking for our biggest pension funds have managed to present their profession as a highly specialised art form where the performers are not ordinary mortals, but investment gurus able to walk on water,' one financial journalist (Jeremy Warner) justly observed. 'A mystique built up around Ms Galley, her company and her industry which, as we now know, was scarcely deserved.'[5]

Almost certainly there was more than incompetence involved in the case of John Rusnak, the Baltimore-based trader who in February 2002 was discovered to have notched up losses amounting to an impressive $750 million on behalf of Allfirst, the US subsidiary of Allied Irish Banks. In a sense, the story seemed no more than Nick Leeson revisited: an inadequate management failing to identify and then take out a greed-driven trader who had got himself into ever-deeper trouble. But one commentator, Peter Martin, went back to first principles and argued that the underlying cause of these periodic high-profile disasters – and many others that never came to public light because they were hidden within otherwise profitable trading books – was the sheer volume, velocity and volatility of the markets themselves. Given that daily turnover in the foreign exchange markets (in which Rusnak came a cropper) was by this time running at some $1,600 billion, while simultaneously some $760 billion was traded in over-the-counter currency and interest rate derivatives, he surely had a point – especially given that the great majority of trading in these 'superliquid' markets was trading for its own sake. Was there a remedy for this ramping up of systemic risk in the financial system? 'Shareholders must impose a valuation penalty on financial institutions that rely too heavily on trading,' Martin suggested as much in hope as in expectation. 'Managers must lessen the value of the trader's option. And we must persuade our sons and daughters that there is nothing glamorous about the trading life.'[6]

Meanwhile, the after-shocks of the sheer cumulative folly that was the dotcom mania of the late 1990s continued to reverberate. Few were surprised that corporate financiers, on both sides of the Atlantic and even in the most prestigious investment banks, had more or less abandoned all pretence at quality control, shovelling out rubbishy new issues to the avaricious, day-trading public as the bull market roared towards its peak; but there was significantly more consternation that the once respectable profession of investment analysis – pioneered in the US and exported to Britain in the 1950s – had forsaken objectivity and succumbed to the quick buck. The specific charge was that investment analysts in the major investment banks had feebly succumbed to pressure from corporate finance departments – where the really big money was to be made during the bull market – and rigged their research and recommendations in order to suit both their colleagues and their colleagues' corporate clients. The outcome, unimpeded by calls for caution from such analysts (some of whom enjoyed considerable éclat in the investment world at large), was a spectacular misallocation of resources. When in February 2002 US regulators announced new rules designed to ensure the independence of analysts from the companies they cover, the feeble thud of a stable-door being belatedly shut was all too palpable.

Yet even as the implications were being digested of the huge amount of capital that had been sucked so wastefully into internet stocks and telecom companies, history – like fate in *Gentlemen Prefer Blondes* – kept on happening. 'It's hard to overstate the enormity of the impact of Enron's implosion,' Madeleine Bunting wrote in the *Guardian* in January 2002, shortly after that energy giant's sensational fall from grace. 'The biggest corporate collapse in US history is now dragging politicians, banks, accounting firms, other corporations, pension funds, investment analysts, the reputations of so-called business experts and millions of investors into an astonishing vortex where they risk losing billions of dollars and some of the most trusted reputations in corporate America.'[7] Some of the most blackening headlines were targeted at Andersen – apparently responsible for shredding key Enron-related documents – but the deeper worry was that there suddenly seemed no reliable basis for evaluating capitalist enterprise. The reported words of Stephen Roach, Morgan Stanley's chief economist and perhaps the most highly respected on Wall Street, reflected disillusion as well as disbelief: 'This was America's most-admired company, and it was worthless and run by crooks. And none of us spotted it.'[8]

There remains, moreover, the fundamental question of whose history it is anyway. The world's citizens – or the world's footloose, bonus-hungry investment bankers? In 2001 the *Financial Times* carried a striking – and strikingly emblematic – full-page advertisement. The top half comprised a dramatic colour photograph of the Berlin Wall being pulled down, above a quotation from Thomas Mayer of Goldman Sachs, Germany: 'After all those years, we were dismantling the wall with our own hands. It was an incredible feeling.' Below, the main text began:

> *The people of Germany began tearing down the Wall in 1989. As they did so, it somehow signalled a new era for Europe, one in which other, less physical barriers also began to disappear. In this exciting marketplace, with all its new freedoms and opportunities, Goldman Sachs has played a leading role ...*[9]

It was a breathtakingly arrogant piece of self-aggrandisement – in effect, an appropriation of history, a misrepresentation that the people of Berlin had risked so much in order to make the world even more profitable that it had been already for the partners of Goldman Sachs. It certainly gave a new twist to 'Ich bin ein Berliner.'

Yet in truth there was nothing inevitable, certainly in a British context, about the rise and rise of the markets. The party of the Left did not have to abandon its traditional egalitarian goals; elected politicians did not have to cede monetary policy to unelected central bankers; the maximisation of shareholder value was not the only rational corporate ambition. Nevertheless, as we have tried to show, there were powerful reasons why these crucial things happened. None of those reasons will, to put it mildly, go away overnight. If the future remains as contestable as the past always has been, it will also continue to be heavily influenced by that past. More than blasts on the trumpet will be required before the walls come tumbling down of this particular City State.

Notes

Preface – A Foreign Country

1 *Economist*, 7 October 1995.
2 *Observer*, 5 August 2001.
3 *Times Higher Education Supplement*, 8 February 2002.

1 Not in Bratislava

1 Paul Ferris, *The City* (1960), p. 16.

2 Conspicuous by its Absence

1 Richard Roberts and David Kynaston (eds.), *The Bank of England: Money, Power & Influence, 1694–1994* (Oxford, 1995), p. 226.
2 Ibid., p. 230.
3 *Financial News*, 12 January 1917.
4 Roberts and Kynaston, p. 235.
5 Sidney Pollard, *The Development of the British Economy, 1914–1980* (1983), p. 396.
6 Ranald C. Michie, *The London Stock Exchange: A History* (Oxford, 1999), pp. 419, 521.
7 William M. Clarke, *Inside the City: A Guide to London as a Financial Centre* (1979), p. 38.
8 Roberts and Kynaston, p. 25.
9 Alec Cairncross, *The Wilson Years: A Treasury Diary, 1964–1969* (1997), p. 297.
10 A.J.P. Taylor, *English History, 1914–1945* (1965), pp. 222, 166.

11 David Kynaston, *The City of London, Volume I: A World of Its Own, 1815–1890* (1994), p. 20.

12 William Cobbett, *Rural Rides* (1948 edition), p. 104.

13 Alfred Kazin (ed.), *The Essential Blake* (1968), p. 412.

14 E.T. Cook and Alexander Wedderburn (eds.), *The Works of John Ruskin: Volume XVII* (1905), pp. 389–90.

15 John Ruskin, *Praeterita* (1949 edition), p. 5.

16 William J. Barber, *A History of Economic Thought* (1967), p. 56.

17 Asa Briggs (ed.), *William Morris: Selected Writings and Designs* (1962), p. 264.

18 G.D.H. Cole, *The Next Ten Years in British Social and Economic Policy* (1929), p. 246.

19 J.M. Keynes, *The General Theory of Employment, Interest, and Money* (1936), p. 161.

20 Andrew Shonfield, *Modern Capitalism: The Changing Balance of Public and Private Power* (1965), p. 66.

21 *Financial Times*, 17 September 1970.

22 E.P. Thompson, *The Poverty of Theory and Other Essays* (1978), pp. 35–91.

23 See, for example, Stuart Holland, *The Socialist Challenge* (1975), a seminal text of the period.

24 Tony Benn, *Arguments for Socialism* (1979), p. 17.

25 Nicholas Davenport, *Memoirs of a City Radical* (1974), p. 149.

26 David Kynaston, *The City of London, Volume IV: A Club No More, 1945–2000* (2001), p. 155.

27 Frances Partridge, *Hanging On: Diaries, December 1960–August 1963* (1990), p. 87.

28 BBC Written Archives Centre (Caversham), R28 files.

29 Paul Ferris, *The City* (1960); Anthony Sampson, *Anatomy of Britain* (1962), pp. 345–414.

30 A rare exception is Richard Whitley, 'Commonalities and Connections among Directors of Large Financial Institutions', *Sociological Review* (November 1973), pp. 613–32.

31 *Investors Chronicle*, 13 June 1975.

32 Michael Collins, 'English Bank Development within a European Context, 1870–1939', *Economic History Review* (February 1998), pp. 13–17.

33 Cole, pp. 244–5.

34 The argument is fully set out in Geoffrey Ingham, *Capitalism Divided? The City and Industry in British Social Development* (Basingstoke, 1984).

35 Margaret Thatcher, *The Downing Street Years* (1993), p. 44.

3 Money — New Lingua Franca?

1 Mass-Observation Archive (at University of Sussex Library), Spring Directive 1990 (2): Retrospective on the Eighties. In order of appearance in the text: B 690; B 1426; C 2185; F 2133; L 2352; L 2393; S 2191; C 1786; B 1392; C 1539; K 1515; W 2117; C 2149; C 1832; C 1548; S 2209.

2 Ian Jack, *Before the Oil Ran Out: Britain 1977–86* (1987), pp. 95, 99.

3 Peter York and Charles Jennings, *Peter York's Eighties* (1995), p. 109.

4 *Financial Times*, 19 March 1987.

5 *Sunday Times Magazine*, 14 April 1985.

6 Paul Ferris, *Gentlemen of Fortune* (1984), p. 189.

7 *Economist*, 20 July 1985.

8 *Listener*, 20 March 1986.

9 *Economist*, 20 July 1985.

10 *Institutional Investor*, June 1986, p. 118.

11 *Sunday Express Magazine*, 26 October 1986.

12 Michael Lewis, *Liar's Poker* (1989), p. 242.

13 *Futures World*, 17 January 1985.

14 *Financial Times*, 27 October 1986; *Sunday Express Magazine*, 26 October 1986.

15 York and Jennings, p. 118.

16 *Euromoney*, April 1986, supplement, p. 13; *Sunday Times Magazine*, 1 November 1987.

17 *Naked City* (Blakeway Productions), BBC 2, 30 October 1996.

18 Michael Lewis, *The Money Culture* (1991), pp. 121–2.

19 Lewis, *Liar's Poker*, p. 241.

20 *Sunday Times*, 25 October 1987.

21 York and Jennings, p. 108.

22 Thomas Frank, *One Market Under God: Extreme Capitalism, Market Populism and the End of Economic Democracy* (2001).

23 John Curtice, 'Political Partisanship' in Roger Jewell et al. (eds.), *British Social Attitudes: The 1986 Report* (Aldershot, 1986), p. 52.

24 Roger Jewell and Richard Topf, 'Trust in the Establishment' in Roger Jewell et al. (eds.), *British Social Attitudes: The 5th Report* (1988), p. 116.

25 *Sunday Times*, 14 June 1987.

26 *New Society*, 19 June 1987.

27 *Daily Telegraph*, 21 October 1987.

28 *Daily Mail*, 21 October 1987; *Sunday Telegraph*, 25 October 1987.

29 *Sunday Times*, 25 October 1987.

30 *Capital City* (Euston Films), ITV, 3 October 1989 (first episode).

31 *New Statesman*, 17 November 1989.

32 *The Times*, 23 November 1990.

33 For an analysis that suggests that job insecurity did *not* increase in the early 1990s across the British population as a whole, but that it did increase among the professional classes, whose squeals were picked up and magnified by the media, see Francis Green, Alan Felstead and Brendan Burchall, 'Job Insecurity and the Difficulty of Regaining Employment: An Empirical Study of Unemployment Expectations', *Oxford Bulletin of Economics and Statistics* (December 2000), p. 879.

34 *The Times*, 20 January 1997.

35 Will Hutton, *The State We're In* (1996 Vintage edition), p. xxvii.

36 York and Jennings, p. 7.

37 *Independent*, 8 April 1997.

38 *Sunday Times*, 4 March 2001.

39 *Financial Times*, 9 February 1999.

40 *Financial Times*, 15–22 December 1999.

41 *Financial Times*, 4 January 2001.

42 *New Statesman*, 23 October 2000.

4   Getting and Spending

1 *Financial Times*, 11 January 1992.

2 *Sunday Times*, 7 March 1999.

3 *Sunday Telegraph*, 7 March 1999.

4 Ibid.

5 *Sunday Times*, 7 March 1999.

6 *Financial Times*, 26 January 2001.

7 *Independent*, 4 October 1995.

8 *Financial Times*, 26 January 2001.

9 Quoted ibid.

10 *Sunday Times*, 28 September 1997.

11 *Sunday Times*, 7 March 1999.

12 *Financial Times*, 8–9 September 2001.

13 *Financial Times*, 26 January 2001.

14 *Sunday Times*, 18 March 2001.

15 *Financial Times*, 26 January 2001.

16 *The Times*, 7 July 2000.

17 Lombard Street Research, an economic consultancy, estimates that in 1995 the

wages and salaries of London's money-centre workforce of 250,000 people totalled £7.5 – £9 billion. A more up-to-date yardstick is the government's New Earnings Survey for the year 2000, that gives £45,400 as the average size of a City pay-packet. Multiplied by the money-centre labour force of 335,000, this gives a total of £15.2 billion. The Centre for Economics and Business estimates the City's gross output as £22 billion. Our estimate of staff remuneration of £13 billion is consistent with industry cost-revenue ratios.

18 *Spectator*, 13 December 1997.

19 Philip Augar, *The Death of Gentlemanly Capitalism: The Rise and Fall of London's Investment Banks* (2000), p. 261.

20 *Evening Standard*, 14 December 1997.

21 Corporation of London, *City Research Project: Final Report (1995)*, pp. 7.27–7.29.

22 *Independent*, 13 June 1996.

23 *Financial Times*, 1–2 February 1997.

24 *Independent*, 13 June 1996.

25 *Financial Times*, 22 February 2001.

26 *Financial Times*, 1–2 February 1997.

27 *Spectator*, 13 December 1997.

28 Ibid.

29 *Financial Times*, 1–2 February 1997.

30 *Evening Standard*, 29 January 1998.

31 *Financial Times*, 1–2 February 1997.

32 *Spectator*, 13 December 1997.

33 *Sunday Times*, 29 November 1999.

34 *Independent*, 9 December 1999.

35 *Financial Times*, 10 April 2000.

36 *Independent*, 9 December 1999.

37 *Financial Times*, 29 November 2000.

38 *Financial News*, 12–18 February 2001.

39 *Financial Times*, 1–2 February 1997.

40 Ibid.

41 *Sunday Times*, 17 December 2000.

42 *Financial Times*, 1–2 February 1997.

43 Ibid.

44 *Spectator*, 13 December 1997.

45 *Sunday Telegraph*, 19 December 1999.

46 *Evening Standard*, 18 December 2000.

47 *Evening Standard*, 10 April 2000.

48 *Evening Standard*, 18 December 2000.
49 Ibid.
50 *Sunday Times*, 17 December 2000.
51 *Evening Standard*, 28 February 2001.
52 *Spectator*, 13 December 1999.
53 *Evening Standard*, 29 February 2000.
54 FDPSavills, *Residential Research Bulletin* (autumn 1998).
55 *Evening Standard*, 10 April 2000.
56 *The Times*, 19 December 2000.
57 *Financial Times*, 26 January 2001.
58 *Financial Times*, 2 November 2000.
59 *Financial Times*, 22 December 1999.
60 *Guardian*, 23 March 2001.
61 *Sunday Times*, 6 January 2002.
62 *Evening Standard*, 7 January 2002.
63 *Evening Standard*, 27 December 2001.
64 *Evening Standard*, 22 March 2001.

5   Markets, Markets, Markets

1 Sources: Lombard Street Research, *Growth Prospects of City Industries* (1998), Appendix 2; Centre for Economic and Business Research, *The City's Importance to the European Union Economy* (November 2000; November 2001). Missing data points filled by linear extrapolation and estimation.
2 Lombard Street Research, *Growth Prospects of City Industries* (1998), p. 20.
3 Centre for Economic and Business Research, *London's Contribution to the UK Economy* (July 2001), p. 46. The data is for 1999.
4 *Spectator*, 13 December 1997.
5 Source: *New Earnings Survey*, annual data.
6 Source: ibid.
7 *New Earnings Survey* (2000), table A21: 'Full Time Employees of Both Sexes on Adult Rates'.
8 Lombard Street Research, *Growth Prospects of City Industries* (1998), pp. 9, 40.
9 Source: based on Centre for Economic and Business Research, *The City's Importance to the European Union Economy* (November 2000), p. 10; (November 2001), p. 7; and Lombard Street Research, *Growth Prospects of City Industries* (1998), p. 30. These estimates have been adjusted in the light of a variety of other evidence.

10 Data on City activities in Tables 5.2 to 5.7 is derived from: International Financial Services, London, *International Financial Markets in the UK* (November 2001).

11 International Financial Services London, *International Private Wealth Management* (January 2002), p. 4.

12 Lloyd's of London Press Release, 5 July 1999.

13 Pat Bowman, *Handbook of Financial Public Relations* (1989), p. xiv. Interview with Neil Mainland, co-ordinator of the City Group.

14 *Evening Standard*, 22 December 2000.

15 Neil Harris, *Getting into The City* (1997), p. 55.

16 *City View* (July 2000), p. 6.

17 Centre for Economic and Business Research, *London's Contribution to the UK Economy* (July 2001), p. 46.

18 International Financial Services London, *The City Table 2001* (October 2001), p. 1.

19 Lombard Street Research, *Growth Prospects of City Industries* (1998), p. 40.

6   The World's Playground

1 Information from individual banks. See also *Sunday Business*, 11 March 2001.

2 *Economy Info*, Economic Development Unit of the Corporation of London, September 2000, p. 1.

3 Philip Ziegler, *The Sixth Great Power: Barings, 1762–1929* (1988), p. 85.

4 *Financial News*, 28 July 1941.

5 *Economist*, 4 August 1945.

6 Ronald Grierson, *A Truant Disposition* (1992), p. 31.

7 *Banker* (November 1986), p. 69.

8 Ron Chernow, *The House of Morgan: An American Banking Dynasty and the Rise of Modern Finance* (New York, 1990), p. 544.

9 Samuel L. Hayes and Philip M. Hubbard, *Investment Banking: A Tale of Three Cities* (Boston MA, 1990), appendices tables.

10 Richard Roberts, *Take Your Partners: Orion, the Consortium Banks and the Transformation of the Euromarkets* (2001), p. 173; authors' interview.

11 *Guardian*, 24 October 1979. John Plender and Paul Wallace, *The Square Mile: A Guide to the New City of London* (1985), p. 20.

12 *Financial Times*, 25 October 1979.

13 Richard Roberts, 'Setting the City Free: The Impact of the U.K. Abolition of Exchange Controls', *Journal of International Financial Markets* (August 2000), p. 136.

14 W. A. Thomas, *The Big Bang* (Liverpool, 1986), p. 157.

15 For 1890: Richard Roberts, *Schroders: Merchants & Bankers* (1992), p. 151; Stanley Chapman, *The Rise of Merchant Banking* (1984), pp. 55, 61; Bo Bramsen and Kathleen Wain, *The Hambros 1779–1979* (1979), p. 323; Niall Ferguson, *The World's Banker: The History of the House of Rothschild* (1998), p. 808. For 1990: Shearson Lehman Brothers, *UK Merchant Banks Annual Review* (1991). Arguably, it was nine out of twelve, if Seligmans (acquired by Warburgs in 1957) is included.

16 *Banker* (November 1986; November 1989).

17 Harvard Business School, 'Morgan Stanley and S.G. Warburg: Investment Bank of the Future' (March 1997).

18 *Independent*, 17 February 1995 (Jeremy Warner).

19 Philip Augar, *The Death of Gentlemanly Capitalism* (2000), pp. 247, 249.

20 *Daily Telegraph*, 6 October 1997.

21 Augar, p. 265.

22 Ibid., p. 269.

23 NatWest Securities, *Merchant Banks: End of an Era?* (February 1995).

24 *Financial Times*, 17 December 1997; 18 December 1997; 30 April 1998.

25 Augar, p. 286.

26 *Financial Times*, 24 January 2000.

27 *Financial Times*, 19 January 2000.

28 *Daily Telegraph*, 8 October 1997.

29 *Banker* plus authors' research.

30 *Financial Times*, 17 March 1997; 8 October 1997.

31 Alastair Ross Goobey, 'A Long Farewell to Wimbledon, EC2', *Spectator*, 6 October 2001.

32 *Sunday Business*, 24 October 1999.

33 Information from Association of British Insurers.

34 *Financial Times*, 22 February 2000.

35 *Sunday Telegraph*, 18 March 2001.

36 *Financial Times*, 19 September 1997.

37 *Economist*, 22 February 2001.

38 Augar, p. 322.

39 Citigroup, *2000 Annual Report* (2001), p. 3.

40 *Independent on Sunday*, 16 July 1995.

41 *Independent*, 13 March 2000.

42 Augar, p. 324.

43 Ibid. p. 326.

44 *Spectator*, 18 September 1999.

45 *Financial Times*, 21 December 2000.

46 Authors' interview.

47 *Financial Times*, 26 January 2001.

48 *Financial Times*, 18 August 2000.

49 *Financial Times*, 17 November 1999.

50 *Financial Times*, 27 October 1999; Edward Chancellor, 'Millennial market', *Prospect* (November 2001).

51 Authors' interview.

52 *Financial Times*, 21 December 2000.

7 The Mighty Markets

1 John Major, *The Autobiography* (1999), p. 318.

2 Ibid.

3 Ibid., p. 326.

4 Ibid., p. 329.

5 Norman Lamont, *In Office* (1999), p. 249.

6 *Black Wednesday*, BBC 1, 16 September 1997.

7 Ibid.

8 Ibid.

9 Lamont, p. 255.

10 Sources for the figures in this paragraph: Jeffry A. Frieden, 'Invested Interests: The Politics of National Economic Policies in a World of Global Finance', *International Organisation* (autumn 1991), p. 428; A.C. Chester, 'The International Bond Market', *Bank of England Quarterly Bulletin* (November 1991), pp. 524–5; Richard Roberts, *Inside International Finance* (1998), p. 28.

11 See especially chapters 4 and 5.

12 Steven Solomon, *The Confidence Game* (New York, 1995), p. 40.

13 *Financial Times*, 9 July 1985.

14 David Cobham (ed.), *Markets and Dealers: The Economics of the London Financial Markets* (Harlow, 1992), p. 14.

15 Bank for International Settlements, *63rd Annual Report* (Basle, June 1993), p. 196.

16 Solomon, p. 40.

17 William Keegan and Rupert Pennant-Rea, *Who Runs the Economy?* (1979), p. 131.

18 Tony Benn, *Conflicts of Interest: Diaries 1977–80* (1990), p. 305.

19 Adrian Hamilton, *The Financial Revolution* (1986), p. 50.

20 Philip Stephens, *Politics and the Pound: The Conservatives' Struggle with Sterling* (1996), p. 86.

21 Ibid. p. 93.

22 Nigel Lawson, *The View from No. 11: Memoirs of a Tory Radical* (1992), pp. 1059–60.

23 Margaret Thatcher, *The Downing Street Years* (1993), p. 706.

24 Lawson, p. 868.

25 *Financial Times*, 29 January 1988.

26 Jeffry A. Frieden, *Banking on the World: The Politics of American International Finance* (New York, 1987) pp. 114–15.

27 *Central Banking* (summer 1990), p. 11.

28 Major, p. 154.

29 Ibid., p. 160.

30 *Financial Times*, 6 October 1990.

31 *Marxism Today* (November 1987), 'City Supplement', p. i.

32 This analysis of the 'prawn cocktail offensive' owes much to Mark Wickham-Jones, 'Anticipating Social Democracy, Preempting Anticipations: Economic Policy-Making in the British Labor Party, 1987–1992', *Politics and Society* (December 1995), pp. 476–86.

33 *Financial Times*, 16 May 1990.

34 *Financial Times*, 4 April 1992.

35 *Economist*, 7 October 1995.

36 *Financial Times*, 4 January 1995.

37 *Financial Times*, 19 August 1995.

38 Michael King, 'The Politics of Central Bank Independence', *Central Banking* (February 2001), p. 51.

39 *Central Banking* (spring 1996), p. 5.

40 Stephens, p. 267. The fullest account of the path in the 1990s to Bank of England independence is Michael King, 'The New Lady of Threadneedle Street: The Triumph of Ideas over Interests?', *Central Banking* (May 2001).

41 *Financial Times*, 30 October 1992.

42 Centre for Economic Policy Research, *Independent and Accountable: A New Mandate for the Bank of England: The Report of an Independent Panel* (1993), pp. 48–9.

43 Treasury and Civil Service Committee: The Role of the Bank of England, *Minutes of Evidence* (1993–4, HC–II), qq. 241–96.

44 Major, pp. 675, 682.

45 *Financial Times*, 14 April 1994.

46 Robert Elgie and Helen Thompson, *The Politics of Central Banks* (1998), p. 92; *Financial Times*, 16 July 1996.

47 *Central Banking* (August 2000), pp. 23, 27.

48 *Financial Times*, 28 September 1994; 23 May 1995.

49 Mark Wickham-Jones, 'Social Democracy and Structural Dependency: The British Case', *Politics and Society* (June 1997), p. 257.

50 *Financial Times*, 12 July 1996.

51 *New Statesman*, 3 May 1996.

52 *Financial Times*, 5 July 1996.

53 For a forceful statement of the argument, see Colin Hay, 'Blaijorism: Towards a One-Vision Polity?', *Political Quarterly* (October–December 1997), pp. 372–8.

54 *Financial Times*, 4 April 1997.

55 *Financial Times*, 7 May 1997.

56 *Independent*, 7 May 1997; *Daily Telegraph*, 7 May 1997.

57 Will Hutton, *The State We're In* (1995), p. 291; *Guardian*, 7 May 1997.

58 *Daily Telegraph*, 7 May 1997.

59 *Central Banking* (February 2001), p. 8.

60 *Financial Times*, 3 February 2001 (Martin Wolf).

61 *Financial Times*, 2 March 2001.

62 Niall Ferguson, *The Cash Nexus: Money and Power in the Modern World, 1700–2000* (2001), p. 184.

63 Layna Mosley, 'Room to Move: International Financial Markets and National Welfare States', *International Organisation* (autumn 2000), p. 737.

64 *Financial Times*, 24 March 2001.

65 *Central Banking* (February 2001), pp. 9–10.

66 *Independent*, 17 December 2001.

8   City 1 Industry 0

1 Charles Handy, 'What Is a Company For?', *RSA Journal* (March 1991), pp. 238, 241.

2 Records at Centre for Tomorrow's Company (19 Buckingham Street, London WC2N 6EF).

3 John Littlewood, *The Stock Market: 50 Years of Capitalism at Work* (1998), p. 355.

4 *Financial Times*, 28 January 1985.

5 John Banham, *The Anatomy of Change: Blueprint for a New Era* (1994), pp. 247–8.

6 *Financial Times*, 4 November 1989.

7 *Guardian*, 9 March 1989.

8 Derek Ezra and David Oates, *Advice from the Top* (1989), pp. 106–7.

9 Sir Hector Laing, *A Parting Shot* (1990), pp. 3, 11–12, 14.

10 DTI, 'Innovation & Short-Termism Conference', 25 June 1990. Proceedings, 9.4.

11 *Financial Times*, 26 June 1990.

12 *Financial Times*, 8 September 1990.

13 Paul Marsh, *Short-Termism on Trial* (1990), pp. 40, 44, 101–2.

14 Joel M. Stern, 'Preface' in G. Bennett Stewart, *The Quest For Value: The EVA™ Management Guide* (New York, 1991), p. xix.

15 Allan A. Kennedy, *The End of Shareholder Value: The Real Effects of the Shareholder Value Phenomenon and the Crisis It Is Bringing to Business* (2000), p. 210.

16 Stewart, pp. 1–8.

17 *Financial Times*, 8 March 1991.

18 David Rogers, *The Big Four British Banks: Organisation, Strategy and the Future* (Basingstoke, 1999), p. 46.

19 Lloyds Bank plc, *Report and Accounts 1985* (1986), p. 9.

20 Coopers & Lybrand Deloitte, *Shareholder Value Analysis Survey* (spring 1991), unpaginated.

21 John Kay, *Foundations of Corporate Success* (1993), p. 367. See also *Financial Times* 26 March 1993 (Guy de Jonquières).

22 *New Statesman*, 29 March 1996 (Ben Webb).

23 *Financial Director* (November 1992), p. 33.

24 *Economist*, 12 February 1994.

25 James Taggart, Peter Kontes and Michael Mankins, *The Value Imperative* (New York, 1994), p. 205, quoted in Mark Goyder, *Living Tomorrow's Company* (Aldershot, 1998), p. 23.

26 Will Hutton, *The State We're In* (1996, Vintage edition), p. 5.

27 Ibid., p. 298.

28 *Financial Times*, 16 March 1995.

29 *Financial Times*, 27 March 1995.

30 John Plender, *A Stake in the Future: The Stakeholding Solution* (1997), p. 12.

31 *Independent*, 15 January 1996.

32 *Financial Times*, 1 February 1996.

33 Meghnad Desai, 'Debating the British Disease: The Centrality of Profit', *New Political Economy* (March 1996), p. 92.

34 *Financial Times*, 17 January 1996.

35 *New Statesman*, 29 March 1996.

36 Ibid.

37 *New Statesman*, 12 July 1996.

38 *New Statesman*, 21 March 1997.

39 RSA, *Tomorrow's Company* (June 1995), p. 2.

40 *Financial Times*, 26 August 1996.

41 *Management Today* (January 1997), pp. 42–4; (March 1997), pp. 48–52.

42 PA Consulting Group, *Managing for Shareholder Value* (1997), p. 4.

43 *Financial Times*, 27 October 1997.

44 *Financial Times*, 22 December 1997.

45 *Financial Times*, 16 February 1998.

46 Cadbury Schweppes, *Annual Report 1997* (1998), pp. 1, 11.

47 *Financial Times*, 14 May 1998.

48 *Financial Times*, 27 April 1998.

49 Tony Golding, *The City: Inside the Great Expectation Machine* (2000), pp. 176–81.

50 *Management Accounting* (March 2000), p. 42.

51 *Independent*, 31 March 2000.

52 *Financial Times*, 28 October 2000.

53 *New Statesman*, 6 November 2000.

54 *Financial Times*, 12 February 2001.

55 Andrew Black and Philip Wright, *In Search of Shareholder Value: Managing the Drivers of Performance* (2001 edition), p. xi.

56 *Financial Times*, 5 April 2001.

57 *Financial Times*, 27 November 2000.

58 *Financial Times*, 6 February 2001; 31 March 2001.

59 *Financial Times*, 29 January 1999.

60 *Financial Times*, 29 January 2001.

61 *Financial Times*, 22 June 2000.

62 *Management Today* (July 2000), p. 63.

63 *Independent*, 21 March 2001 (Jeremy Warner).

64 *Financial Times*, 20 January 2001.

65 *Financial Times*, 15 March 2001.

66 *Financial Times*, 8 January 2001.

67 Plender, p. 71.

68 *Financial Times*, 4 April 2001; 7 April 2001.

69 *Financial Times*, 8 September 2001.

70 *Financial Times*, 18–21 January 2002.

71 *Financial Times*, 6 January 2001.

72 DTI, 13.2.

73 *Financial Times*, 2 February 2001.

74 *Independent*, 2 February 2001.

75 *Evening Standard*, 27 February 2001.

9 Public Places, Private Finance

1 David Conn, *The Football Business* (Edinburgh, 2001 edition), p. 162.

2 Ibid., pp. 66–7.

3 Ibid., p. 179.

4 *Financial Times*, 22 December 2000.

5 Nicholas Timmins, *The Five Giants: A Biography of the Welfare State* (1995), p. 349.

6 Ibid., pp. 402–3.

7 Nigel Lawson, *The View From No. 11: Memoirs of a Tory Radical* (1992), p. 222.

8 Simon Deakin and Stephen Pratten, 'Quasi Markets, Transactions Costs, and Trust: The Uncertain Effects of Market Reforms in British Television Production', *Television & New Media* (August 2000), p. 326.

9 Timmins, p. 442.

10 Steven Barnett and Andrew Curry, *The Battle for the BBC* (1994), p. 185.

11 *Investors Chronicle*, 24 July 1998.

12 Francis Terry, 'The Private Finance Initiative – Overdue Reform or Policy Breakthrough?', *Public Money & Management* (Jan–March 1996), p. 13.

13 George Monbiot, *Captive State: The Corporate Takeover of Britain* (2000), p. 86.

14 Terry, p. 13.

15 *Financial Times*, 18 October 1996.

16 *Project & Trade Finance* (February 1997), p. 44 (Richard Holliday).

17 *Financial Times*, 18 October 1996.

18 *Project & Trade Finance* (February 1997), p. 23.

19 Will Hutton, *The State We're In* (1996 Vintage edition), p. 339.

20 *Financial Times*, 16 July 1996.

21 *Financial Times*, 18 October 1996. See also Monbiot, chapter 1, 'The Skye Bridge Mystery'.

22 *BMJ*, 10 August 1996.

23 *BMJ*, 26 April 1997.

24 Ibid.

25 Raymond Plant, 'Blair and Ideology', in Anthony Seldon (ed.), *The Blair Effect: The Blair Government, 1997–2001* (2001), p. 558.

26 *Project Finance* (December 1997), p. 33.

27 Ibid., pp. 34–6 (Rupert Bruce).

28 See Monbiot's account, pp. 88–90.

29 *Project Finance* (January 2001), p. 28.

30 *Financial Times*, 29 November 2000.

31 *Private Finance Initiative Journal* (March–April 2001), pp. 44–5, 46–7.

32 *Observer*, 11 March 2001.

33 *Financial Times*, 26 February 2001.

34 *Financial Times*, 10 April 2001.

35 *Independent*, 28 March 2001.

36 *Evening Standard*, 9 March 2001.

37 *Evening Standard*, 13 March 2001.

38 *Director* (April 2001), p. 42.

39 These remarks about state education by spring 2001 derive from *Financial Times*, 26 February 2001 (Nicholas Timmins) and *Times Education Supplement*, 13 April 2001 (Jeremy Sutcliffe).

40 *Daily Telegraph*, 1 March 2001.

41 *Observer*, 11 February 2001.

42 *Financial Times*, 17 April 2001.

43 *The Times*, 11 September 2001.

44 *Financial Times*, 24 February 2001.

45 *Times Higher Education Supplement*, 26 March 1999.

46 *Guardian*, 15 February 2000.

47 *Financial Times*, 1 December 2000; 7 December 2000.

48 *Financial Times*, 15 December 2000.

49 *Financial Times*, 15 November 2000.

50 *Times Higher Education Supplement*, 2 February 2001.

51 *Financial Times*, 24 November 2000; 25 November 2000.

52 *Financial Times*, 20 March 2001.

53 *New Statesman*, 13 November 2000.

10   Global Portal

1 *Financial Times*, 14–15 April 2001.

2 Saskia Sassen, *The Global City: New York, London, Tokyo* (1991), chapter 4.

3 Corporation of London, *Global Powerhouse* (2000), p 37.

4 *Financial News*, 14–20 June 1999.

5 *Evening Standard*, 20 August 2001.

6 Healey & Baker, *European Cities Monitor* (2000).

7 Richard Roberts, *Take Your Partners: Orion, the Consortium Banks and the Transformation of the Euromarkets* (2001), pp. 297–308.

8 *European Cities Monitor* (2000).

9 Information from Frankfurt Industrie und Handels Kammer.

10 *Financial Times*, 8 February 2002.

11 *Evening Standard*, 6 February 2002.

12 *Spectator*, 18 September 1999.

13 *Evening Standard*, 6 February 2002.

14 *Financial Times*, 9 June 1997.

15 Anglo-German Foundation, *Comparing London and Frankfurt as World Cities: A Relational Study of Contemporary Urban Change* (2001), p. iv.

16 Bank of England, *Practical Issues Arising from the Euro* (November 2000).

17 Centre for Economic and Business Research, *The City's Importance to the European Union Economy* (November 2000 and December 2001).

18 *Independent*, 10 May 2001 (Hamish McRae).

11   A Triumphal Note?

1 *Spectator*, 18 September 1999.

2 *Independent*, 23 May 2001.

3 *The Times*, 15 May 2001.

4 *Independent*, 25 May 2001.

5 *Independent*, 7 December 2001.

6 *Financial Times*, 12 February 2002.

7 *Guardian*, 28 January 2002.

8 *Sunday Times*, 10 February 2002.

9 *Financial Times*, 23 January 2001.

Acknowledgements

For permission to quote from archival material, the authors are grateful to the Trustees of the Mass-Observation Archive, University of Sussex, and to the Centre for Tomorrow's Company. The Mass-Observation Archive material is reproduced with the permission of Curtis Brown Group Ltd, London and is copyright Trustees of the Mass-Observation Archive. We also wish to thank the many people who have assisted us, including numerous people in the public affairs departments of City banks and institutions. We are especially grateful to Kath Begley, Tim Congdon, Nick Davison, Andrew Franklin, Mark Goyder, Anthony Harrison, Amanda Howard, John Howard, William Keegan, Lucy Kynaston, Peter Lees, John Littlewood, Neil Mainland, David Marsh, Paul Marsh, Hamish McRae, Layna Mosley, Sir Geoffrey Owen, John Plender, Dilwyn Porter, Mark Pragnell, Sarah Robson, Dorothy Sheridan, Rob Skinner, Henry Snell, Daniela Strebel, Nicholas Timmins, Alison Turton, Ian de Vanna, John Wakefield, Stephanie Watson and Julia Williams. None of the above bear any responsibility for the views expressed.

Index

Numbers in *italics* indicate
Figures; those in **bold**
indicate Tables.

A

3i Group 83, 156
A1(M) upgrade funding 170
A13 Thames Gateway 173
Aaronovitch, David 162
Abbey National 173, 178
Abdulaziz, Prince al-Waleed bin
    Talal bin 43
ABN Amro 107, 186
accountancy **68**, 75, 76, 83, 104, 105
acquisitions 50, 58, 63, 109, 135,
    139, 154
actuarial consultants 78
advertising 77
AIG 103
aircraft broking 62
Akroyd & Smithers 84
Albert, Michel: *Capitalism
    Against Capitalism* 144
ALCOA (Aluminium
    Corporation of America) 87
Alexander, Henry 89
All About Making Money
    magazine 33
Allen & Overy 43, 83
Allfirst 199
Allianz 189
Allied Irish Banks 199
'Aluminium War' (1958–9) 87
American Express Bank 114

American General 103
Americanisation 22, 23, 31
Amis, Martin: *Money* 12
Amsterdam 4, 195
analysts 45, 71, 74, 134, 135, 156,
    159, 200
Anglo-German Foundation 190
annuity policies 75, 103
Antonioni, Michelangelo 12–13
Antony Gibbs 85, **94**
Antwerp 194
Arbuthnot Latham 85
The Archers (radio series) 22
Arthur Andersen 83, 104, 175,
    176, 200
Aspen, Colorado 58
assets, diversification of 114
associates 45
Aston Villa Football Club 164
A.T. Kearney 48
Augar, Philip 46, 99, 101, 106, 194
Austria 185
Autostrade 88
Aventura, L' (film) 12
aviation insurance 74–5, 75, 103
Axa 103

B

baby bonds 35
Baker, Kenneth 167
balance of payments 79, 88
balance sheets 68, 91
Balls, Ed 127
Baltic Exchange 76, 83

'bancassurance' 75
Banham, Sir John 136
Bank of America 113, 171, 173
Bank Charter Act (1844) 17
Bank of Credit and Commerce
    International (BCCI) 30
Bank of England 11, 38, 43, 102,
    195
    and Barings 86, 97–8
    and Black Wednesday 112, 113
    and British Aerospace 166
    corporate communications
        staff 77
    Court of Directors 85
    the dominant note-issuer 5
    established (1694) 5
    Exchange Control
        Department 93
    the government bank 5
    independence 118–21, 125, 126
    interest rates 74, 127, 129
    and LIFFE 103
    manages the National Debt 5
    monetary policy 7, 74, 118
    nationalisation of (1946) 7,
        10, 86
    'nexus' with the City 16
    reports to the Treasury
        Select Committee 129
    and short-termism 147
Bank for International
    Settlements 62, 115
Bank of London and South
    America 88

Bank of Scotland 156
Banker 70
Bankers Trust **96**, 99, 107, 189
banks
    central 124, 126, 127, 132
    clearing 7, 15, 89, 90
    commercial 72, 89
    consortium 90
    continental 96
    foreign 68, 69, **69**, 83, 89, 102–3
    international 90
    investment 24, 35, 37, 39, 45,
        47–8, 51, 59, 67, 70–71, 72,
        82, 89, 95, 100, 108–9, 110,
        116, 164
    lending policies 14
    major British 82
    merchant 49, 84–8, 90–92,
        94–5, **95**, 96, 102, 106
Banque de France 187
Barbican development 38
Barclays 43, 82, 89, 94, 98, 99,
    100, 107, 110, 144, 147, 156, 178
Barclays Capital 44, 99, 102–3
Barclays Life 103
Barclays Merchant Bank 98
Barings 17, 84, 85, 89, **94**, **96**,
    97–8, 101, 107, 109, 186
Barings crisis (1890) 86
Barrett, Matthew 156
Barry, Jim 173
Bates, Sir Malcolm 172
BBC (British Broadcasting
    Corporation) 167, 168
BBC 2 34
BBC Broadcast 168
BBC Production 168
BBC Radio 13–14
Bear Sterns 82, 107
Beeson Gregory 83, 178
Belgravia 54
Benefits Agency 174
Benn, Tony 117
    Arguments for Socialism 12
Berkshire 54
Berlin Wall 201
Bertelsmann 158
Biederman, Howard D. 159–60
Big Bang (1986) 19, 21, 22, 23, 25,
    30, 46, 67, 93–6, 101, 113, 142
Billingsgate 39
bills of exchange 6, 85, 86
Birmingham Chamber of
    Commerce 173

Birmingham Northern Relief
    Road (BNRR) 173
Bisgood 84
Black, Andrew and Philip
    Wright: *In Search of
    Shareholder Value* 157
Black Wednesday (16 September
    1992) 111–13, 114, 123, 124, 131
Blair, Tony 33, 127, 128, 148–52,
    164, 177
    Singapore speech (1996) 148,
        150, 151
Blake, William 9
Bloomberg 77
Bloomer, Jonathan 103
Blue Arrow scandal 30
Blue Circle 161
Blunkett, David 177
BNP 157
BNP Paribas 82, 107
Bodker, Christopher 25
Boer War 6
bond markets 115, 124, 127
bonds **68**, 70–73, 81, 85, 131
    drop-lock 115
Bonfield, Sir Peter 158–9
bonuses 44–53, 56, 57, 59, 108–9,
    196
Boots 153
borrowing 123, 124
bought deal 91
Bovril 6–7
Boyle, Séan 171
Bracken House 38
brands 154
Branson, Richard 27–8
Brazil 80
Brent Crude 76
Brent Walker 138
Bretton Woods Conference
    (1944) 63, 113
Bretton Woods system 11, 63, 113,
    115, 116, 119, 184
Bridget Jones's Diary (film) 33–4
Brit Awards 34
British Aerospace 166
British Airports Authority 166
British Airways 166
British Empire 4, 6, 183
British Medical Journal (*BMJ*)
    171
British Petroleum 38, 119, 166
British Rail 23

British Social Attitudes 28, 31
British Steel 166
British Telecom (BT) 20, 21, 158,
    159, 166
Britoil 166
Brittan, Samuel 150
Broad Street Station 39
broadcasting 167
Broadcasting Act (1990) 167
Broadgate building project 39
Bromley 171
Brown, Cedric 32
Brown, George 116
Brown, Gordon 33, 79, 127–31, 151
    Where There Is Greed 197
Brown family 85
Brown Shipley **94**
Bryant, Arthur 8
Bucklersbury House 38, 39
Buiter, Willem 124
'bulge bracket' 107, 108, 196
bull markets 21, 29, 35, 50, 59,
    109, 135, 152, 156
'bulldog bonds' 93
Bundesbank 112, 118, 120
Bunting, Madeleine 200
business recovery 76
business schools 168
Butlers Wharf 56
BZW (Barclays de Zoete Wedd)
    23, 42, **96**, 97–8, 101, 102, 126

C
Cable & Wireless 166
Cadbury, Dominic 154
Cadbury Schweppes 154
Cairncross, Sir Alec 7
Calderdale 171
Callaghan, James 15, 117, 122, 127
Canada 125
Canary magazine 43–4
Canary Wharf 37, 40–44, 54, 56,
    60
Capital City (ITV drama series)
    31
capital market 166, 186
    and *Das Kapital* 10
    expands in range (late
        C19th) 6–7
capital repatriation scheme 122
capitalism 11, 143, 146, 147, 148,
    151, 158, 160, 161
    'gentlemanly' 101
    global 106

models 144
  popular 21, 28
  shareholder 135, 139, 149, 150
  stakeholder 149, 150
Carlton 34
Carlyle, Thomas 9
cartels 49, 113
Carville, James 124
cash nexus 9, 27
Cassel, Ernest 5
Cassidy, Michael 42, 175
Cazenove 84, 93, 107, 163
CBI (Confederation of British
  Industry) 58, 136
Cedel 91
Central Banking magazine 120,
  125
Central European financial crisis
  (summer 1931) 86
centralisation 65
Centre for Dispute Resolution
  183
Centre for Economic and
  Business Research 191
Centre for Tomorrow's
  Company 133
CGNU 83, 103, 105
CGU 103
Channel Four 167
Channel Tunnel 182
Channel Tunnel Rail Link 170,
  171
charitable foundations 72
Chartered Institute of Bankers 78
Charterhouse **94**, 170
Charterhouse Securities 107
Chase Manhattan Bank **96**, 100,
  101, 102, 107, 140
Checkland, Michael 167
Chelsea 53, 54, 56
Chelsea Football Club 164
chief executive officers (CEOs)
  155, 157
China 80
Churchill, Caryl: *Serious Money*
  22, 30
Churchill, Sir Winston 8
CIBC Wood Gundy 170
Citibank Canada 40, 44
Citicorp 71
Citigroup 43, 71, **96**, 100, 101, 105
City Airport 41, 181
City Corporation 38, 39, 40, 42,
  78, 175

Policy and Resources
  Committee 42, 79
City University Business School
  78
City/industry relationship
  14–15, 139, 155, 161
Clarendon, Chantal 52
Clarke, Kenneth 112, 126, 127, 170
Clarke, Mark 113
Clarke, Peter: *Hope and Glory,
  Britain 1900–1990* 8–9
clearing banks 15, 89
  cartel 113
  head offices in the City 7
Cleaver, Sir Anthony 143
Clifford Chance 43, 83, 104
Clinton, Bill 124, 125, 177
Close Brothers 53, 83
Co-op 33, 99
Cobbett, William: *Rural Rides* 9
Coca-Cola 140, 142
Cohen, Norma 43, 44
Cold War 88
Cole, G.D.H.: *The Next Ten
  Years in British Social and
  Economic Policy* 10, 16
commercial banking 67–8, **68**, 99
commercial law 76
commercial revolution 6
Commercial Union 38
commercialism 9
Commerzbank 186
commodities **68**, 76, 77
commodity markets 15
Common Market 185
communications 81, 113, 144,
  181–2
communications revolution 63
communism 144, 198
companies 133, 143–4, 158
competition 11, 64, 89, 96, 134, 162
computers 78, 81
Condé Nast 44
Conigm, Michael 54
Conn, David: *The Football
  Business* 163
Connect Communications
  Cable Network 173
Conservative government
  and the ERM 138
  and the manufacturing
    industry 138
  and the 'stop-go' cycle 7–8
consulting 76

contracts, short-term 168
convertibility crisis (1947) 7
Coopers & Lybrand 104, 142,
  143, 168
Corbridge, Mark 164
Corby, Sir Brian 126
corporate finance **68**, 75–6
corporate financiers 49, 156
corporate fund-raising 109
corporate law 76
Corus 161–2
County Bank 89
Cox, George 48
Credit Suisse 107
Credit Suisse First Boston 33, 37,
  40, 42, 51, 82, 99, 100, 107, 196
credits 88
Crimean War 5–6
Cripps, Sir Stafford 127
crisis of affluence 58
Crosland, Anthony: *The Future
  of Socialism* 11–12
cross-border deals 108
CSFB 35, **96**
Cunliffe Brothers 85
currency deals 81
Curtice, John 28

D
Daily Express building 39
Daily Mail 29
Daily Telegraph 43, 129
Daimler-Benz 145
Daiwa Securities 38
Dalton, Hugh 127
  Principles of Public Finance
    13
Daniela (a fund manager) 1–3
David Sheppard and Partners 23
Davies, Sir Howard 65
Davies, Linda 25
de Mallet Morgan, Tommy 25
de Zoete 84
de Zoete & Bevan 98
debt issues 87
Defence, Ministry of 170
  Whitehall Building 173
deflation 131
Delamuraz, Pascal 157
*Delivering Shareholder Value
  Through Integrated
  Performance Management* 156
Deloitte Touche Tohumatsu 83,
  104

demand management,
Keynesian 116
demutualisations 153
denationalisation 166
deregulation 22, 113
derivatives 64, **68**, 72, 99, 115, 190
derivatives traders 49
Desai, Meghnad: 'Debating the
British Disease: The
Centrality of Profit' 150–51
Deutsche Bank 1, 2, 35, 47, 48,
82, 95, **96**, 102, 105, 107, 110,
134, 186, 189
Deutsche Börse 187–8
Deutsche Morgan Grenfell 47,
99
devaluation 123
September 1949 7
Dickens, Charles: *Dombey and
Son* 12
Dickinson Robinson group 136
Dickson, Martin 160, 161
discount market 5
discounted cash flow 141
diseconomies of scale 65
dispute resolution 76
Distillers 135
Dixon, Thomas 9
Docklands Light Railway 41
dollar, the 87
Donaldson, Lufkin & Jenrette
50, 107
Donoughue, Lord Bernard 122
Dorset 25
dot.com sector 34, 50
downsizing 143
Draft Local Plan (November
1984) 39
Dresdner Bank **96**, 97, 105, 107,
186, 189
Dresdner Kleinwort Benson 105,
172, 173
Dresdner Kleinwort Wasserstein
82, 107
Drexel Burnham 110
drop-lock bonds 115
Drucker, Peter 116
Dunlop 6–7
Dyson, Mike 42, 44

E
Earned Income Group 177
East Asia financial crisis 49
economic analysis 68

economic consultants 78
economic development
and emerging countries 63
and the growth of financial
services 61–2
Economic Development Unit 79
economic growth 80, 124, 151
economic value added (EVA)
140, 141, 153
economies of scale 64, 65, 80, 191
economies of scope 64, 65, 80,
191
Economist, The 77, 86, 145–6
economists 78
Edinburgh University 178
education system 167, 168–9, 175,
176–7
educational endowments 72–3
EF Hutton 110
egalitarianism 21
Eliot, T.S.: *The Waste Land* 12
Elizabeth I, Queen 4
English Heritage 54
English language 182
Enron 200–201
enterprise zone allowance 41
Environment, Transport and
the Regions, Department for
the (DETR) 174
equities 63, **68**, 70, 71, 73, 87, 99,
129, 190
equities trading 71, 81
ERM *see* Exchange Rate
Mechanism
Ernst & Young 83, 168
EU withholding tax 13
Eurex 188
euro, the 81, 190, 195
Euro notes 88, 190
Eurobond markets 62, 72, 88, 89,
91, 114, 185–6
Euroclear 91, 188
Eurocurrency markets 88–9, 91
Eurodollar market 113
Euromarkets 88, 90, 91, 102, 115,
182
Euromoney 77
Euronext 104, 187
European Central Bank 124, 130,
187, 190
European Medicines Evaluation
Agency 42
European Monetary System 111,
117

European monetary union 190
European Union 42, 53, 184,
191–2
Eurostar rail services 182
Evening Standard 46, 48, 55, 59,
162, 175
Excelsior Industrial Holdings
138
exchange controls 17, 21, 92–3,
113, 122, 151, 167, 184
exchange rate mechanism
(ERM) 31, 111, 112, 115, 117, 121,
123, 124, 125, 138
exchange rates
excessively high 138
fixed 11, 63, 121, 184
floating 113
exchange trading 62
expense ratios 109

F
Fabian Society 10, 127
Federal Reserve Bank of New
York 184
Federal Reserve Board 120
Felsmann, Jürgen 189
Ferris, Paul 1, 14
Fildes, Christopher 43, 98, 102
finance directors (FDs) 155
financial assets 61–2
financial liberalisation 118
Financial News 86
financial services
and commercial sectors 51
and economic development
61–2
mainstream 60
Financial Services Authority 43,
74, 77, 81, 110
Financial Times 2, 11, 33, 34, 38,
43, 77, 101, 106, 108, 115, 119,
121, 123, 125, 127, 132, 135–6, 138,
141, 147, 150, 151, 153, 155, 160,
170, 173, 177, 180, 193, 201
Financial Times building 39
The Financial World Tonight
(Radio Four programme) 14
Finanzplatz Deutschland 187–90
fire insurance 75, 103
First Boston 107
First Boston Real Estate 40
First Hydro Finance 170
First World War 4, 6, 86, 183, 195
fixed commission rates 93

fixed exchange rates 11, 63
Flemings **94**, **96**, 100, 101, 102
flipflop perpetual notes 115
football 163–5
Football Association 163, 165
Foreign & Colonial 103
foreign banks 68, 69, **69**
foreign companies: listed on
  exchanges 71, **71**, 93
foreign exchange market 7, 114,
  117
foreign exchange trading 68, **68**,
  69, **70**, 124, 190
foreign ownership 102–7
'Foresight Panels' 168
Forster, E.M.: *Howards End* 12
Fortune 'Global 500' companies
  184
Foxtons 53
FPDSavills 53
France
  economic growth 151
  loss of overseas colonies 185
franchises 49
Franco-Prussian War (1870) 195
Frank, Thomas 27
Frankfurt 184, 186–90
Frankfurt stock exchange 187–8
Frankfurter Allgemein Zeitung
  190
Franklin, Roland 136
Frederick Huth **94**
free markets 105, 106, 175
free trade 17
French Wars (1793–1815) 5, 84,
  185
Freshfields 104
Freshfields Bruckhaus Deringer
  83
Friedman, Milton 11
Friends of the Earth 173
FTSE 100 153, 155
FTSE 250 162
FTSE 350 159
FTSE 500 153
fuel crisis (September 2000) 131
Fulham 54
fund management 63, **68**, 72–4,
  73, 93, 137
fund managers 73–4, 108, 156
Fund Managers Association 103
Furman Selz 107
Furse, Clara 103
futures 72, 115

Futures and Options
  Association 48

G
Galley, Carol 199
Gamages 56
Gamble, Andrew 152
Gartmore 102
Gatwick Airport 181
GCHQ Building 173
GEC 160
General Elections
  June 1987 28
  June 2001 174, 196, 198
General Electric 140, 142
'general' insurance 75, 83
General Post Office 39
Générale de Banque 100
George, Sir Edward 105, 112, 126,
  127–8, 130, 147
Germany
  established as a nation state
    185
  growth 151
  loans 86, 87
  stock market turnover rates
    139
  success of 135
  supervisory boards 145–6
Gideon, Samson 5
gilts 129, 130
  increase in value 6
  long-term 131
  sales to the market 6
  ten-year gilt yields 127
Gladstone, William Ewart 31
global economy 4, 10
Global Investor column
  (*Financial Times*) 153
globalisation 101, 105, 114, 143,
  152, 198
Gloucestershire 54
Go-Ahead Group 161
Goizueta, Roberto 140
gold and silver trading 76
gold standard 7, 8, 10, 16, 86
Golding, Tony 155, 156
Goldman Sachs 35, 46, 47, 48,
  50, 58, 71, 82, 95, 100, 107, 108,
  110, 116, 173, 201
Goodhart, Professor Charles
  126, 130, 132
Goodhart, David 122
Goodison, Sir Nicholas 21, 92

government bonds 71
government broker 6
government/industry
  relationship 14
GP fundholders 168
Great Education Reform Bill
  ('GERBIL') 167
Great Fire (1666) 38, 39
Greed (television show) 197
Green paper on education
  (February 2001) 176
Greenspan, Alan 120, 125, 132
Grierson, Ronald 87
Gross Domestic Product (GDP)
  53, 79, 192
Gross National Product (GNP)
  6, 114, 168
Group 4 168, 174
growth markets 154
Grunfeld, Henry 87
GT 103
guaranteed bonus 47, 50
Guardian 33, 129, 200
Guardian Royal Exchange 103
Guinness 6–7, 28, 30, 95, 135
Gyllenhammer, Pehr 103

H
Hambro family 85
Hambros 33, 87, 89, 94, **95**, **96**,
  99–100, 101
Hampshire 25, 54
Hampstead 54
Handy, Professor Charles: 'What
  Is a Company For?' lecture
  133, 139
Hanson, Lord 137
Hanson Trust 135, 145
Harding, James 129
Harold Wincott Memorial
  Lectures 11
Harris, Martyn 29
Harvard Business School 97
Harvey-Jones, Sir John 161
Hawkpoint Partners 83
headhunters 23, 48, 52, 77–8
Healey, Denis 7, 126, 127
Healey & Baker 186
Heath, Sir Edward 15, 87, 169
Heathrow Airport 42, 181
Heathrow Express 44
hedge funds 109–10, 115
Hemmings, David 12
Henderson, Giles 178

Hermes 158
Heron Quays, Canary Wharf 43, 44
Herstatt 90
high net worth individuals 74
higher education 168–9, 177–8
Highways Agency 174
Hill Samuel 94, 95, 101
Hillards 136
Hilton, Anthony 59, 77, 162
Hobson, J.A. 14
holidays 55–6
Holland 185
Holland Park 54
Holliday, Sir Fred 161
Home Office 167
Horlick, Nicola 32, 34
Houlder, Vanessa 38
House of Fraser 56
house prices 26, 53, 54, 57–8
Howe, Geoffrey 129
HR Owen car dealership 56
HSBC 43, 44, 82, 132, 176
HSBC James Capel 129
Hughes, Beverley 174
human resources 68, 83
Hutton, Will 129–30, 148, 150–51, 152, 156–7, 162, 171, 175
    The State We're In 32, 129–30, 146–7, 156–7, 171

I
Iacobescu, George 43, 44
IBM United Kingdom 143
ICI 138, 144–5
I'm All Right Jack (film) 24
Imperial 135, 136
income-generating investment portfolios 35
Independent 50, 97, 129, 148, 162, 196
Independent Broadcasting Authority 167
Independent newspaper group 42
India 80
Indonesia 80
industrial interventionism 123
Industrial Reorganisation Corporation 87
industrial revolution 6, 9, 193
Industrial Society 162
industrialisation 9
inflation 118, 120, 124, 125, 126, 129, 131, 138

information 77
information technology 77, 83, 174
infrastructure development 6
ING 96, 98, 107, 186
ING Barings 82, 107
insolvency 76
Institute of Chartered Accountants 78
Institute of Directors 152, 175
Institute of Education, University of London 177
Institutional Fund Managers Association 139
Institutional Shareholders Committee 144
insurance 15, 62, 68, 72, 74–5, 83, 103–4, 105, 166
Intercapital 83
interest rates 88, 111, 126, 127, 129, 130, 138, 147
international bonds 63
international capital market 76
International Dispute Resolution Centre 183
international financial flows 62, 63
International Financial Services, London (IFSL) 79, 80
International Monetary Fund (IMF) 7, 62, 116
International Petroleum Exchange (IPE) 76
international trade 62
internationalisation 10
internet 34, 50, 178, 200
Investec 96, 100
investment
    internationalisation of 62, 63
    long-term 138
investment banking 67, 70–71, 76, 82, 99, 101, 110
investment banks 24, 35, 37, 39, 45, 47–8, 51, 59, 67, 70–71, 72, 82, 89, 95, 100, 108–9, 110, 116, 164
investment policies 75, 103
Investors Chronicle 169
'invisibles' 80
ISAs 35
Isle of Dogs, London 37
ISMA (International Securities Markets Association) Centre, University of Reading 78
isolationism 128

IT consultants 78
Italian Central Bank 110
Italy
    established as a nation state 185
    government 112

J
Jack, Ian: 'The Return of the Bright Young Things' 21
Jackson, Tony 153, 154–5
Jacomb, Sir Martin 166
Jaguar 166
James-Crook, James 25
Japan
    growth 151
    investment rate 137
    stakeholders 145
    stock market turnover rates 139
    success of 135
Jenkins, Clive 15
Jenkins, Simon 30
Jewish merchant banks 86
job insecurity 143
job losses 59, 61
John D Wood (estate agents) 54
Johnson, Dr Samuel 178
    Dictionary of the English Language 9
Johnson Matthey affair (1984) 119
joint ventures 90
Jones Long Laballe 189
Jones, Vanessa 54
JP Morgan Chase 58, 82, 107, 188
JS Morgan 94
Jubilee Line extension 41, 42, 43, 44
junior traders 45
Jupiter 103

K
Kay, John 159, 161
    Foundations of Corporate Success 143–4
Keegan, Kevin 164
Keegan, William and Rupert Pennant-Rea: Who Runs the Economy? 116–17
Kelly, Gavin 152
Kennedy, John F. 89, 111
Kensington 53, 54
Kent, Rod 53

Kenwood 145
Kerr, Ian 50–51
Keynes, John Maynard 11, 162
   *The Economic Consequences
   of the Peace* 32
Keynesianism 11, 150
Kidder Peabody 110
Kidderminster Hospital 198
Kiley, Bob 175
King, Mervyn 125
King, Stephen 132
Kingfisher 158, 159
King's Fund 171
Kinnock, Neil 28, 31, 121, 123
Kleinwort Benson 22–3, **94**, **96**,
   97, 166, 186
Kleinwort, Sons **94**
Kleinwort family 85
Knight Frank 53, 54
Knightsbridge 54, 56
KPMG 83, 104, 170–71
Kyte, David 24

L
L. Messel & Co 23
Labour governments
   of 1945–51 6, 86
   of 1964–70 87
   and education 176, 177
   fall in 1931 financial crisis 87
   landslide of 1997 33, 35
   loses election in 1987 28–9
   spending 130–31
   and sterling 11, 16, 116
labour markets 31, 49, 128
Labour Party
   and PFI 171–2
   public expenditure
      programme 123
   Road to the Manifesto 128–9
   socialism-in-one-country
      ambition 121–2
Lafarge 161
Laing, Sir Hector 136, 137, 161
   A Parting Shot 137
Lakhani, Kinner 48
Lamont, Norman 112, 113, 125,
   126, 169, 170
lastminute.com 34
Latin American debt crisis 142
Lawson, Nigel 29, 35, 117–21, 166
lawyers **68**, 75, 104–5
Lazard family 85
Lazard Frères 128

Lazards 84, 87, **94**, 107, 185
LDC (less developed countries)
   debt crisis 120
Leach, Graeme 175–6
Leeson, Nick 97, 107, 199
Left, the 10, 11, 12, 15, 28, 196
Legal and General 103
legal services 75–6, 104–5
Lehman Brothers 39, 43, 48, 82,
   101, 107
Leicester City Football Club 164
Leigh-Pemberton, Robin 118–19,
   120–21
Lenin, Vladimir Ilyich:
   Imperialism 10
Levene, Sir Peter (later Lord) 42,
   190
Lewis, Michael 26, 27
   Liar's Poker 23, 116
Lex column (*Financial Times*)
   136, 147
life assurance companies 31, 75,
   103
Limehouse Link 41
Link 175
Linklaters 58, 104
Linklaters & Alliance 83, 104
Livingstone, Ken 175
Llanwern steel plant 162
Lloyd, John 152
Lloyds Bank 42, 89, 99, 126, 142,
   153
Lloyd's of London 5, 74, 75, 83
Lloyds Merchant Bank 39
Lloyds TSB 82
Lloyds TSB Life 103
local education authorities
   (LEAs) 176
local financial centres 65
London
   accounting and related
      services 76
   American expansion 26, 96,
      184
   as a business location 186–7
   the foremost international
      financial centre 61
   as a global city 180–82
   international cross-border
      bank lending 69
   international legal services
      75–6
   the leading foreign exchange
      market 69

London Bridge City
   development 39
London Bullion Market
   Association 76
London Business School 78,
   139
London Commodity Exchange
   76
London Court of International
   Arbitration 183
London Docklands
   Development Corporation 37
London International Financial
   Futures and Options
   Exchange (LIFFE) 24, 29, 33,
   48, 72, 76, 103–4, 187, 188, 190
London Maritime Arbitrators
   Association 183
London Metal Exchange (LME)
   76
London School of Economics
   10, 78
London Stock Exchange
   anti-competitive and costly
      commission structure 92
   bull market (1982) 21
   established (1801) 5
   and Eurobonds 91–2
   expansion of the capital
      market 6–7
   flotation of Canary Wharf
      (March 1999) 43
   foreign companies listing 71
   gilt issues 6
   and LIFFE 103–4
   restrictions on membership
      92
   survey of 1952 13
   women in 8
London Underground 41, 81, 174
London Wall 38, 39
Long-Term Capital
   Management (LTCM) 49, 109
'long-term' insurance 75, 83
Lord Mayor 78–9
Lothian 171
Louvre Accord (February 1987)
   117
Lovells 83, 104
Lower Thames Street
   development 39
Luftwaffe 87
Luton Airport 181
Luton plant 162

M

Maastricht Treaty 111, 124
MacDonald, Lord 174
MacDonald, Ramsay 7, 16
Macmillan Committee on
  Finance 14
'Macmillan gap' 14
McKenzie, Duncan 80
McNeany, Kevin 176
McRae, Hamish 105, 196
macroeconomic policy 129
Magan, George 135
Magnus, George 128
Mais Lecture (May 1995) 128
Major, John 31, 111, 112, 126, 131,
  168, 169
Major government 113, 125, 127
Mallinckrodt, Sir George 100
Management Accounting 156
Management Today magazine 153
managing directors 45–6
Manchester United 164
Mannesmann 108, 157
Mansfield College, Oxford 179
Mansion House 48
Manufacturers Hanover Trust 42
manufacturing industry
  borrowing facilities 7
  and Conservative
    government 138
  and financial services 51
Marconi 160–61
marine insurance 74–5, 103
marine services 68, 76–7
market economics 29
market populism 27
market research 77
market value added (MVA) 141
marketisation 165, 168, 172, 179
markets
  and players 17
  power of 17, 113
Marks & Spencer 144, 158, 159, 160
Marquand, David 148–9, 152,
  178–9
Marsh, Paul: Short-Termism on
  Trial 139
Martin, Lord Mayor Clive 79
Martin, Peter 153–4, 199–200
Marx, Karl: Das Kapital 10
Marxism Today 122
Mass Observation survey 18, 31
Mastercard 34
Maxwell, Robert 31, 55

Mayer, Thomas 201
Mayo, John 145, 160–61
medium-term lending 15
Mellon Bank 102
Mercers livery company 176
merchant banks 49, 84–8,
  90–92, 94–5, 95, 96, 102, 106
Mercury Asset Management 96,
  102, 199
mergers 50, 58, 63, 81, 103–5, 109,
  135
Merrill Lynch 34, 35, 49, 71, 82,
  95, 96, 97, 100, 102, 107, 110, 176
Merrill Lynch Investment
  Managers 199
Metallgesellschaft 145
metals trading 76
Mexico crisis 124
Meyer, Bernhard 48
Michael Page City 50
Middleton, Sir Peter 126
Midland Bank 134
Midlands Expressway Limited
  173
Milan Stock Exchange 12
Millennium Exhibition 171
millionaires
  dollar 47, 51
  sterling 50–51
Milne, Alasdair 167
minimum wage 123
Mirror Group 158
Mirror newspaper group 42
Mitterrand, François 111, 120, 122
Moffat, Sir Brian 162
monetarism, Friedmanite 117
monetary policy 7, 74, 130
Monetary Policy Committee
  128, 129
Money Management magazine
  33
Money Observer magazine 33
money-centre activities 60, 61,
  61, 72, 77, 78, 80, 82, 83, 103,
  107, 187
Moneywise magazine 33
Montagnon, Peter 115
Montague, Adrian 172, 174
Montgomery, David 158
Monty Python's Flying Circus:
  'The Dull Life of the City
  Stockbroker' 12
Morgan, Rhodri 162
Morgan family 85

Morgan Grenfell 32, 84, 94, 95,
  96, 135, 166, 186, 189
Morgan Grenfell Asset
  Management 102
Morgan Guaranty 21, 89
Morgan Stanley 35, 40, 42, 46,
  48, 53, 58, 71, 82, 95, 96, 100,
  107, 196, 201
Morgan Stanley Dean Witter
  107
Morris, William: News from
  Nowhere 10
Morton, Sir Alastair 170
Mosley, Layna 131
motor industry 102, 103
motor insurance 75
Moulton, David 54
Mowlam, Mo 122
Mulcahy, Sir Geoff 159
Mullens 6, 84
multinationals 12, 90, 182
Munich Re 189
mutual funds 73, 74
Myerson, Brian 145, 158

N

Naked City (television series) 25
'names' 75
Napier Scott 181
Nathan, Stephen, ed.: Prison
  Privatisation Report
  International 174
National Air Traffic Services
  (Nats) 174–5
National Bank of Switzerland
  118
National Bus Company 166
National Debt 5, 6
National Grid 170
National Health Service (NHS)
  6, 167, 168, 171, 198
National Lottery 34
National War Bonds 6
National Westminster 156
nationalisation 7, 10, 128
Nationwide Mutual 102
NatWest 82, 89, 94, 99, 100, 102,
  107
NatWest Markets 46, 96, 99,
  100, 164
NatWest Tower, off Bishopsgate
  38
negative equity 31
Nestlé 136

Neuer Market 188
New Change 38
New Industrial Compact 155, 156
New Labour 33, 128, 152, 176, 179, 197–8
New Left 12
new Right 179
New Society 29
New Statesman 152
New York 58, 75, 87, 88, 106–7, 180, 191, 192
New York Stock Exchange 145
New York University 58
New Zealand 125
Newcastle United Football Club 164
Newmarch, Mike 153
Newsnight (television programme) 22
Newton 102
NHS trusts 168, 169
Nikko Securities 102
Nine Years War 5
Nomura 82
Nord Anglia 176
Norman, Montagu 8, 11, 130, 184
North, Lord 8
North Sea oil 92
Northern Trust 43
Northumbrian Water 161
Northwestern University 140
Norwich Union 103, 144
Notting Hill 53, 54
Nottingham Express Transit Line OneSystem 173

O
Oak Administration 159
Oakley, Professor Ann 177
O'Brien, Richard: *Global Financial Integration: The End of Geography* 114
Observer 33
Office of Health Economics 174
offshore banking 64
offshore bonds 64, 72
offshore financial markets 69, 92
offshore transactions 62, 63–4, 80
Ogilvy & Mather 42
oil price shock (1973) 61, 90
Old Labour 7
Olivetti 157

Olympia & York 40, 42
One Canada Square, Canary Wharf 41, 42, 43
options 72, 115
Orion Royal 91
over-the-counter (OTC) 72, **73**
overseas earnings 79, 80
Oxbridge graduates 27
Oxford Senior Executive Finance Programme 157
Oxford University 35, 178
Oxfordshire 54

P
P & O 38
Paddington Basin development 44
Pagano, Margareta 181
Paine Webber 107
Paribas 157
Paris 186
   corporate headquarters in 182
   and the Franco-Prussian War 195
Paris Europlace 187
Parkinson, Cecil 21
Partnership Property Management (PPM) 172–3
Partnerships UK (PUK) 174
Partridge, Frances 13
Passport Agency 174
Paternoster Square development 38, 44
Peacock Committee 167
Pearl Group 172
Pelican History of England 8
Pember & Boyle 84
Pembridge Investments 136
Pembroke College, Oxford 178
Pennant-Rea, Rupert 117
pension funds 72, 93, 103
pensions 31, 165
   personal 31
   stakeholder 35
personal accident insurance 75, 103
Personal Investment Authority 42
petrodollar recycling 90
Phillips & Drew 102, 146, 158
Pierer, Heinrich von 157
Pirelli 153
pit-closure programme 32

Pitman, Sir Brian 142
Plaza Accord (September 1985) 117
Plender, John 106, 110, 124, 159, 160–61
Portugal 185
'prawn cocktail offensive' (1990) 122–3
Premier League 163
Premier Prison Services Refinancing 173
Prescott, John 13, 174
press, the 77
Price Waterhouse 39, 104, 153, 167, 168
price/earnings ratios (P/Es) 136
PricewaterhouseCoopers 58, 83, 104, 157
primary markets 70
Prime Contract 172
Pringle, Robert 125
Priory Clinic 52
Prison Service 168
private banking 74
Private Finance Initiative Journal 174
Private Finance Initiative (PFI) 169–75, 178, 197–8
Private Finance Panel 170
Private Finance Taskforce 172
private sector 169, 175, 176
privatisation 20, 21, 28, 34, 63, 166, 167, 169, 174–5
productivity 81
profits 133
project finance 76
Project Finance 172–3
property booms 26, 29, 38
property insurance 75, 103
property slumps 42
proprietary trading 71, 116
Protection and Indemnity (P&I) clubs 74
Prowse, Michael 177
Prudential 83, 103, 105, 126, 134, 153, 178
Prudential-Bache International 102
Public Money & Management journal 170
public relations 68, 77, 83
public sector 58, 169, 175, 197
public-private partnership (PPP) 172–5, 178, 197

Pünder Volhard Weber & Axter 104
Purves, Libby 196–7

Q
Quantum Fund 115

R
Radio Four 14
Railtrack 175
Randall, Jeff 33
Rappaport, Alfred
    Creating Shareholder Value 140
    Information for Decision Making 140
RBC Dominion Securities 107
real estate 73
real output per head 80
recession
    mid-1970s 61
    1981 21
    1990 138
    1991 31, 42, 96
recruitment 77
Rees-Mogg, Wlliam 32
Regan, Andrew 33
regional financial centres 65
regulatory compliance 68
Reichmann, Paul 40–41, 42
Reichmann brothers 40
reinsurance 75
rental sector 54–5
research councils 168
Reserve Bank of New Zealand 126
retail banking 100, 107
Reuters 48, 77
Richelieu, Duc de 84
Right, the 11
Riley, Barry 141–2, 151
Roach, Stephen 201
Road Management Group 170
'rocket scientists' 72
Rogers & Wells 104
Rohatyn, Felix: 'Recipes for Growth' 128
Roll, Lord Eric 125
Rolls-Royce 166
Romans 4
Ross Goobey, Alastair 25, 170, 171
Roth, Martin 190
Rothschild, Nathan 5, 56, 85
Rothschilds 48, 84, 85, 89, **94**, 107, 187

Roux Brothers 37
Rover Group 166
Rowe & Pitman 84
Rowntrees 136
Royal & Sun Alliance 103
Royal Academy 33
Royal Bank Group 82
Royal Bank of Canada 91
Royal Bank of Scotland 82, 156
Royal Exchange 24, 56, 130
Royal Society for the Encouragement of Arts, Manufactures and Commerce 133, 139, 143, 145, 152
Ruskin, John 9–10
Rusnak, John 199
Russia 185
    default of 49, 110

S
St Paul's Cathedral 38, 60
salaries 22–3, 25, 44–7, 53, 57, 65, 66, 67, 96, 108, 109
salesmen 45, 71, 78
Salomon Brothers 23, 27, 39, 40, 48, 116
Salomon Smith Barney (Citigroup) 71, 99, 100, 107
Sampson, Anthony 14
Samuel Montagu 89, **94**
Sandland, Mike 144
Sassen, Saskia: *The Global City: New York, London, Tokyo* 181
Savings Bonds 6
SBC 184
Schiro, Jim 104
Schlesinger, Dr Helmut 112
Schmengler, Thomas 189
Scholl 145
Schroder family 85
Schroder Salomon Smith Barney (Citigroup) 82
Schroders 94, **95, 96**, 100–101, 103, 166, 185
Schweppes 6–7
Scrimgeour 84
Scudder 189
Second Severn Crossing 170
Second World War 6, 85, 87, 184
secondary markets 70
securities **68**, 70, 82
Securities and Investment Board 48
securities brokerage 71

securities houses 106
securities markets 114, 185
securities sector 93
securities trading 63, 109
Security Pacific 39
Seelig, Roger 135
Seifert, Werner 188
Seligmans **94**
Seligman family 85
Sellers, Peter 24
senior traders 45
senior vice-presidents 45
SERPS (state earnings-related pensions scheme) 165–6
services 135
SG Hambro 82
share-buying 20, 29
shareholder value 10, 138, 140–43, 153–61
Shareholder Value Analysis Survey (Coopers & Lybrand) 142–3
shareholder value analysis (SVA) 142–3
shareholders 133, 134, 135, 139, 144, 146, 154, 156, 165
Shearson Lehman 23
ship broking 62
shipbuilding industry 102
shipping 15
Shonfield, Andrew 11
short-term contracts 168
short-term loans 88
short-term rollover credits 15
short-termism 135, 138, 139, 142, 143, 147
Short-Termism and the State We're In (Institute of Directors report) 152
Shurety, Mike 57
Sieghart, William 21
Siemens 157, 158
Signet 145
Simpson, Lord 160
Singer & Friedlander 83, **94**
single market 96
Skadden Arpos Slate Moagher & Flom LLP 43
Skeoch, Keith 129
Sky television 163
Skye bridge 171
Slater, Jim 15
Slaughter and May 83, 178
Smith, John 121, 122, 123